About Frith

"I knew when I was in his [Schuon's] presence that I was in the presence of a true saint and also the spiritual master that I was seeking. When I say 'true saint', I don't mean just a saintly man but a true saint of the first magnitude, such as one cannot expect to meet in the twentieth century. I mean a saint of the magnitude of St. Bernard, St. Francis, or St. Augustine in Christianity; of Ibn Arabi or Rumi in Sufism; of Shankara in Hinduism; and of Milarepa in Buddhism. I knew this with a certainty."

—**Martin Lings**, author of *A Sufi Saint of the Twentieth Century: Shaykh Ahmad al-'Alawi*, describing his first meeting with Schuon

"[Schuon is] the most important religious thinker of our century. . . . [He] is the only person I have known who invariably made me feel on leaving him that I had been in the presence of a different order of human being."

—**Huston Smith**, author of *The World's Religions* and *Why Religion Matters*

"I think that he [Schuon] is a great man. . . . I know that people come over here to see him from other countries—from all over the world. I regard him as a holy man. . . . Considering this and because he is a good friend, I did something well worth doing by adopting a great man into [my] family."

—**Thomas Yellowtail**, Crow Medicine Man and Sun Dance chief, speaking about adopting Schuon as his brother

"His face was bright with the light of inner illumination. He possessed a regal bearing . . . but he was at heart so humble, simple, and loving. . . . The love in his heart was manifest on his face. . . . The tall and stately figure of the Sufi saint stood out in great prominence above us all—a very prince among saints."

—**Swami Ramdas**, from the chapter "Visit to a Sufi Saint" in his book *World Is God*

"Knowing Schuon created for many of us all over the world a fraternity. We often met for the first time in his name and became fast friends. Humanly he created a cosmopolitan international fraternity, which reaches far beyond the circles that any one of us individually knows. . . . For this enrichment of our lives at so many levels, from the practical to the social, the intellectual and above all, the spiritual, thousands of people all over the world will remain truly grateful."

—**Mudumbaï Ramachandran**, a Hindu admirer and disciple of the 68th Jagadguru of Kanchipuram

"I have met with no more impressive work in the comparative study of Oriental and Occidental religion."

—**T. S. Eliot**, Nobel laureate for literature, on Schuon's first book, *The Transcendent Unity of Religions*

"Schuon seems like the cosmic intellect itself impregnated by the energy of divine grace surveying the whole of the reality surrounding man and elucidating all the concerns of human existence in the light of sacred knowledge."

—**Seyyed Hossein Nasr**, The George Washington University, author of *Knowledge and the Sacred*

"[Schuon] is, without doubt, one of the most penetrating philosophical minds of the twentieth century, if not well beyond."

—**Keith Critchlow**, Professor Emeritus, The Prince's School of Traditional Arts, and President of the Temenos Academy

"Frithjof Schuon is one of the greatest exponents ever of perennial wisdom; his unique feature is that, amongst all the great sages, he is the only one who is equally at home—and in a masterly fashion—in all of its many and varied historic forms: Vedānta, Taoism, Platonism, Palamitism, Scholasticism, and Sufism."

—**William Stoddart**, author of *Remembering in a World of Forgetting*

"[Schuon is in] possession of 'the gift of tongues', the ability, that is to say, both to speak and understand the various dialects through which the Spirit has chosen to communicate itself to men in their diversity and therefore, in practice, also the ability to communicate clearly with one's fellows across the religious frontiers. . . . [He] exemplifies the power to penetrate all traditional forms as well as to render them mutually intelligible."

—**Marco Pallis**, author of *A Buddhist Spectrum* and *Peaks and Lamas*

World Wisdom
The Library of Perennial Philosophy

The Library of Perennial Philosophy is dedicated to the exposition of the timeless Truth underlying the diverse religions. This Truth, often referred to as the *Sophia Perennis*—or Perennial Wisdom—finds its expression in the revealed Scriptures as well as the writings of the great sages and the artistic creations of the traditional worlds.

Letters of Frithjof Schuon: Reflections on the Perennial Philosophy appears as one of our selections in the Writings of Frithjof Schuon series.

The Writings of Frithjof Schuon

The Writings of Frithjof Schuon form the foundation of our library because he is the pre-eminent exponent of the Perennial Philosophy. His work illuminates this perspective in both an essential and comprehensive manner like none other.

Books by Frithjof Schuon

The Transcendent Unity of Religions (1953, 1984)
Spiritual Perspectives and Human Facts (1954, 1970, 1987, 2007)
Gnosis: Divine Wisdom (1959, 1978, 1990, 2006)
Language of the Self (1959, 1999)
Stations of Wisdom (1961, 1980, 1995)
Understanding Islam (1963, 1972, 1986, 1998, 2011)
Light on the Ancient Worlds (1965, 1984, 2006)
Treasures of Buddhism (In the Tracks of Buddhism) (1968, 1989, 1993, 2018)
Logic and Transcendence (1975, 1984, 2009)
Esoterism as Principle and as Way (1981, 1990, 2019)
Sufism: Veil and Quintessence (1981, 2006)
Castes and Races (1982)
From the Divine to the Human (1982, 2013)
Christianity/Islam: Perspectives on Esoteric Ecumenism (1985, 2008)
Survey of Metaphysics and Esoterism (1986, 2000)
In the Face of the Absolute (1989, 1994, 2014)
The Feathered Sun: Plains Indians in Art and Philosophy (1990)
To Have a Center (1990, 2015)
Roots of the Human Condition (1991, 2002)
Images of Primordial and Mystic Beauty: Paintings by Frithjof Schuon (1992)
Echoes of Perennial Wisdom (1992, 2012)
The Play of Masks (1992)
Road to the Heart: Poems (1995)
The Transfiguration of Man (1995)
The Eye of the Heart (1997, 2021)
Form and Substance in the Religions (2002)
Adastra & Stella Maris: Poems by Frithjof Schuon (bilingual edition) (2003)
Songs without Names, Volumes I-VI: Poems by Frithjof Schuon (2006)
Songs without Names, Volumes VII-XII: Poems by Frithjof Schuon (2006)
World Wheel, Volumes I-III: Poems by Frithjof Schuon (2006)
World Wheel, Volumes IV-VII: Poems by Frithjof Schuon (2006)
Primordial Meditation: Contemplating the Real (2007)
Autumn Leaves & The Ring: Poems by Frithjof Schuon (bilingual edition) (2010)

Anthologies of Frithjof Schuon's Writings

The Essential Frithjof Schuon, ed. Seyyed Hossein Nasr (1986, 2005)
Songs for a Spiritual Traveler: Selected Poems (bilingual edition) (2002)
René Guénon: Some Observations, ed. William Stoddart (2004)
The Fullness of God: Frithjof Schuon on Christianity, ed. James S. Cutsinger (2004)
Prayer Fashions Man: Frithjof Schuon on the Spiritual Life, ed. James S. Cutsinger (2005)
Art from the Sacred to the Profane: East and West, ed. Catherine Schuon (2007)
Splendor of the True: A Frithjof Schuon Reader, ed. James S. Cutsinger (2013)
Towards the Essential: Letters of a Spiritual Master, ed. Thierry Béguelin (2021)
Letters of Frithjof Schuon: Reflections on the Perennial Philosophy,
ed. Michael Oren Fitzgerald (2022)

Letters of Frithjof Schuon

Reflections on the Perennial Philosophy

Edited by
Michael Oren Fitzgerald

Introduction by
Catherine Schuon

Letters of Frithjof Schuon: Reflections on the Perennial Philosophy
edited by Michael Oren Fitzgerald

Library of Congress Cataloging-in-Publication Data

Names: Schuon, Frithjof, 1907-1998, author. | Fitzgerald, Michael Oren, 1949- editor. | Schuon, Catherine, 1924- writer of introduction.
Title: Letters of Frithjof Schuon : reflections on the perennial philosophy / edited by Michael Oren Fitzgerald ; introduction by Catherine Schuon.
Description: Bloomington, Indiana : World Wisdom, [2022] | Series: The library of perennial philosophy | Includes index.
Identifiers: LCCN 2021059103 (print) | LCCN 2021059104 (ebook) | ISBN 9781936597727 (paperback) | ISBN 9781936597734 (epub)
Subjects: LCSH: Schuon, Frithjof, 1907-1998--Correspondence. | Religion--Philosophy. | Tradition (Philosophy)
Classification: LCC BL51 .S4631513 2022 (print) | LCC BL51 (ebook) | DDC 194--dc23/eng/20220127
LC record available at https://lccn.loc.gov/2021059103
LC ebook record available at https://lccn.loc.gov/2021059104

Cover:
Frithjof Schuon in Marrakech, Morocco, c. 1965

Printed on acid-free paper in the United States of America

For information address World Wisdom, Inc.
P.O. Box 2682, Bloomington, Indiana 47402-2682
www.worldwisdom.com

CONTENTS

to deal with many of the specific dangers to be found in our modern technological society.

In the third category are letters that relate to various aspects of Schuon's life, most of which are written to his closest friends. These shed light on such things as his struggles of youth; his search for a spiritual master; his military experiences; his travel impressions; his relationship with the American Indian world; some of his mystical experiences, including his relationship with the Virgin Mary; his guidance of a spiritual order, a *Tarīqah*; his artistic activities and intentions; his moving to a new land; his reflections on growing old; and his reactions to the passing of close friends. The result is an intimate view of certain key moments in the course of Schuon's life.[3]

Taken as a whole, it is our hope that the present collection will offer insights into the content of Frithjof Schuon's message—his exposition of the perennial philosophy—as well as a glimpse into his life as messenger of that philosophy.[4]

—— ·⁝· ——

Schuon once noted that there are times when "one may have the inclination to enter into an author's thinking by a conscientious exploration of one of his books", while at other times one may prefer "a less laborious and somehow carefree exploration".[5] We anticipate here that certain readers will prefer something closer to this second mode of assimilation, and will repeatedly dip into the compilation for inspiration, rather than attempt to read it cover-to-cover. Whichever mode is chosen, a table at the end of the book can help the reader discover or revisit letters of particular interest by listing the date and place of

[3] For a more complete understanding of Schuon's life and its meaning, see our previous *Frithjof Schuon: Messenger of the Perennial Philosophy* (Bloomington, IN: World Wisdom, 2010) and Jean-Baptiste Aymard & Patrick Laude, *Frithjof Schuon: Life and Teachings* (Albany, NY: SUNY, 2004).

[4] For a valuable anthology of Schuon's writings, approved by the author himself, see Seyyed Hossein Nasr, *The Essential Frithjof Schuon* (Bloomington, IN: World Wisdom, 2005); and for a helpful guide to Schuon's writings, see Harry Oldmeadow, *Frithjof Schuon and the Perennial Philosophy* (Bloomington, IN: World Wisdom, 2010).

[5] *Echoes of Perennial Wisdom*, p. x.

writing, the name or relationship of the recipient, and a word or short phrase taken from the letter indicating the general subject matter.

Excerpts from nearly 200 letters appear within these pages. The vast majority were written in French or German, with a few composed in English. The presentation is chronological and each chapter title identifies a prominent theme associated with the respective period of Schuon's life. Many of these letters are several pages long, thus substantial editing was often required so as to be able to touch upon a diversity of subjects. In order not to distract readers, editorial ellipses are not shown. Many of the foreign language phrases and quotations have been translated into English, and readers may consult the glossary for those that remain. Editorial footnotes contain some brief comments and explanations as well as citations to scriptural and other references.

This book of Schuon's letters was only made possible because so many of his correspondents instinctively safeguarded his original letters for decades. In addition, several individuals deserve mention for the particular role they played in preserving this material. The first of these is Lucy von Dechend, one of Schuon's earliest childhood friends and a frequent correspondent, who acted for several decades as Schuon's secretary, typing his handwritten articles for publication and also important excerpts from many of his letters, copies of which she retained. Whitall and Barbara Perry[6] were Schuon's next-door neighbors from 1955 until his death in 1998, and in that time they assisted him in various ways, among them copying many of Schuon's papers during the late 1950s and '60s and all of his letters from the 1970s onwards. In the early 1980s, Patrick Casey, who in America served as an aide and secretary to Schuon, approached him with the idea of collecting all of the letters he had sent out over the years. With the author's approval, Casey began a process that resulted in the collection of over 1,200 letters; excerpts of some of these have since been published in various works, while many appear for the first time here below. The translations are the work of William Stoddart, Barbara Perry, Mark Perry, Gillian Harris, and Joseph Fitzgerald.

[6] Whitall N. Perry (1920–2005), compiler of the monumental *A Treasury of Traditional Wisdom* (London: George Allen & Unwin, 1971; Louisville: Fons Vitae, 2000) and his wife, Barbara (1923–2015), were among the few people who had close personal relationships with Ananda K. Coomaraswamy, René Guénon, Titus Burckhardt, and Frithjof Schuon—the four most important writers of the perennialist school.

Schuon's correspondence with René Guénon merits particular mention, as they are the two originators of the perennialist school of thought. Their correspondence began in early 1931 and continued for two decades until Guénon's death in 1951. Unfortunately, the archive of Schuon's letters currently includes relatively few of those he wrote to Guénon, thereby limiting our ability to feature them here.

—— ·:· ——

Special thanks are owed to the late Catherine Schuon for her contribution to this volume, whose publication she eagerly anticipated but did not live to see.[7] Her touching and informative reminiscences about her husband's life provide a helpful context within which to read some of his more biographical letters. Elsewhere, in an interview, she has also provided the apt observation that "[Schuon's] function in the world is really to bring people back to practice their religion . . . to bring them back to a path that leads to God." She continued, "[M]any people have gone back and practiced their religion very seriously after having read his books. He wants to help us to go back to where we belong."[8] Her view accords with that of Schuon himself, who writes in the preface to one of his books:

> [E]verything has been said already, though it is far from being the case that everyone has always understood it. There can therefore be no question of presenting "new truths"; however, what is needed in our time, and indeed in every age as it moves away from the origins of Revelation, is to provide some people with keys fashioned afresh—keys no better than the old ones but merely more elaborated and reflective—in order to help

[7] Madame Schuon's Introduction is based upon her article "Frithjof Schuon: souvenirs et anecdotes", published in *Le Dossier H: Frithjof Schuon* (Lausanne: Les Éditions de l'Āge d'Homme, 2001), pp. 367–81, and published in English translation as "Frithjof Schuon: Memories and Anecdotes" in *Sacred Web* 8 (2001):35–60.

[8] Film interview 2006, quoted in *Frithjof Schuon: Messenger of the Perennial Philosophy*, p. xxii.

> them rediscover the truths written in an eternal script in the very substance of the spirit.[9]

May these extracts from Schuon's personal correspondence provide just such fresh keys to those eternal truths.

Michael Fitzgerald
Bloomington, Indiana

[9] *Understanding Islam: A New Translation with Selected Letters* (Bloomington, IN: World Wisdom, 2011), p. xvii.

INTRODUCTION

From the outset, I must warn the reader that when speaking of Frithjof Schuon I always say "the Shaykh", for I never addressed him otherwise than by this title; I used his first name only in the presence of my family members, and even then I avoided doing so, as it seemed to me totally inappropriate. During our fifty years together, I never ceased to be filled with a reverential awe in his presence and with a veneration that ever deepened as his spiritual and moral greatness unveiled itself to me by the reading of his books and by the qualities he manifested.

I met him for the first time in the spring of 1947. He was then living in a small one-room apartment in Lausanne (Switzerland), on a quiet lane without traffic, bordered on one side by a beautiful property planted with cedars and blooming trees and on the other side by a row of buildings whose entrances were adorned with little gardens. I was accompanied by one of the Shaykh's representatives who had lent me the most important books of René Guénon and who, seeing my enthusiasm and the seriousness of my intentions, had consented to talk to me about Frithjof Schuon and his role as spiritual master, and of his confraternity.

We rang the doorbell on the fourth floor, and the Shaykh, dressed in a brown caftan, opened the door. My heart, which had been beating very hard, calmed down immediately at the sight of this man whose great dignity was coupled with an affability that at once put one at ease, and whose voice was astonishingly soft and clear. He beckoned me to sit down on a cushion; he himself sat down on a low divan covered with a Turkmen blanket, while the visitor sat on the floor next to him. He was there, like a mountain of strength and serenity, his beautiful hands lying on his knees, his eyes half-closed. On the wall behind him hung a beautiful Indonesian fabric. The room was divided in two by a golden curtain behind which one could guess was the space reserved for prayer; the larger part, which looked out on a balcony, was furnished with the divan and a Gothic chest on which stood a Romanesque statuette of the Virgin Mary in majesty. The whole room was covered with nomadic Afghan rugs. Next to the divan, near the window, a ficus tree and two azaleas added a welcoming note to the sober and peaceful beauty that reigned in this place.

After a moment of silence, the Shaykh asked what my reasons were for being attracted to the spiritual life and whether I had any particular problems. Of course I had problems, but through the mere presence of this Master and by some of his words, they had as it were evaporated. Then he asked me: "Do you know how to make coffee? Could you prepare us a cup of coffee?" Delighted to be of service, I went to the kitchen. An old desk was wedged in between the door and sink by the window; on the opposite side, between the cooking stove and a closet, stood a table with piles of books and folders stacked on top of it and beneath it. A glass door gave onto the same small balcony, where an oleander was growing and flower boxes were waiting for geraniums to bloom. Everything was clean and neatly arranged so that it was easy for me to find what was needed to make coffee. I brought the coffee pot and two cups on a tray which I put before the Shaykh, happy to be able to show my respect by kneeling before him and by serving him the coffee. I refused as politely as I could his offer to drink also. He then turned to my companion and asked among other things: "How is your cat?" This disciple, in fact, owned a beautiful Persian cat and he recounted that he liked to blow soap bubbles to watch the cat trying to catch them. The Shaykh said with a slight smile: "I wonder whether you bought the bubbles for your cat or for yourself?" I do not remember anything else, except the fact that the Shaykh did not drink all his coffee and poured the rest into the pot of the ficus tree. Later I learned that this was his habit, and the plant was indeed thriving.

After this interview I went back home, my heart filled with a sweet joy. I had expected a severe interrogation, but everything had been so simple and natural. The sound of his soft voice continued ringing in my ears and I could not forget his deeply mysterious gaze; (for a long time I believed that his eyes were black, whereas in reality they were gray-blue).

A few days later, from the tramcar in which I was returning from work, I saw the Shaykh in the street: he was carrying a net filled with groceries, walking with an energetic gait that stood in contrast to the recollected expression of his face. Like so many times thereafter, I was struck by this fascinating combination of irresistible strength and serene inwardness.

But I began to ask myself some questions: how was it possible that a man, who for more than ten years had been the head of a *Tarīqah* with numerous disciples, that such a man was living in the tiniest apartment, had to open the door himself for his visitors, had to do his own shopping, his cooking and who knows what else? Also, it seemed to me that he did not look well. Did he have any health problems? Was he well nourished? The answers came to me only later.

Soon after my first encounter with the Shaykh, I was invited from time to time to prayer meetings together with other friends. After a simple meal—rye bread, cheese, fruit, and tea—taken in silence, the Shaykh would speak of doctrine and the spiritual life and would answer questions. On these occasions, I would invariably feel a powerful breath of benediction coming out of his mouth; it was almost as if I could see rays of light emanating from him. He was seated on his divan in Moroccan dress, as were his disciples who were sitting on the floor in a half circle, the women in the rear. The traditional garment, which the Shaykh insisted upon, gave dignity to each one. Two Moroccan lamps of finely chiseled copper cast delicate lace patterns on the ceiling and walls, and while we were performing the rites, incense filled the air. All was sacred beauty and peace, and I would walk home after these evenings as if drunk with the wine of truth.

One day Lucy von Dechend (an old friend of the Schuon family and herself a disciple) who used to type the Shaykh's articles, asked me whether I could take over this job since she had to leave for a few months, and she handed me the manuscript of the article "Microcosm and Symbol" which was later to appear in *The Eye of the Heart*. I was to deliver my work on a Wednesday at six o'clock in the evening and fetch another article, thus having the privilege of seeing the Shaykh quite regularly. Each time he would ask me whether I had understood everything; so I acquired the habit of putting myself in the place of the reader and if a passage seemed a bit too difficult to understand, I would indicate it to the Shaykh who, to my great astonishment, would change the phrasing. I was astonished indeed that such an intelligent man would listen to a young "beginner" like myself, but humility was at the base of his character—it could not be otherwise—and he liked to ask for advice from his friends on many a question. He would write his articles in one stroke, in a few days, and would recast them only once they were typewritten; then one had to recopy them so that everything would be clear for the publisher, though his handwriting and his corrections were always very clear.

About one year after our first meeting, he asked me whether I could come and cook for him once a week. I tried my best to cook wholesome meals, to which he invited me without exception—an offer I had not expected. After the meal, he would read to me mystical poems of St. John of the Cross and St. Theresa of the Child Jesus. He loved this young saint very much, saying that her greatness consisted precisely in her holy littleness, and he lent me *The Story of a Soul.* He was at that time absorbed in the reading of the Church Fathers and the Christian mystics; it was then that he wrote "Christic Mysteries", an article which helped me to understand Christianity in depth, like everything he would later write on this subject.[3]

Another book which was lent to me was *Black Elk Speaks*, the dictated autobiography of a sage and holy man of the Sioux, who in his youth experienced the heroic resistance of his people against the whites and who at the same time received visions in order to help his neighbors spiritually and medically. I knew practically nothing about the American Indians, and this book was an opening into a totally unsuspected world. The Shaykh himself was so impressed by it that he suggested to one of his American disciples, Joseph Epes Brown, future professor of ethnology, to travel out West to try and find this sage in order to obtain more ample information about his religion. Brown found him and stayed with him for almost a whole year, during which Black Elk confided to him all his knowledge on the seven essential rites of his people; the result was the book *The Sacred Pipe* and a friendship with Benjamin, Black Elk's son, who would open many a door to us during our travels in the American West.

—— ·:· ——

When we were engaged, we would on weekends go for walks by the lake. The Shaykh loved this lake which, with its calm surface and the majesty of the mountains in the distance, had become like an extension of his own soul. He used to go early in the morning to the Quai

[3] The French article "Mystères Christiques" first appeared in the journal *Études Traditionnelles* (Paris, July-August 1948), but remains unpublished in English; portions of this early article were, however, incorporated into Schuon's subsequent books, notably *The Transcendent Unity of Religions* (London: Faber & Faber, 1953) and *Gnosis: Divine Wisdom* (London: John Murray, 1959).

d'Ouchy to breathe in deeply the Presence of God. He would but rarely meet other pedestrians, also in search of solitude, as for example King Alfonso XIII of Spain, the venerable Bey of Tunis, or a then well-known orchestra conductor, or General Guisan of the Swiss army. He would greet them with a nod and they would respond to his greeting. During our walks the Shaykh explained to me the different meanings of the Islamic testimony of faith, the *Shahādah* ("there is no god but the one God"), saying that one could replace the word "god" by any positive quality: there is no beauty but *the* Beauty, there is no justice but *the* Justice, and so on, and finally: there is no reality but *the* Reality. He spoke much of the "metaphysical transparency of phenomena" and it was obvious that he saw God in everything and everything in God. For me, who until then had conceived of God as dwelling in a far-off Beyond, these conversations were like a revelation that allowed me to intuit the nearness of the divine Presence.

The respect which the Shaykh had for all creation manifested itself in little things. For example, when crossing a meadow, he would avoid stepping on the daisies, or if sparrows were picking up crumbs on a sidewalk, he would wait until they flew away or make a detour not to disturb them. He would never kill an insect: if a spider or centipede showed up in his room, he would get a drinking glass, put it upside down over the beast, glide a postcard under it and throw the thus imprisoned insect out of the window. He loved cats and would not tolerate that one disturb them during their sleep or in their contemplative states; when our cat lay down on the Shaykh's desk to prevent him from writing—he seemed to be jealous of the attention given to the pad—that was a real problem! I would be called to come to the rescue and lift our little feline off his forbidden couch. After we had moved into our new house in Pully, the Shaykh was helping me plant flowers in the garden, when suddenly he stopped, turned pale, and said: "I cannot go on with this task—with the spade I have cut a worm in two . . ."

Some animals would respond to this love and this respect. Dogs often would follow the Shaykh, wagging their tails, or they would stop barking when he walked by a house they were supposed to guard. At the zoo in Rabat (Morocco), all the sleeping male lions suddenly got up and roared powerfully at the exact moment that the Shaykh entered the half-circle of their cages. The lions wished to greet him! This impressive salute lasted a few seconds and then the silence of the felines' nap reigned again. A similar thing happened during a visit to the menagerie of the Knie Circus in Switzerland where four adult elephants, who were peacefully swaying their trunks, suddenly lifted their trunks in salutation when the Shaykh passed near them!

As a child, little Frithjof had the habit of praying throughout the half-hour walk to school. During a lesson of Biblical history, his teacher had spoken about the injunction to "pray without ceasing", an injunction the child took very seriously. Now one day as he was walking home talking to God, a big black dog with a vicious look attacked him, threw him to the ground and threatened to bite his throat when a beautiful German shepherd appeared, chased away the black beast and accompanied the little boy all the way home.

Much later—the Shaykh had already been for some years the head of a flourishing *Tarīqah*—his mother, who had not the slightest understanding of her son, was criticizing him bitterly for not having studied law or medicine, asserting that he was a failure in life, etc., when a little cat appeared, jumped onto the Shaykh's lap and started dancing with its forepaws, gazing at him with its big eyes and purring loudly. Mrs. Schuon, who liked cats too, seeing this manifestation of love for her son, stopped on the spot and dared not continue her, at the very least, unwarranted diatribe.

(Once, however, Mrs. Schuon was proud of her son. She had, after a stroke, lost the ability to speak. The Shaykh brought her his statuette of the Virgin and said to his mother: "Look at this statue and try to say '*Ave Maria*'; if you persevere, you will be able to speak again." And this is what happened: after three days, she could speak normally and was telling everybody that her son had cured her—whereas the Shaykh knew very well that it was the Virgin who did so.)

As for human beings, they generally reacted towards him with respect or with a respectful inquisitiveness. His dignity and his recollected expression could not but attract the attention of certain persons. He walked as if he were carrying within himself a sacred object, and in fact, this treasure was the perpetual remembrance of God. People would ask him who he was, or tell him that he had a strong radiance or that they felt a state of well-being in his presence. The Jews took him for a rabbi, the Russians for a *staretz*, the Orthodox for a pope, the Muslims for a great *shaykh*, and some Western Americans for an Indian chief!

During a stay in Morocco, we were once invited to lunch by a merchant who was living in the middle of the medina of Fez. We went there dressed in traditional garments and the Moroccans started to follow us through the narrow lanes of the old city, forming an ever longer line behind us. The Shaykh accelerated his pace in order to escape them, but to no avail; they pursued us to the very door of our host and settled themselves, imperturbable, in front of it in the hopes of seeing us when we left. We had to wait until the time of the afternoon prayer, when everyone would go to the mosque, in order to be able to return to our hotel without hindrance.

His respectful affability also attracted the sympathy of simple people. After our engagement, the Shaykh introduced me to all the shops where he had been going during the last seven or eight years. The grocer, the butcher, the baker's wife, the proprietress of the laundry, all expressed their congratulations in the most cordial way. It was touching. Perhaps they had had a kind of gentle pity for this man who seemed as it were wrapped up in his solitude.

The caretaker of the building where the Shaykh was living, and who would come once a month to clean his apartment, had a true veneration for him. One day she begged him to please bless her and her family. The Shaykh could not but agree and one Sunday morning Mrs. G., her husband, and her daughter came and knelt before him. He prayed the "Our Father" with them and put his right hand on their heads while reciting a prayer of benediction, and the little family left overflowing with gratitude.

But the presence of the sacred can also generate hatred. Thus, the Shaykh had to suffer the painful experience of people who rebelled against him and heaped false accusations upon him. In the street it could happen that young rowdies would insult him with abusive language; usually the Shaykh would pay no attention, but once on Piccadilly Circus in London, he stopped and fixed his gaze on a group of youths who were mocking him, and he shouted in French: "Qu'est-ce que vous vous permettez?" ("How dare you?") The young people remained rooted to the spot, unable to move, and when I looked back after having crossed the square, I saw them still motionless in the same place. Exactly the same thing happened in Cambridge, Massachusetts, where a man at the passage of the Shaykh stood at attention with sneering laughter. The Shaykh stopped, fixed him with his gaze without a word, and went his way. The man remained there, frozen, unable to take down his hand from the visor of his cap until we had turned a corner, as a friend walking behind us had observed. Thanks be to God, such incidents were extremely rare.

It was most touching when little children would come spontaneously to greet him, sometimes running away from their parents or nurse to do so. With the Red Indians, where the beard is unknown, they would ask him if he was Santa Claus, and he knew very well how to put himself at their level.

Some time after our marriage, my little twin sisters, who were then eight years old, came to see us in our new apartment. The Shaykh fetched from his closet a box filled with toys and took out of it a large humming top which he made spin by pushing down several times the spring traversing it; it would then emit a mysterious sound which he described as "the music of the spheres"; then he took out of the box a child's rattle which sounded like a Balinese gamelan and of which he said that it was the "music of the angels". My two sisters listened with delight to this celestial concert and, entering into the spirit of the game, one of them spun the top and the other shook the rattle. The Shaykh watched them for a moment and then retired, not without first having brought us some illustrated books on Bali and India. My sister Anne, future Carmelite, said afterwards: "I like your husband, he knows how to please little girls." This was so true that he once did not hesitate to take with him in the train from Lausanne to Basel a blue balloon for the little daughter of a friend, because he knew she liked balloons of this color. And how many times we played ball with our neighbor's children, just as we did with Dr. Martin Lings and his wife when they would visit us in the summer!

The Shaykh knew also how to entertain little boys; he would show them his collection of Red Indian objects: a bow and arrows, a peace pipe, a necklace made of bear claws, a tomahawk and pouches and ornaments embroidered with porcupine quills or beads; he would recount to them heroic deeds of an Indian chief, which moreover he was perfectly able to illustrate with humorous little drawings.

In a general way, he liked to give pleasure, not only to children but to adults as well, and he yielded easily to requests if they were reasonable.

The Shaykh would elicit tenderness by his childlike and sometimes almost too benevolent side. With a disconcerting purity of heart, he would believe what was told him and he preferred to ignore the fact that persons with spiritual aspirations could be hypocrites or even liars. Concerning holy naivety, he often quoted the story of St. Thomas, whom a monk had summoned to the window to see a bull flying; when the monk mocked the saint for having believed him, St. Thomas answered: "I would rather believe in a bull that flies than in a monk that lies." The Shaykh would react in the same way.

—— ·:· ——

As a child, I had seen beautiful pictures of the Swiss National Park in the Canton of Grisons, and I had always wished to visit that place. Thus, I asked the Shaykh whether we could spend some time there after our marriage. He agreed; we arrived at the moment of the opening of the season so that during one week we were the only guests at the hotel and had the whole big park entirely to ourselves. Every day we went for lengthy walks, enjoying the flower-covered meadows and resting by rushing streams, observing the deer running and frolicking on the mountain pastures and the marmots playing like children in front of their burrows. For the Shaykh, who had always lived in cities, it was a wonderful experience. I felt that he was drinking in with all his being what was offered to his senses. We almost always walked in silence.

We had discovered by the side of a stream, in the middle of a pine forest, a large flat boulder where the Shaykh liked to sit and meditate. Wrapped in his cape, his eyes closed, deeply absorbed, he looked like a sage in a Taoist landscape. He was seated cross-legged, his hands on his knees, unshakable, infinitely majestic, and it seemed to me that the more I looked at him (I was sitting on the opposite side of the stream), the more his image was growing and finally merging into the grandeur of the surrounding nature. For me there was no doubt that he was one with God. I have only rarely seen the Shaykh like this, for in the presence of other people he tried to hide his spiritual states, and he always withdrew into his room when he was meditating—this is obvious—but this most majestic expression often showed on his face during sleep, and I wondered how such a man upon awaking could bear to live in a world like ours.

One day we had reached a place far above the limit of the trees, with a magnificent view on the snow-covered mountains; the Shaykh his military service he read, among other things, the life of Milarepa and the life of Ramakrishna, and he wrote down his thoughts which he communicated to his friends by mail; this was the beginning of his first book, written in German: *Leitgedanken zur Urbesinnung* (Guiding Thoughts for Primordial Meditation). Like an icebreaker in the night, he tried to clear the way towards the light of which he knew the truth by intellection and in which he wanted his neighbor to partake.

When he lost his job as a fabric designer in Paris, it was for him a sign: he had to leave Europe forever—thus he thought—and flee to the Orient, putting himself wholly in the Hands of God who would show him the path to follow. And destiny directed him to Algeria and the venerable Shaykh al-Alawi. During his three-and-a-half months' stay in the company of this great saint, many a wound began to heal; but the French police were harassing him as well as the old Shaykh because of his presence at the *zāwiyah*, so that he felt obliged to go back to France.

A few years later, when he left for India with the secret hope of disappearing there forever, World War II broke out and he was obliged to return to be drafted into the army. It was obvious that the Almighty willed that the gifts He had put into this young man should be turned to account in the West, rather than be lost in the sands of the Sahara or the waters of the Ganges. "I wished to be carried towards the Divinity on the wings of exterior as well as interior beauty, without any self-deception and in a profoundly serious and sacred manner, and thus not outside of the Truth and what it imposes on us", he wrote to a friend; and it was finally he himself who had to create about him, and with those who understood and assimilated his writings, the world of his aspirations which, precisely, was a world of truth, beauty, and greatness of soul.

—— ·⁞· ——

After our sojourn in the Grisons mountains we moved into a new apartment with three rooms on the top floor of a building, with a view on Lake Geneva. My family, who only knew that Schuon was a writer, had opposed my marriage outright ("one does not marry a man without name, without money, who has written an incomprehensible book and who, on top of it all, has the face of a prophet!");

but at last they showed themselves to be generous and we were able to afford some Berber rugs and blankets and the necessary minimum of rustic furniture in light wood of which we were dreaming. The Shaykh was leading a highly disciplined life, punctuated by the times of prayer; ever hard on himself, he was on the contrary indulgent with his disciples, taking into account the difficult work conditions of the modern world. He never changed his habits during all the years we lived together. He would get up at dawn and perform his prayers. "As long as one has not said one's prayers, one is not a human being." After a simple breakfast, he would walk down to the lake alone, as he had always done before his marriage. He had a strict need for these hours of solitude outdoors. At ten o'clock, he would receive visitors and in the afternoon, after having retired for an hour, he would write articles or letters. He answered all his mail with admirable patience and generosity, not hesitating to fill more than a dozen pages if necessary, to shed light upon all angles of a problem. Often, he would write until late at night and would get up to go back and forth in his room, less to ponder what he wished to express than to remember God. Every day he would read at least one page in the Koran (in Arabic) and he also loved to read the Psalms—Psalms 23, 63, 77, 103 and 124 were his favorites, depending on circumstances.

We would eat either sitting on the floor at a small Moroccan table or in the kitchen, in silence. "One should respect the food", and in fact the Shaykh would always eat with recollection. He could not tolerate that people have intense conversations at table, and when I answered visitors out of courtesy he would say: "Let them eat", which sufficed to impose silence on everybody. When seated, he would never lean back, and in any case we owned no chairs, only two stools, one for his desk and one for the kitchen; apart from this, we had a few Moroccan poufs. For visitors who were not accustomed to life *à l'orientale*, we had acquired two folding garden chairs which could be quickly produced from their nook. It was only during the last years of his life that the Shaykh consented to sit in an armchair to receive his visitors, but he would avoid doing so as often as possible. He would always walk in a straight, upright fashion, even during the last months of his life, weakened though he was by three heart attacks. He would wash only with cold water; to take a hot bath occurred to him as little as to smoke a hookah! If it is true that some of his habits stemmed from the fact that he had always been poor, they corresponded on the other hand to his ascetic nature. Everything he did, he would do well, without hurry, with recollected mien. One of his habits was to wash his cup or glass immediately after each meal; he also made his bed as soon as he was through with his morning prayers.

When he wanted to be informed on a subject of which he wished to treat, he would go to his bookseller friends, borrow a book and bring it back after a day or two, or he would read what he needed at the bookstore itself. He had the gift of falling immediately on the pages he needed for his information; it was as if an angel would open the book for him. This way he was not wasting his time in searching and in reading what was not useful to him. But he would also fall on errors and, with the sword of his discernment ever vigilant, he would combat them without mercy. "There is no right superior to that of the truth", seemed to be his chief motto, and his frankness did not of course attract towards him friends only. Sometimes he would buy a newspaper to know what was happening in the world; but the errors committed by the politicians would irritate him so much that he preferred to turn away from this domain. We would in any case always be informed in one way or another of the most important events.

In the 1950s, the Shaykh started to paint again. It lay in his nature to always wish to give; he would give through his books, his letters, his guiding texts for his disciples, his poems; he never ceased to give and to open inward and heavenward doors for us. Through his paintings he wished to express virtues or communicate states of being. As models, he took mainly on the one hand the Plains Indians of olden times, among whom summits of virile nobility can be found (Guénon, to whom the Shaykh had sent a dozen photographs of such Indians, wrote back: "These are indeed remarkable faces"); and on the other hand the Holy Virgin under her universal aspect of Mother of the Prophets or of the feminine Logos, who represents the summit of feminine sanctity. The paintings of the Shaykh could therefore have an ennobling and interiorizing effect for people receptive to this kind of manifestation.

The talent the Shaykh had for drawing allowed him, from the age of sixteen, to earn a living for his mother and himself as a fabric designer, while occasionally selling a painting. An art merchant in Paris, having seen some works of the young Schuon, said to him: "Young man, you have millions at the tip of your fingers." But this young man was not dreaming of an artistic career and had on the contrary at that moment decided to leave Europe forever, to withdraw from the world into a cave in the Sahara Desert or the Himalayas, while waiting, in a total annihilation of his individual will, for God's guidance. "One cannot know God's Will except in the annihilation of one's own desires; it is not for us to create an intellectual elite, it is for God to do so, if such is His Will", he wrote to a friend. "I would prefer to die rather than do something that is not the will of Heaven." In the same sense he said once to me that a *Shaykh al-barakah* is born from the ashes of his own ego.

—— ·⁝· ——

From time to time, we allowed ourselves the luxury of seeing a beautiful exotic show: the ballets of Bali, Kabuki theater, Hindu dancing; or a beautiful film on the Middle Ages or on the life of a saint. And the Shaykh did not prevent his disciples from doing the same: indeed, in a world of ugliness and triviality, the soul could learn much through the concrete vision of beauty and the expression of noble and elevated sentiments, and could thus be encouraged in the effort towards virtue. "One cannot enter the sanctuary of the Truth but in a holy manner, and this condition entails above all beauty of character." He wished us to cultivate beauty of soul and dignity of comportment, language, and dress—all qualities that threaten to disintegrate in a world where carelessness and slovenliness are almost becoming the fashion; and at that period—the fifties and the beginning of the sixties—the corrosive influence of psychoanalysis had not yet been able to creep into all manifestations of the dramatic arts.

Sometimes we listened to music; we possessed only a few records, but they were well chosen for the interiorizing and uplifting power of the melodies. In addition to records of Hindu, Japanese, or Balinese music, we had some classical pieces of which the Shaykh said they were true inspirations and like doors opening upon Paradise; for example, the "Lullaby" of Sibelius, the Moonlight Sonata, the second movement of Beethoven's Seventh Symphony, the first movement of the Concerto of Aranjuez by Rodrigo, "Goyescas" by Granados, "In the Steppes of Central Asia" by Borodin. And Gypsy music! We never tired of listening to it. The Shaykh's father was a violinist and had given concerts in Russia and Scandinavia; he had specialized in the Eastern European composers and he himself could play like a Gypsy. Curiously, when we would go to a restaurant where Gypsies were playing, they seemed to feel an affinity with the Shaykh, for the *primas* would always come to our table and make his violin vibrate close to our ears.

—— ·:· ——

The number of visitors was increasing year after year, and life in our little apartment became almost untenable. Thus it was a true gift from Heaven when one of my family members, who had joined the Path and realized our difficult situation, offered us the means to buy a piece of land and build a house on it. We found in the vicinity of Lausanne an old abandoned orchard amidst vineyards, with a view on the lake and mountains. We could not have dreamt of anything better; it was a true little paradise that offered the Shaykh the peace and space necessary for his activities.

Friends of ours, Mr. and Mrs. Whitall Perry, bought the land next to us, which brought many advantages to us—among others, to have access to a telephone close by. The idea of having such a device in his house occurred to the Shaykh as little as having a typewriter, and we were going to do without it just as in the past, when I had to go to town to make necessary calls. The Shaykh was a man of another age, and he seemed to live more in the world of ideas than in that of everyday facts. He was like the incarnation of the verse of the Song of Songs: "I sleep, but my heart waketh",[6] or of what he says himself in a text: "God is Being, and what he loves in us is the aspect of being; we must, when we think of God, repose in being." However, he was always aware of what was going on around him. While traveling with friends, we were sometimes engaged in conversation in which he did not take part. But it sufficed that someone utter a stupidity for him to swoop down like an eagle to correct the error. It was the same when he was asked a question: the answer would spring forth without the slightest hesitation. He used to carry with him a little notebook in which he would jot down ideas or phrases for his articles. Not long ago, I found in one of these booklets the following sentence, which had impressed me

[6] Song of Sol. 5:2.

when I read the chapter on the Koran in *Understanding Islam*: "The seeming incoherence of [sacred Scriptures] always has the same cause, namely the incommensurable disproportion between the Spirit on the one hand and the limited resources of human language on the other; it is as if the poor and coagulated language of mortal man would break under the formidable pressure of the heavenly Word into a thousand fragments, or as if God, in order to express a thousand truths, had but a dozen words at his disposal and so had to use ellipses, abridgements, and symbolical syntheses."[7] If ever he had forgotten his notebook he would ask me to remind him of such or such a sentence or word; thus one day he said: "Remind me of the word 'boomerang' when we are back home." "Boomerang?" "Yes, boomerang." Intrigued, I went in the evening to read what on earth he could have written, and I read: "To the question of knowing why man has been placed in the world when his fundamental vocation is to leave it, we would reply: it is precisely so that there would be someone who returns to God; this is to say that All-Possibility requires that God not only project Himself, but also realize the liberating beatitude of return. . . . Just as the boomerang by its very form is destined to return to him who has thrown it, so man is predestined by his form to return to his divine Prototype; whether he wills it or not, man is 'condemned' to transcendence."[8]

The Shaykh again and again surprised me by his presence of mind or his practical sense. If it happened that he dropped an object, he would catch it midway, before it reached the ground; when a candle had left spots of wax on the rug, he would put one or two blotting papers on the spot, heat some water in a flat cooking pot which he would put on the blotting paper, and in no time the wax would be absorbed. Or again: we had dug in our orchard a flat space in order to be able to pitch the tipi we had brought back from the American West; now the birds came by the dozens to peck the grains I had sowed to have grass grow on the freshly prepared patch, and I complained about this to the Shaykh. "Go and ask our neighbor for some hay and cover the area with it", he said, as if he had always been an agriculturist, and the system proved efficacious.

[7] *Understanding Islam*, chap. "The Quran" (Bloomington, IN: World Wisdom, 1994), pp. 40–41.

[8] *The Play of Masks*, chap. "Man in the Cosmogonic Projection" (Bloomington, IN: World Wisdom, 1992), pp. 19, 20.

The Shaykh loved thunderstorms and he would watch them from his balcony. The more lightning flashes and thunderclaps, the happier he was. "The Wrath of God consoles me and makes me breathe." There was in his character, besides his great goodness, a volcanic trait that made one think of Beethoven. He suffered from the fact that he could never throw someone out the door, as any spiritual master in the Orient could do with impunity; in the West, this was not possible and it was one of the reasons that made him ill. Thunderstorms were for him a manifestation of the divine Justice, which he knew some day would strike.

The years went by, our trees blossomed and gave us fruit, the meadow with its many wildflowers and the birds with their variegated songs gave us delight. All could have been beauty and harmony if the Evil One had not constantly been on the lookout to torment the Shaykh; the defections, treasons, calumnies followed one upon another, and for a man like the Shaykh, who was faithfulness and rectitude incarnate and who had an almost superhuman capacity for forgiveness, these disappointments, *a priori* inconceivable to him, ended by breaking down his physical resistance; he became gravely ill with asthma and earnestly thought of no longer accepting new postulants to the Path and retiring somewhere in the mountains, far from the world.

But Heaven intervened and sent him its most gentle and most beautiful Messenger, the Virgin Mary, for whom the Shaykh had always had a great veneration; She gave him courage and renewed strength. After a stay of one month in Morocco, which was full of blessings, our life continued as before and a whole river of young aspirants came to knock at our door.

Fifteen more years went by, interrupted by fruitful trips to the East and West and restful stays in the Swiss mountains, when one day the Shaykh received an absolutely certain sign from Heaven to emigrate to America. This sign was so imperious that when I told the Shaykh, after a visit to the American Consulate, that there was no possibility for us to immigrate, he had a crisis of asthma and said in that case we should try Canada or Mexico. Fortunately, thanks to the help of an American friend who was a lawyer, the obstacles could be removed and it is thus that we left for the forests of Indiana.

I was anxious to tell this episode because there have been many erroneous speculations about our departure from Switzerland. In fact, the Shaykh would never have undertaken such a change in his life—he was then already seventy-three years old—without being sure it was the divine Will. Already a few years before, it had been suggested to us that we move to Morocco; we were shown very tempting properties near Tangier, but he said: "To take such an important step, I must have a sign from Heaven."

Thanks to the foundation of a publishing company specializing in the publication of the Shaykh's writings, which we helped to translate into English, the work of Frithjof Schuon became more and more well known. All his life the Shaykh wanted one thing only: to express the Truth, to draw to the Truth, and to live the Truth. Is the goal he proposes too high?

In a letter addressed to his friend, Titus Burckhardt, he writes: "Greatness is the necessary condition for the return to God, for God is great and only what is great can reach the great. This greatness is above all union of the soul with God. To him for whom this union is inaccessible, fervor may be accessible, and to him for whom fervor is out of reach, perseverance or faithfulness is certainly accessible, because this is a greatness accessible to any spiritual person."[9]

In the last two-and-a-half years of his life, the Shaykh wrote over 3,000 poems, didactic as well as lyrical—a testament, as it were, in which he distills to the last drop his wisdom and his soul in verses which go straight to the heart for whoever can read them in the original German.[10]

After arising for his prayers, he passed away at dawn on May 5, 1998, seated in his armchair, invoking the Name of God.

[9] Letter dated May, 1944.

[10] For more on Schuon's poetry, see *Frithjof Schuon: Messenger of the Perennial Philosophy*, chap. 23, "A Profusion of Songs".

Already as a child, I read the *Bhagavad Gītā* and was deeply moved by Indian and Buddhist art; there, I found the whole Truth on the one hand and the most direct expression of the Sacred on the other. In Hinduism, I felt completely at home, it was for me the homeland of pure metaphysics as well as primordial spirituality and thus also sacred nudity; it contains indeed every spiritual possibility, from the simplest to the most finely-shaded and complex.

And in addition to this, I had from childhood a special relationship with the American Indian world: boundless virgin nature; eagle and sun; metaphysics of the directions of space; the all-transcending and at the same time all-pervading Great Spirit. Then the ideal of self-mastery, of transcending oneself, of dignity; the eagle soaring towards the sun, relived in the Sun Dance.

November 4. My relationship with Islam results from the fact that Islam is founded on the confession of Unity; then from the fact that everyone is his own priest, and also that Islam could offer me an initiation and a spiritual method; and finally from my providential encounter with an Islamic saint.

The most important—and therefore altogether decisive—thought in life is the consciousness that God is the Sovereign Good, to which all earthly values bear witness. Then come two fundamental attitudes: surrender to God's Will and trust in God's Goodness; one must resign oneself to the unavoidable, and this without ever doubting God's Mercy, which indeed has the last word for us and which is contained in the supreme Name.

Our right relationship with the world results from our right relationship with God; from this second relationship, which in reality is the first, come also the essential virtues; and these are at the same time a condition of that relationship.

The primordial thought that God is the Sovereign Good silences—by its very nature—all the mental din of the world; its preeminence in the soul constitutes the spiritual nobility of man, and thus also the right relationship to the world around him.

Wherever we are conscious of God, there always is the Center, and there also is the essence of our happiness.

1. Something Great Spoke to Me
Ages 18–20

"*Interactions of Spirit and Body*"
Mulhouse, France, late 1925 to Lucy von Dechend

On receiving the transcripts of my lecture, I was struck by your energetic goodwill. I thank you with all my heart for your work. Your offer to transcribe one of my plays is also a pleasant surprise, and I have already selected the phantasmagorical play "Light".

Things are not going so badly with my paintings, but I am not satisfied with "The Poet" or "The Cross". I could actually paint frescoes much more easily. On the other hand, the Isa[1] portrait, the Buddha head, and the Lama have turned out quite well.[2]

I would like to say a further word about intuition. My article says that intuition, intelligence, and experience are one. I have never spoken of an essential difference between these three *gunas*, but I have spoken of a different application of this unity. Intuition is the grasp of the objective existence of things that arises in our sensibility. It cannot be "clothed", if you will, in explanatory words, but rather in unconscious sounds or colors in an artistic creation, for as soon as it enters into consciousness it ceases to be intuition. I will give you a concrete example: I once reflected upon the interactions of spirit and body. Thanks to my intuitive gift, I beheld with my spiritual, visionary eye a rising on one side and a sinking on the other. I was completely penetrated by this feeling.

How would I have arrived at this if my intuitive gift had not brought intelligence-experience into play? How would intelligence-experience have arrived at this without intuition, which in plain German we like to call understanding of the world?

[1] Isa is the Islamic name for Jesus.

[2] Schuon painted throughout his life. See *Frithjof Schuon: Messenger of the Perennial Philosophy*, chap. 18, "An Artistic Dimension".

Sunday. I have just painted a portrait. I will bring it with me next time. Perhaps along with the other pictures, though I am not entirely satisfied with them, since they represent a striving after form. I have now managed to arrive at a mystical poverty of color.

—·⁝·—

"*My Credo*"
Mulhouse, January, 1926 to Lucy von Dechend

I am enclosing for you my attempt to conceive of a possible translation of my credo, whose form is open to question; as I said, I make no claim to linguistic correctness, for this is beyond my capacity.

Here is my attempt to coin English "equivalents" for my German formulations: "I believe in the divine primary Self and its singleness, in the infinity of itself in its utterances, in the sempiternity of self, in the inconstancy of individual appearance, and the efficacity of every single thing in the universe; in inner event as the reality and in beauty as its completion; in the Will of the Divine throughout existence, in the manifestation of the godlike intellect and the aspiration of finished beings; in the postulation and fulfilment through the microcosmic event of Self; in the eternity of consciousness, the development of the Unique in the Self and the spiritualizing of the World; the ultimate bliss of fulfilment and the Path of Radiancy; in the tree of degeneration . . ."[3] The last sentence seems to me to enter too much into what is individual, contingent, whereas in fact the expression should be as absolute and universal as possible.

—·⁝·—

"*The Great Stillness*"
Mulhouse, April, 1926 to Lucy von Dechend

You write in your last letter that you would be happy to die for what is Great; it seems to me that it is more valuable, and at the same time

[3] This statement is written in English in the original letter.

more difficult, to live even one day for it. Dying is the least part of devotion; death is the smallest thing in life.

For me there is nothing great in expecting nothing from life, fearing nothing in life, for I know that everything that happens to me does so because it must; otherwise how could it happen? What influences my destiny decisively is what I alone must overcome, it is my own original problem; and it becomes clear from this why suicide in order to escape a situation is so senseless and foolish; surely every being who is exposed to the cycle of interactions must unfailingly empty every chalice it had passed by with ashen face—be it here or there; and how well known it is to life's initiate that the first cup is always the easiest, and that every rejected cup returns, whatever form it may assume. Who is to be feared in this other than we ourselves?

Whoso wishes to enter the great Stillness must become identical with the geometrical point. Alluring splendor is earthly, God's Beauty is veiled, it has nothing seductive about it, it is silent. But to whom am I saying this! Would it not be preferable to write nothing? Everything noble is outwardly cold and inwardly hot.

What does talent matter? Everything is a matter of attitude, of the way talent is used. No one is great through talent, but through the way he handles it. The virtuoso, the natural actor who belongs in the marketplace and in the world of appearances, is accustomed to wearing his heart upon his sleeve; he becomes outwardly hot and inwardly cold.

—— ·:· ——

"*Something Great Spoke to Me*"
Mulhouse, July, 1926 to Lucy von Dechend

Perhaps in the near future I will come to speak of a question of faith that separates us, namely your pitiful and abominable spiritism, to which I unfortunately submitted myself despite grave reservations and suspicions at a time when my soul's distress robbed me of my mind. As this letter is in any case already long, I will say only one thing for now: that since the great miracle came to me, I have an infallible touchstone against all false gold, and was granted an insight that is well able to distinguish the signs of darkness.[4] No contract based on reciprocity is possible between me and spiritism, and you will one day have to choose between my spirit and the dark bequest of my unfortunate father, unless you were to find the promised land of your yearning somewhere else altogether.

Evening. But Lucy, now that the evening has come over me, so marvelous and deep blue, other tones are also resounding in my soul, and I want to recount other things to you; all my evenings are so wonderful, as austere and strange as a secret and yet so full of sweetness. I often accompany a young apprentice to the station and chat with him, then turn to my own paths, which appear desolate and cheerless to others, but are full of magic for me because here something Great spoke to me. I often stroll for an hour in the woods or lean against a tree, when the branches murmur and whisper in the darkness and night winds lay their cool hands on my countenance. Then I no longer know when and where I am living, it could be in Manchuria or Persia or the land of the Blackfeet, it could have been a hundred or thousand years ago; tall, bare trees, starry sky with the moon, weaving twilight; that is all.

———

"*Respect for Chinese Culture*"
Mulhouse, November 14, 1927 to Jakob Jenny

My journey to Belgium was very instructive.[5] The Trappist monastery is said to be one of the most important that exists; the monks are very cultivated, even urbane. My brother's[6] reserved, ascetic nature seems to have found its home there; he has fully found his way in his mode

[4] Schuon never spoke of this "great miracle" (*grosse Wunder*) in his later life and we thus have no additional information about the event; the German *Wunder* can mean "miracle", "wonder", or "marvel".

[5] Schuon's brother was a Trappist monk living at the Abbey of Notre-Dame de Scourmont, Belgium. This letter was written shortly after Schuon returned from a visit to the monastery in Belgium.

[6] Eric Schuon, Father Gall.

of life and his faith. And I would be the last to cast aspersions on his ideal of religious life.

I had an interesting talk with the Prior, as was to be expected without agreement: the Theosophists and Krishnamurti were mentioned in passing, as were Tagore and Gandhi. More stimulating for me was my conversation with a young Chinese man I met in the hotel, who has in the meantime written to me; his explanations concerning the state of affairs in the Middle Kingdom were particularly valuable for me; he himself belongs to the Nationalist Party of Nanking. He remarked among other things that those who were stronger were always the more civilized, when China was once strong. When I confided to him my opinion regarding the shamefulness of the unequal treaties[7] and my respect for Chinese culture, the mask of legendary "inscrutability" fell from him and he became positively cordial. He also showed me my errors in writing Chinese characters and we parted with deep mutual esteem.[8]

Anyone who understands Taoism must admit that it is peerless and unique; such an understanding is extraordinarily rare, particularly today, not to mention that it has always been difficult, since to be able to approach such doctrines, a man must as it were change himself by rising above himself. Hovelacque compares Lao Tzu with the English poet Wordsworth, and thinks he can understand Taoism better through Swedenborg, Blake, Coleridge, Shelley, Schelling, Fichte, Hegel, and Schopenhauer. Claude Farrère goes furthest of all, calling Lao Tzu the "father of spiritism" and wondering whether spiritism and metaphysics—the highest and ultimate knowledge—might not be "close relatives". It is to be hoped that René Guénon,[9] perhaps the only one in modern times whose vocation it is to understand Eastern thought, will write a book on Taoism as he has done on the *Vedānta*; namely with ruthless objectivity, without fine words, without far-

[7] A series of treaties made in the nineteenth and early twentieth centuries between China and various Western powers, in which China was forced to concede much of its sovereignty.

[8] Several of Schuon's letters, including this one, contain his Chinese calligraphy of verses from sacred texts.

[9] This is the first surviving letter with a reference to René Guénon, whose ideas had influenced Schuon and his friends after Lucy von Dechend gave him a copy of Guénon's *Orient et Occident* (East and West) in 1924. See *Frithjof Schuon: Messenger of the Perennial Philosophy*, chap. 4, "Introduction to Guénon".

fetched and simple-minded fantasies à la Henri Massis, and above all without artificial systematization, without "philosophy"; I shudder at the thought of the superficial foreword in Payot's translation of the *Tao Te Ching*, which compares Lao Tzu with Rousseau and considers him inferior to the Buddha.

—— ·:· ——

"*My Paintings of Indians*"[10]
Mulhouse/Besançon,[11] 1927 to Lucy von Dechend

On Saturday I spent the whole afternoon in the tent with the Indians, who are performing their war dances here. I showed them my paintings of Indians, which they regarded with interest and unerring insight, and gave them cigarettes. I felt like a child in their midst; they were a good bit taller than me, except for one who laid his hand on his chest and said, "I am a Delaware." He is in fact the most interesting of all, apart from the very old chief: broad-shouldered, with a faintly proud expression, as well as being very typically Indian in all his movements. Another one wears his hair loose and has something mistrustful in his nature; a third is a strikingly handsome and noble young man—his brown face came very near me as he lit his cigarette from mine (a "peace cigarette"). Naturally the women also smoked; old Chief Rain Crow was the only one who regarded me coldly and indifferently from his seat and, after observing me briefly, closed his eyes. I did not dare offer him any cigarettes, particularly because the other Indians showed much veneration in his presence, but as a precaution I placed a few on the table; neither did he take notice of the paintings that lay colorfully spread out before him. Our conversation in English went quite well. A portly tribesman introduced his little boy to me and pointed out the resemblance. I told them that I love the red race, that I have relatives over there, etc.[12]

[10] This is Schuon's first meeting with American Indians. See *Frithjof Schuon: Messenger of the Perennial Philosophy*, chap. 16, "The American Indian Spirit".

[11] Written during Schuon's obligatory French military training, which took place in Besançon.

[12] Around the time of his move to America, Schuon wrote: "Fifteen members of my

Last Sunday I fired a gun for the first time; the sergeant yelled at me: "Don't close your eyes, damn it!" He is by the way an amiable Frenchman.

—·:·—

"*To Understand the* Tao Te Ching"
Basel, Switzerland, February 1, 1928 to Jakob Jenny

When I arrived in Basel, I found the German translation of the *Tao Te Ching* by Alexander Ular, or rather his recreation of it, which despite the naive claims of the commentator is anything but irreproachable. First of all, it is wrong to see in Taoism an opposition to the *Vedānta*, a view due merely to the prejudice that literary influences must have taken place whenever discernible intellectual similarities exist, so that whenever one wishes as it were to "save" a sage's honor and establish his intellectual independence—a very relative thing—one must force irreconcilable oppositions onto other teachings. Next, the purely outward, debatable, and disgraceful analogy between Lao Tzu and the imprudent, passionate, misguided, and myopic scribbler Nietzsche is very vexing. Finally, the claim that one must take into account the earlier meaning of ideograms that express abstract concepts, by making them literal and concrete, is nothing more than a meaningless scholarly nicety, given the fact that such possible fluctuations in the meaning of individual characters have no influence on the correct understanding of the *Tao Te Ching.*

To attach any importance to such possibilities—to believe that philological contingencies could encroach upon the understanding of such a profound and universal work—indicates an insufficient capacity to understand Lao Tzu from the start. As far as I am concerned, *Tao* can have meant, twenty-five centuries ago, a "well-trodden path" or a "way", and today may be taken by some to mean "sense" or "reason"

family emigrated to the United States under President Lincoln; the men fought in the Civil War. I knew only two of these relatives, by correspondence, when I was a child and a young man: my great-aunt, Mrs. Emma Klakring-Rau (my grandmother's sister), and her son, Mr. Alfred Klakring. Mr. Klakring was a cartographer for the Smithsonian Institute. . . . They wrote me many letters and told me about life in America and sent me many fine books" ("Affinities with America", unpublished).

or nothing at all: the conceptual gesture of the sentence, "The *Tao* that can be expressed is not the eternal *Tao*"[13] has nothing to do with the words that clothe it. Lao Tzu confirms this himself in the second sentence of his book: "The name that can be named is not the true name." To understand the *Tao Te Ching*, one must bring each and every one of its sentences to bear on itself. The words here express values, and the sentences relationships, much more than they do concepts and ideas. Generally speaking, in the *Tao Te Ching*, as in the *Bhagavad Gītā*, the Gospels, the Koran, and all the profound writings of humanity, every sentence has several meanings that correspond to applications in a given domain. And the form in which the sentence is necessarily expressed—because precisely as a sentence, it must have a form—is no more than a necessary evil, and yet no evil, since he whose vocation it is to understand profound things cannot be hindered in his understanding by anything.

I once rendered the above-mentioned first sentence of the *Tao Te Ching*[14] as: "Definable knowledge is not true knowledge", or in the same way, "Discernible intelligence is not ultimate intelligence". One cannot learn to understand books such as the *Tao Te Ching* simply by reading them: one must in a sense understand them before one approaches them. If I knew Chinese it would not matter if I did not understand individual words, or that I could not "conceptualize" certain maxims, which in any case is not my inclination. The *Tao Te Ching* is for me a corroboration and illustration of the Truth that in other Scriptures is expressed more graphically, literally, and less obscurely, but perhaps for this reason also more one-sidedly or otherwise inadequately. These Scriptures seek to allow latent, purely spiritual capacities to blossom by means of unforeseen inner workings, which can also occur indirectly by means of other experiences whose effects are "realizatory", "disillusioning", "sattvic", or "solar".

—— ·⁝· ——

[13] Quoted in Chinese calligraphy in Schuon's own hand.

[14] Again, quoted in Chinese.

"*Doctrine of Deliverance*"
Mulhouse, early 1928 to Lucy von Dechend

My great work, which will probably be called "The Doctrine of Deliverance", is already thought out in detail and many of its ideas are already essentially written down, but I have no time to perfect it—neither is it yet time.[15] It will perhaps be the only book I will write. First part: "Deliverance through Inner Scripture"; second part: "The Parable"; third part: "Visions and Songs"—philosophical, dithyrambical, and lyrical. But I must live my doctrine up to the last drop, experience in myself its deepest pain and triumph.

[15] Schuon continued to refine and edit this manuscript for several years, eventually publishing his first book, *Leitgedanken zur Urbesinnung* (Guiding Thoughts for Primordial Meditation), in 1935.

2. I Stand At a Crossraods
Ages 20–25

"Servant of Truth"
Mulhouse, February 21, 1928 to Jakob Jenny

I am nothing but the poorest, soberest, simplest servant of Truth, who needs no fame and no luster other than that which does not come from me. I cease to care for myself and forget often who I am and even that I exist; my contemplation of the Infinite will surely make of me what I should be according to its wont, as long as I live as a finite being.

I contemplate the Infinite ceaselessly. During the day it envelops my soul like a deep, distant rhythm coming from the ocean's depths. I do not forget it in sleep; it is like a gaze of the gods that continuously rests upon me with cool stillness. It will transform me, impure vessel, according to its will. Man needs only to close himself to the finite and open himself to the Infinite in order for it to stream into him. I wish my life to be a listening to holy monotony, an ever-present resting in the Ultimate, in the still white heights where no muffled sound, no sultry air, and no flickering of doubt penetrates me any longer. When I tell you that I once wrote in my notes that every willing is a non-willing of God; every feeling, a non-feeling of God; every thinking, a non-thinking of God, you will perhaps, without stumbling upon the unavoidable clumsiness of the words, have a sense of how literally, palpably, and directly I comprehend my ideal, and how little I allow myself to be diverted from my solitary path by people's childish taste.

—— ⁘ ——

"Earnest Longing for the Infinite"
Mulhouse, February 26, 1928 to Lucy von Dechend

I believe that there are only two positions with regard to woman, namely one that takes femininity into account and another that addresses itself

they can only crumble, as if carried away by the breath of an infinitely severe silence.

I do not envy worldly men. Everything must die—not only the body's flower, but also the fortress that man's boundless vanity built on bubbles, the false paradise and false peace that his hollow spiritual pride invented; everything will be dissolved at *Mahādeva*'s feet in whimpering shame.

Death is an expression of Being or a facet of Reality; the "now" is another. This "now" is everything; may we take hold of it! When we die, we look at the world from the point of view of a single present that compensates for our existence and absorbs it into the Immutable.

I am a bridegroom; I, too, am wooing a woman: Parvati.

—·⁝·—

"*Morning of Deliverance*"

Besançon, December 8, 1929 to Jakob Jenny

I have indeed been in error, and have been through the same errors whose effects now darken your world. It had to be: I had to find what I now possess without a master, alone, groping in the darkness; it was my destiny. No man has passed through more severe confusion than I did last winter; and what saved me from destruction, from death, was the fact of my very existence; not my ideas, not my wisdom, shaken and wrung to the core, but rather the superhuman fact of the grace that led me into darkness and raised me out of the darkness.

I come to this subject because you are quite disconsolate; since you consider me healthy and strong—and not without reason, for I am so—perhaps it will not be without value for you if he who is released and affirming speaks of last winter's valley of death and the miracle by which he escaped a thousand-fold ruin. This man, who is now a teacher and master in the Spirit and feels the proximity of the Ultimate in every hour, who stands victorious in the present and has found the deep mystery of joy in the Divine, had to experience in sunless winter days the piece-by-piece paling and freezing of all that constituted the garden of his world; he had to see the icy hand of death strangle his dreams, and suffer the faltering existence of a living corpse.

And then the morning of deliverance, which came to me so soberly and yet with such painful sweetness, like the indifferent countenance of a girl who nevertheless has tears in her eyes; and everything passed through my soul like a roaring vision, and I thought mostly of my earliest childhood. But enough said: I have tasted death and I know how the dying must feel. Then came a time when I tried to realize naked knowledge and naked will, and burned everything that was the content of knowledge or will. I wish to pass over the phases of my recovery; but one thing is certain and bears witness to the omnipotence of ideas, or of the spiritual: had I then been an atheist or a worldly man, I would have fallen into incurable derangement or suicide; what guided and saved me was an idea, which I could not even grasp at that time, but which lay in me and worked liked a healing balm: my faith, my spirituality—Grace.

Evening. The *yogin* is like the flower that manifests the Master's splendor by its blossom, its fragrance. In this also lies the secret of men's yearning for love, for man is the restless, destructive, questioning one, whereas woman is the loving, conserving, protecting one, whose beauty is not rent by any unsettled enigma. To be able to love the Eternal Feminine as such, beyond its expression in the world of forms, is a grace; one cannot obtain a grace by force. So, love in woman the innocence of the divine morning yet untorn by any cry from a troubled human breast. Let the wild waves of your world of thoughts and imagination come to repose, so that God's Stillness may be revealed—the stillness that God in his bounty has prepared for you, for you alone. And if you are suffering now, do not defame your suffering with pathetic envy of those empty shells that call themselves "worlds". God will give you unity of soul and clarity of spirit, though chaos cover you like fog. For "O thou who art covered, arise!"[3] said *Allāh*'s messenger to Muhammad when, on the brink of madness, he wanted to throw himself from a cliff near Mecca. Your confusions will pass, as did mine, because you are a believer. No believer has ever yet perished, not a one. Think of this what you want, but I will remember you when I am with the Master; with Him who was so suddenly and

[3] Koran, *Sūrah* "Wrapped in His Cloak" [74]:1–2. Schuon's German references Friedrich Eberhard Boysen's 1775 translation.

overwhelmingly revealed to me, as that terrible winter left me, and my bones rose from the long grave.

You have understood Guénon—or rather the ideas of India—not incorrectly, but insufficiently. The world is wide. Not human feeling, but the Spirit, inclines me toward you. Give me the joy and honor of being my brother in the Spirit; for what God placed in you, he has not placed elsewhere, and what you have to fulfill according to his Will, his Destiny, no other can fulfill but you alone. God's Bounty is not so paltry that it no longer needs the individual; He lies in the individual with his undivided Infinitude.

Early morning, December 9, 1929. In the night I thought I had not yet said everything that could comfort you in your distress. It seems to me that prayer, which is an inescapable necessity for us, is like a chalice made to collect our sentiments, then unify and transform them into power to be used for the awakening and nourishing of pure spirituality; though in saying this I by no means wish to limit the nature and possibilities of prayer or to diminish its meaning. Christ was the great master of prayer, and his prayer was like a golden cup that closed protectively around the miraculous rose of his spirituality. Every master is at once a *bhakti-*, *jnāna-*, and *karma-yogin*, except that one or another of these qualities predominates in the case of a given master. To Nicodemus,[4] and in his discourses in general, Christ appears as a *jnānin*; as a man, he appears primarily as a *bhakta*; and in his life's destiny, which found its ultimate conclusion on the cross, he appears as a mighty *karma-yogin*.

I have already intimated to you that I feel Hindu, like a branch of this soul or this spirituality, which reaches from the brooding *Gopurams* of the Ganges, to the red-gold shadows of the silent *Gompas* of the Himalayas, to the melancholy splendor of a destroyed Amarapura,[5] up to Angkor Wat and all the Shaivite echoes of Mongolia and Cambodia—and which is even alive in far-away Bali. This kinship is a fact and not a voluntary monomania; it corresponds to natural laws, to an elective spiritual affinity.

[4] See John 3:1–12 for the words of Christ to Nicodemus.

[5] Amarapura is the former capital of Burma, now Myanmar; it was founded in 1787 and is now a township of the city of Mandalay.

You do not know who you are, nor what you are and will be. But you possess a rare sincerity of intelligence and goodness of heart, because of which you stand like a star among all those I know. Do not throw your heart on the base market of doubt, but rend the barriers of the small, bloodsucking denials that would cravenly kill you. "O thou who art covered, arise!"

"*The General Tendencies of Humanity*"
Paris, France,[6] June 14, 1930 to Jakob Jenny

It is neither by chance nor without meaning that we were born into those circumstances that form part of our being; for the Divine, being infinite, seeks to operate in this and other worlds in an infinite diversity of ways, and to resolve an infinite multiplicity of problems through the emanation of its Spirit. Had I been meant to be another, I would have come into the world at another time and among other people; but the Spirit's infinity had to manifest itself thus; we had to be what we are, without fleeing the world, but rather cutting through and overcoming its problems. Were it not necessary for us to stand with our spirit in this atmosphere, then we would not be here; but we have been born in our time so as to bring about the flowering of still-to-be-unfolded possibilities of humanity, no matter how opposed these possibilities may be to the general tendencies of the humanity to which we belong.

Most people live like animals, such that one can ask oneself without exaggeration what distinguishes them so much from animals; they consider themselves far above idolaters, but would not even be capable of worshipping an idol—let alone a god. The things surrounding people have lost all meaning for them; they can neither eat correctly nor sleep properly, other than in the way of animals, but not as befits human beings to whom is given the possibility of rebirth in the Spirit and victory over death. It seems that for them it is due to chance that the sun rises in the morning, that night falls again and

[6] Written while the then twenty-two-year-old Schuon was working as a textile designer in the French capital.

again, that summer follows upon spring, and winter upon autumn; they no longer have a deeper relation to anything—everything is as if suspended in the air, and nothing has any meaning, unless in the same way as for animals.

—·:·—

"*A Recovery of Western Intellectuality*"
Paris, August 23, 1931 to Jakob Jenny

I will relate to you the passages in question, first the one in my letter to Guénon, then the one from Guénon's letter.[7] I wrote: "Several times in your books you have indicated the possibility of a recovery of the Western mentality, of a return to a traditional civilization, and of a reconciliation between East and West, and on the other hand the necessity for the truly intellectual elements in the West to become conscious of themselves through a knowledge of principles, whatever may be the final solution to modern anarchy. But are there not grounds for fearing that those who would be qualified to cooperate in a recovery of Western intellectuality would be readily absorbed by the East, which would have lent them its light, even if indirectly?" Guénon answered me by saying, among others things: "However, if a Western elite were to be constituted, it is very clear that only those who have a Western *mindset* can be part of it, which is not the case for those who, as you say, can be absorbed by the East, because there is no question that that is in fact a possibility, and for this there is more than the question of birth that needs to be considered, especially in an epoch in which neither things nor people are in their true place." You ask me whether there is already a Western elite; this seems to me unlikely since Guénon did not even bring it up.

—·:·—

[7] In early 1931 Schuon initiated a correspondence with Guénon, which would continue until the latter's death two decades later.

"*Everything Depends on the Divine Will*"
Paris, November 15, 1931 to Jakob Jenny

My future is dark like that of us all. Islam is looking at me with gold-tinted pupils; will I plunge into it once and for all, exhausted from battling this foul atmosphere corroding me like a poison?

Everything depends on the divine Will; this is something that some—who want to "do" something in the West!—are so incapable of understanding, when in fact if something is to be done it must come out of our annihilation, and not out of our good pleasure or our human and fallible reasoning. A tradition comes out of blood, I would almost say out of distress—it surpasses and seizes us, it is not we who seize it, or establish it according to theories. It must be raw necessity, not vain and sterile elaboration; better that it were not, than to waste strength in doing nothing. As for myself, I have no interest in whatever it may be. I would like to bury myself in some solitary place without anyone knowing that a being with my name ever existed; but here once more what counts is not my good pleasure, but God's Will; I must be ready for anything, or nothing, without cherishing any prospect of any sort. Leave imagination alone.

I am still writing on doctrinal aspects in aphorisms—which in fact are somewhat too long to merit that designation—or in "*sūtras*"; not knowing Latin, I do so unfortunately in German, since it is a language I master, which is not the case for French.

For speaking, the best language in Europe is Italian; for writing, Latin. But with a language like German, in which hardly any words have a definite meaning, nothing can be done without complications and lyricism.[8]

—·:·—

[8] Schuon closes this letter with "Peace be upon you", written in Arabic; this is the first time he uses an Arabic phrase to close a letter.

"*Writing a Book*"
Paris, January 24, 1932 to Jakob Jenny

I am writing in the "Biarritz" in the boulevard St. Michel, where I have taken my briefcase with metaphysical writings and Arabic books.[9] I have begun writing a book in German (unfortunately not in Latin) in which I have recorded many of my older aphorisms and added new ones, some of which have become rather extensive treatises.[10] The only unity in this work lies in its spirit, not its subject matter, nor its structure. For in it are to be found observations of the most diverse kind—not only those directly related to divine Reality—and the structure consists of nothing but free sequence, the essays being outwardly rather independent and of unequal length, a few taking up several pages and others barely a line; there are thus sections or pieces rather than chapters. I am continuing this book freely as if it had neither beginning nor end.

—⁘—

"*Abandonment to the Divine*"
Paris, February 20, 1932 to René Guénon

On receiving your letter at New Years' time, I very much wanted to respond immediately, but the spiritual difficulties that beset me at the time prevented me from formulating anything that seemed to me worthy of being written to you.

My long and patient attempt at reconciliation with the "world" in which I am obliged to live has failed, so that I now find myself drowned in an isolation and solitude which, given the milieu, is unbearable and pushes me towards a single and radical solution: to an abandonment to the Divine, far from this haunted earth, to a provocation almost, a final plea, a surrender without conditions or expectations to the divine Intention; and such an initiative would

[9] While living in Paris, Schuon studied Arabic first with a Jewish immigrant from Syria and afterwards at the Paris Mosque.

[10] This book was published in 1935 as *Leitgedanken zur Urbesinnung* (Guiding Thoughts for Primordial Meditation).

also be a serious matter for those who believe, perhaps wrongly, that they are acting well in depending intellectually on me, and who, though only seeing me rarely during their visits, have placed their hopes in me and whose attitude depends on mine. I cannot tell you how loath I am to talk thus about myself, who as an individual is wholly unworthy to hold anyone's attention, especially yours; and it is impossible for me to go into more details, unless you desire them, and it is not then too late. Yet I owe you an answer to your letter and it will perhaps be possible, if such things are still relevant, to return to doctrinal considerations, which however seem to me to be insignificant at a time when the world is for me but an atrocious vampire, and when all the efforts of my reason seem to me to be nothing but helpless death gasps in a desert. None of this affects the intellect in any way; but in order not to be affected at all, it would be necessary to partake wholly of the intellect, in such a way that the individual would irresistibly be absorbed by the intellect and would no longer be effectively separate from Before reading your precious books, I lived prey to a confused hatred of the West, and it is they that instilled my thoughts with a serenity that can no longer hate, but can discern, judge, and conclude.

Before reading them, I wished to be passionately Oriental; afterwards, I noticed that I was too much so to be able to function in the modern machine, and that I was like a defective and ill-fitted part that makes the machine creak. If there must have been, according to the nature of things, a sufficient reason for my being born amidst so much suffering and abasement, there should also be one for my escaping these, outwardly, in order then to destroy their inward causes, of which my destiny has been but an "objective" projection. If it is the divine Intention, all the consequences, whatever they may be, will have to participate in conforming to the divine Essence of this intention; yet how devouring the fire of appearances is! Begone intellectual cowardliness, that great rot of the Western mind!

—— ·:· ——

"*Everything Is Finished*"

Paris, February 20, 1932 to Jakob Jenny

Now I can very well say something specific about my future. I have suddenly become jobless. I could look for other positions and, at best, stay for a few months in Basel, or do something for a living in Mulhouse; but I do not want to do that. Everything is finished. I have sufficiently "enjoyed" Europe. It has repelled me like dust. Next week I will already be in Algeria, without the least earthly hope, and even without money. What does it matter? I will give you news from there. What becomes of me is in God's Hands. Until we meet again, here below or in *Allāh*'s garden.

—·:·—

"*I Stand At a Crossroads*"

Paris, early March, 1932 to Jakob Jenny

I stand at a crossroads with three solutions: Basel, Islam, or death. The first solution would merely postpone the other two and allow me to continue writing my German book.

May God give me the courage to want nothing more than suffering, and to enjoy no further happiness—neither the happiness of a sweet fruit, nor a homeland, nor some friendship or love or peace—until I reach Paradise! If I do not weaken before the measureless dread that is opening before me, I know that the only melody of my existence will be suffering and nothing more than suffering, until my senses abandon me, and that I must love suffering like a bride. Even if I were to accept what I am offered in Basel, even if I were to soften before many entreaties on bended knee, this would only postpone my destiny.

No man can do better than to follow the call of the Divine; all of man's works are dust. People are happy to create because they do not know how miserable their creating is, and because they are incapable of understanding the divine Will; and because precisely for this reason the divine Will does not directly oppose their creating.[11]

[11] Schuon signs this letter Abd an-Nur ("Servant of the Light"); this is the first time he closes a letter with an Arabic name.

—— ·:· ——

"*Fleeing from False Peace*"
Mulhouse, April 20, 1932 to Albert Oesch

Outwardly I am "happy"; I could easily find a much more advantageous position than my former one this summer and lead an even more colorful, playful, rich life in Paris. I could follow my relatives' advice and devote myself to painting, I could live free of care for some time in Basel and Mulhouse and then by all means return to Paris and perhaps somehow make a fortune. But it is important to understand that I am not running away from suffering, but from happiness, that I am consciously trampling all possibilities, that I seek suffering and the most bitter homelessness for the realization and glorification of the Spirit, and that in doing this I ascribe no virtue to myself, but rather think that outside the Divine there is nothing good; because for people, to do nothing bad is not good, but simply reasonable.

My spiritual testament[12] has been expressed very inadequately: things that could be said in a few words are minutely explained; there are numerous repetitions; the scope of the individual sections is very diverse. Despite this, there is a copy of it in Basel for you, for which you could write an introduction when I have gone, and to which you could attach your metaphysical aphorisms and theories on art from your time in Paris. Later you could think about publishing the book, and try to explain to Westerners who the author was.

In sum, I have led an unbearable double life for years. Now, not under pressure from events, but voluntarily, I am no longer going along with it. Enough of humiliation and deception, of trampled simplicity. In a few days, I will see my brother for the last time.

I have believed until now in employers, relatives, cities, laws, friends, dreams, words, etc. I want now to believe in God and seal my faith by no longer believing in anything else; compared to my faith in God, my faith in friendship can only be relative. From now on when I believe in something, it must go through the Spirit, as does our friendship.

[12] This is in reference to *Leitgedanken zur Urbesinnung* (Guiding Thoughts for Primordial Meditation).

When I say that I am fleeing from false peace and seeking suffering, I am not denying *a priori* the possibility of a state of soul in which I would be indifferent to the bitterest events. I do not yet understand myself completely. The events towards which I am now growing will bring me to that total understanding and lead me to the certitude without which life is unbearable.

—·:·—

"*The Ultimate, Spiritual, Pure Idea*"

Forges-lèz-Chimay, Belgium,[13] April 22, 1932 to Lucy von Dechend

These last days with my brother are among the most beautiful and perhaps also most painful of my life.

Society is a machine. One must let it go and observe how its wheels turn. One must not consider it from within, as if mingled with it and caught in its ignorance, malevolence, and weakness; rather, one must observe from without, from above, how it jerks and gasps; how it follows its laws obediently and unconsciously when it gives an answer, like water into which one throws a stone.

There is only one thing: the ultimate, spiritual, pure Idea. Outside it there is only suffering and its causation.

—·:·—

"*Last Walks with My Brother*"

Forges-lèz-Chimay, April 25, 1932 to Jakob Jenny

I am writing to you from the land of green meadows, beneath a vast and blue sky; my days are filled with walks with my brother, the last ones no doubt that we will have together. He agrees perfectly with my way of envisioning my future and would do the same as me were he in the world.

[13] This letter and the subsequent letter were written during what Schuon thought would be his last visit to his brother's monastery in Belgium.

May 3. These days are extremely prosperous. I have written more in the last fifteen days than during my entire time in Paris, and if I could stay here longer, I would manage to put together a worthwhile book, whereas in Paris I can only gather fragments of inspiration of very uneven quality.

—·:·—

"*No Distinction between Mecca and Benares*"
Basel, May 25, 1932 to Albert Oesch

Have I ever said that my path to God passes through Mecca? What is that supposed to mean, for a path to God to pass "through Mecca"? If it makes a difference whether the path to God passes through Mecca or through Benares, how can you think I want to come to God "through Mecca", and thereby betray Christ and the *Vedānta*; and if there is no difference between a path to God through Mecca or through Benares, how can you say "moreover, I do not believe that for me the path to God passes through Mecca"? What is the meaning of that? How can the highest spiritual path pass through Mecca or Benares or Lhasa or Jerusalem or Rome? Is the *nirvāna* of Mecca different from the *nirvāna* of Benares because it is called *fanā'*, or is the *fanā'* of Benares different from the *fanā'* of Mecca because it is called *nirvāna*? Why and by what right and in virtue of what could your path lead to God by some other route in preference to Mecca, or, as you seem to determine, exclude Mecca altogether? Perhaps because you are better than the great initiates of Islam, *Sayyidnā* Ali and Abd al-Qadir al-Jilani and Muhyi ad-Din Ibn Arabi? Was Mecca good enough for these greatest spiritual men, whereas you do not wish to follow the path by any lesser route than Benares?

Must I explain to you once again that either we are esoterists and metaphysicians who go beyond forms as such, as Christ walked upon the waters, and consequently make no distinction between Mecca and Benares, *Allāh* and *Brahma*, or else we are exoterists, theologians, and at best mystics, and consequently live in forms like fish in water, and distinguish Mecca from Benares?

—·:·—

"I Pour My Soul"
Lausanne, Switzerland, October 1932 to Jakob Jenny

The thought of writing you has just awoken me from my dreaming, as I was sitting idly and staring out over the silver lake without seeing it, plunged completely in the memory of an old Indian melody I once heard in Paris, which at the time made me think of the Kali Ghat in Benares, of vermilion evenings heavy with gold, in the land of the dancing divinity who dances upon bodies and beats her hand-drum. And I awoke suddenly from the ocean of my love for India, laid aside my hand-drum, over which secret rhythms from Ramakrishna's soul had stolen like the fading murmurs of a dying man, looked at your letter and thought of you, whom I will perhaps not see for a long time or ever again.

Through prayer I pour my soul, which otherwise would drain away into the world of appearances, into the divine vessel; I establish as it were a human relationship between myself and the divine, I speak with Him, for He is real to me like a human being, indeed even more real, since I consider human beings to be but His fragmented and transitory reflected images. Through meditation I recognize myself and the world, I dissolve myself in meditation and it in me and both in the divine. Through breathing I participate in a certain way materially in the divine, I enter as it were bodily into the divine; I do not think the spirit, I live it, I become the breathing of the spirit, the flowing of the world soul. I perform a fast weekly, withholding food and drink from myself every Saturday. Rhythmization[14] is a connecting link between prayer, meditation, and breathing: while sitting on or above the ground or while standing, I establish a two- or three-part rhythm, using my hand-drum or body or arm movements or words, and surrender myself to one of the divine Aspects, the transforming, conserving, or creating, or the corresponding emanations or *Shaktis*—or to particular aspects of these, such as Reality or Omnipotence or Strength or Destruction, or Infinitude or infinite Beauty. My book will give you many indications; it is in the meantime the basis of my spiritual method.

[14] These terms are written in German and then in French. "Rhythmisation" is the French formulation, while the German word he uses, "Durchschwingung", has the sense of "permeation by vibration".

3. My Spiritual Father
Ages 25–27

"*Marseilles!*"
Marseilles, France, November 12, 1932 to Albert Oesch

Marseilles! In the early morning, at five o'clock, I leave the train in the bleak, sooty station and immediately have the impression of neglected, grimy surroundings, a new world awaiting me. A few rather miserable Arabs stand there, clad in a mixture of Eastern and Western rags. I then descend the stairs towards the city and when I reach the bottom look for a long time at the monument to "the Asian colonies", which portrays a beautiful Indochinese woman, naked, resting, mysterious. I wander further in the dawn until I come to the Canebière and finally to the Old Port, which smells of salt water, fish, oysters, and tar, and where dock workers, fishermen, sailors, voluptuous women, and charming children loiter. I pass narrow, raw alleyways, which defy all description, and finally reach the great ships on the dark sea, some of which bear Arabic names: Oued Tiflet, El Beit, Sidi Aissa. Then Japanese steamers, Buyo Maru and Yasukuni Maru, and a Chinese one, Shun Foong; bright Chinese characters glow on the black hulls of these ships, sacks of tea and coal are being unloaded with cranes. Sirens hoot, cries grow loud; I stroll on a wide, fortress-like mole that separates the port from the open sea, and let my gaze glide over all the ships; among them I discover also a Spanish one, a Turkish, a Dutch, and a Polish. As I continue to walk the length of the endless docks, a sallow Arab offers himself as a guide. Since it is by now midday, the Arab takes me into an inn, speaking Arabic with me on the way; he shows me his papers, his name is Hajj Shuti Muhammad, having been once to Mecca; he talks about Oran, giving me valuable information, and speaks to me of a saint who lives there, Shaykh Hajj Ahmad [al-Alawi],[1] whom the French kept under house arrest by soldiers as a

[1] Shaykh Ahmad al-Alawi (1869–1934) was the head of the *Shādhilīyyah-Darqawiyyah Tarīqah*, a Sufi order dedicated to meditation and prayer; the honorific *Hajj* indicates that he had performed the pilgrimage in Mecca.

dangerous "fanatic" and whom I should visit; my guide says he has performed several miracles.

Some ten days have passed since this meeting. I shrink from nothing any longer in Marseilles, I go through the most impoverished, light-deprived alleyways, squeeze past hoarsely-shouting Arabs and speak with them; some have retained full native dress. Most of the numerous Muhammadans here are Kabyles,[2] from whom the Arabs are distinguished sharply by their more striking facial features, yellowish or swarthy skin color, and a different expression. Yesterday, for the first time, I saw Chinese in their traditional dress. Every day I meet Hindus, some of whom retain only the turban, others nothing but the knot of hair on the back of their heads; also black men with scarification and brightly-colored scarves, Nubians, Arabs from the Red Sea, Abyssinians, gypsies, and Jews stroll through the lanes by the Vieux Port. I have found a room in the Rue Bernard du Bois, Hôtel Julien, with a wide but desolate view, opposite a long, roofed fountain and three horse stalls; to the left, at some distance, stands a triumphal arch. I have already had the visit I was expecting from Basel,[3] and am now alone again; tomorrow I will seek out Hajj Shuti so that he can help me with my departure.

I spend every morning in conversation with God; the consciousness that for the spiritual man there can be nothing but submission of his spirit to the Love of God, that everything else is error, ignorance, abasement, betrayal of oneself, and betrayal also of society, that we should keep our spirit pure and devote it exclusively to its highest possibilities, whatever the cost and the circumstance—this certitude is becoming increasingly distinct, obvious, and compelling for me, and that in turn provides a previously unknown and unexpected clarity and unity. Also, that to want the Spirit means to want nothing but the Spirit: this is plainer than ever to me.

—— ·:· ——

[2] The Kabyle people belong to the Berbers of North Africa and are native to the Djurdjura Mountains of Algeria.

[3] His friend Lucy von Dechend came to visit him.

"*Received in the* Zāwiyah"
Mostaghanem, Algeria, early December, 1932 to Jakob Jenny

"No man, having put his hand to the plough, and looking back, is fit for the kingdom of God."[4] Those who cannot break with themselves do not consider that death will break with them, that this clinging to their narrow dream world will not prevent death from shattering it. When we die, our dream fades away through God's Will; but we can also die while living, through our will, which is then a much more direct manifestation of the divine Will; we dissolve our life-dream, and transform it into strength of knowledge. For the ordinary man, reality is the enemy who annihilates him; death is the messenger of reality. For the spiritual man, unreality is the enemy whom he annihilates; the ego is the center of unreality.

My voyage has not been a simple exchange of Western multiplicity for Eastern multiplicity, nor a flight from one kind of pastime to another, but a voyage from multiplicity to unity—a voyage across the sea. At last, I find myself again as I was during my best and rarest hours in Besançon and Paris—myself as I was eternally, already in Paradise.

I thank you for your letter, all the more so because it is the first I have received here. As you have had little news of me since before I set sail, I want to tell you the essential things. As you probably know, in the final days of my stay in Marseilles, my Algerian guide introduced me to two Yemeni dervishes of the *Alawiyyah* order, who not only advised me to visit their Shaykh in Mostaghanem before my journey to Morocco, but also gave me a letter and wrote to Oran so that one of their companions would know to expect me. On the evening before my voyage, I met an Indian from Peshawar at an Arab coffeehouse frequented by the Yemenis. He had just come from Mostaghanem and congratulated me that I, too, had the possibility of visiting Shaykh al-Hajj Ahmad bin Mustafa al-Alawi; he said this Shaykh was one of the greatest Sufis in Islam and a spiritual leader whose influence reached as far as Mecca. When I departed, I did not have to concern myself with anything, the Arabs took care of everything for me and loaded me with abundant provisions for the journey.

[4] Luke 9:62.

My voyage lasted from Wednesday at five o'clock in the evening to Friday at five o'clock in the morning. During the night I stood alone on the foredeck and looked out on the wide black sea that rushed and sobbed monotonously; above stood the eternal stars; the water foamed white on the bow, the immense black funnels thrust themselves into the night; the engine barked like a dog. Then the sun rose and flooded the sea with silver. A splendid day followed. Large seagulls with crooked beaks fly resolutely after the ship, like vultures that pursue their prey with tremendous tenacity. On our left, we saw the Balearic Islands rearing up out of the sea, then on the right came the Spanish coast, on which we could discern houses and trees. For one more night, we thus glide on like a ghost ship. It is still dark when we see from afar the lights of Oran.

In Oran, I breathe the first sepulchral air of Islam. As in Mostaghanem, the Arab houses look poor, deserted, small, the women wander about like corpses in their shrouds. The houses are often yellowish or reddish, like the sandy earth, and painted over their doors are often hands[5] or crescent moons. Donkey carts jolt between automobiles and trams; beside European suits and uniforms you see billowing burnouses, wide jellabas, turbans of all shapes. Now and then wild, black-brown, sharp faces are to be seen, then again the pale, sweet faces of the Moors; the majority is made up of the "yellow" Arabs. The landscape here is so unlike that of yours in the north! Everything seems altered, even if one only sees palms now and then, and more often cacti.

Mostaghanem is ninety-five kilometers from Oran; when I arrived there I let myself be led by a small boy to the *zāwiyah* of Shaykh al-Hajj Ahmad bin Mustafa al-Alawi.

I have been received in the *zāwiyah*. The same evening the Shaykh sends me word that he is pleased at my coming. My Arabic name is written down and I am called by it;[6] they ask me questions, bring me peppermint tea and couscous; the *muqaddam* and five other dervishes sit on the mats in my room and speak with me. The next day the Shaykh's representative comes again and makes a sign for me to

[5] The protecting "Hand of Fatimah", daughter of the Prophet Muhammad.

[6] This was the occasion at the beginning of his stay in Mostaghanem when Schuon formally entered Islam and received the Arabic name of Isa (Jesus). See *Frithjof Schuon: Messenger of the Perennial Philosophy*, chap. 6, "The Shaykh al-Alawi".

follow him. We climb a small staircase and reach the Shaykh's cell. He is seated on some blankets on the ground, wearing a white turban and brown burnoose; the deep, mysterious, and infinitely noble expression of his lean and white-bearded face causes me intense emotion; never before have I have seen such a being. His words sound softly; they come almost drop by drop with long pauses between. When I am back in my cell, the *muqaddam* comes to tell me I should stay with them; if I want to go to Fez, they would not hold me back, but I may stay here as long as I want—a year or more, or only a few months if I am pressed for time—and may always return later. I then proposed three months, but will perhaps travel to Fez even earlier.

I am sitting in the corner of my room, which is furnished solely with mats and a few rugs. Through the window I have a view into the interior of the mosque, where the dervishes are kneeling, swaying their bodies and singing their sustained, swelling and fading, "*Allāh — Allāh*"; their voices fall in confusion like waves of sound.

Sometimes they dance.[7] They form a circle and hold one another's hands, their bodies stiff, their heads leaned back; then like spell-bound corpses they move up and down in wild, racing rhythm—their feet never moving from the spot—all the while gasping and rattling in time so that it sounds like the roar of a giant saw. Their eyes are closed, some faces are painfully distorted; in the center of this strangely noisy circle that moves up and down there stands a singing dervish, who by his monotonous, soothing, and yet rousing singing and hand-clapping, and at times by shrill cries, moves the dancers to rapture beyond the senses. The Shaykh sits during this and stares through it all with wide-opened eyes, as if seeing nothing; sometimes an enigmatic quiver crosses his face. When the dervishes stop, exhausted, and sink down on the carpets, hoarse gurgling sounds and cries escaping their throats as if being strangled, the Shaykh begins to speak in a soft voice, so softly that most hear only his whispering, but nevertheless remain leaning forward devotedly.

That roaring, ear-splitting gasping in the dance has been explained to me thus: one sees the world with one's eyes, but *Allāh* with the heart—similarly in the *dhikr* one speaks the Name *Allāh* with the heart, not with the lips that speak many diverse things; hence the

[7] The dance of the dervishes is a type of invocatory prayer that can take on various forms in the different Sufi orders.

rhythmic gasping and the dance, which tear physical consciousness away from the divided waking state and rock it to sleep in the Unity of *Allāh*.

The *Alawiyyah zāwiyah* is situated at the end of the Arab town, quite close to the sea. Upon stepping out the door, one finds oneself on a wide plain of sand and stones that is strewn with bones, rams' horns, and all sorts of shells and broken pottery, with here and there a bit of green. There is also a Muslim cemetery, with the snow-white dome of a saint's tomb that in the evening light turns pink, when the sky takes on a violet-blue hue and the whole landscape becomes golden as in a dream. To the left is the sea and the port with ships. On the way down to the sea, the path goes through some very tall reeds, so that one might almost think one was in the jungle. Another, and smaller, *zāwiyah* also belonging to our Shaykh is situated right on the seashore, at some distance from the port; this little *zāwiyah* is the most beautiful *āshram* one can imagine; in the background there are high, red rocks, then the land falls steeply to the dark blue sea. It is completely isolated, this little hermitage; far and wide, nothing can be seen but golden-red slopes and ravines, and finally the port which one sees in the distance. Access to the little *zāwiyah* is also difficult, as one must cross a chasm—albeit not a wide one—in order to reach it.

When I think of the Parisian boulevards or the large streets of Basel, the Arab town seems to me like a sort of graveyard. In the narrow lanes one sinks into yellow sand that already makes one think of the dead-ocean of the Sahara. The low houses, which remind one of stables and barns, are much cleaner than the houses in Marseilles.

We are having the most splendid autumn weather here, the sky is almost cloudless, though not a deep blue. And even so this whole region is desolately barren, a sunny death.

On the roof above me the muezzin is calling us to prayer. At five o'clock in the morning, when it is still dark, his song sounds unspeakably sad, exactly as Loti[8] has described it: like the howling of a wolf falling into the void—lamenting, lonesome, almost despairing, as if the sea were breaking against a desert island, or as if a chalice were shattering.

[8] Pierre Loti is the pen name of Julien Viaud (1850–1923), a widely traveled ship's officer and prolific novelist, who wrote many romances about the Orient.

Islam and Christianity must stand in outward contradiction to one another because both express Unity, and there cannot be two Unities. The same truth has been reflected twice, but the circumstances are not the same, and the point of view is different in each case. With Christ, the original Semitic concept of the Godhead was endangered, because Christ was divine, a descent of the divine Principle who absorbed in himself the idea of God that he proclaimed; hence the Islamic reaction, which had to come from an Old Testament Prophet like Muhammad. In Islam, no expression of the Godhead comes down to earth, God is not limited by a person as in the case of Christ, namely the Father by the Son, but rather a person is amplified by God, namely the Prophet by *Allāh*. Muhammad is the man who is assailed by Unity, who with human means, but under divine protection, asserts among men the idea of Unity, which does not belong to him and which inundates him. Islam means resignation; resignation of the seven "gates", namely the hands, feet, eyes, ears, tongue, stomach, and genitals—resignation in *Allāh*, who encompasses within Himself *Apara-Brahma* and *Para-Brahma*. More about this later.

I have just received a letter from Guénon in which he advises me to visit the Shaykh in Mostaghanem, without knowing that I am with him. The letter was sent to me here from Basel; Guénon is on terms of friendship with our Shaykh, and I am to introduce myself to the Shaykh in his name.

I will now probably stay longer in Mostaghanem, or return to Mostaghanem after some months in Fez.

"*France Has Spoken*"

Mostaghanem, late December, 1932 to Jakob Jenny

To understand Islam, one must regard as a unity the doctrine that found its first and essential expression in Moses, realized itself anew in Christ, and manifested its final possibility of formulation in Muhammad; one must understand how Christ broke through the limits of the outward Law in the name of pure spirituality and how Muhammad was the reaction to this breaking of limits—as it were, the Mosaic reaction to Christ who, as avataric superman, had jeopardized the Mosaic doctrine of God. From the Jewish point of view, or rather for Jewish doctrine, Christ was the esoterist who ruthlessly broke through the limits of the outward teaching. Such admittedly irregular breaking of limits by esoterism is sometimes necessary; this is no sacrilege in terms of the primordial doctrine, but only from the point of view of its diminished and transcended form. Thus, whereas the breaking through the limits of the existing tradition had, for example, no sufficient reason in terms of the primordial doctrine in the case of the Sufi Al-Hallaj, in the case of Christ this breach was a necessity stemming from the primordial doctrine itself. Christianity can be regarded as an aspect of Jewish esoterism, one that has become exoteric in its turn because applied to the social order; if the Mosaic concept of God was to live on—not just in the spent shadow of Jewish doctrine still present within Christian dogma—then Muhammad had to come in order to disengage Abraham's doctrine from the figure of Christ, into whom it had been absorbed, and so to restore the concept of an unconditionally free Divinity, bound to no particular destiny; for what Muslims reject in Christianity is the way in which God participates in the history of humanity and is intimately bound up with it; however, in order to establish this rejection exoterically, Muhammad had to deny to Christ what in his case had been the cause of the narrowing of the concept of God, namely his divinity and his crucifixion; if Muhammad had accepted these two things, which from an esoteric point of view would have offered no barrier to God's Infinity, then he would not have been able to establish the non-historical concept of God, a concept independent of the appearance of Christ. The terrible wound that Christ inflicted on the Abrahamic-Mosaic doctrine naturally called for a compensating reaction, and this was Islam; this already emerges from the fact that Islam is the third form of this doctrine, and three is the number of equilibrium and harmony, whereas two is the number of contradiction, alternative, and incompatibility; thus in order to preserve the purity of the Abrahamic doctrine of God and at the same time the sanctity of Christ, Muhammad admitted Christ into Islam as a prophet; in this way, the surpassing figure of Christ could no longer absorb into itself the pure doctrine of God, as a magnifying glass concentrates and strengthens the light of the distant sun; and on the other hand the free and pure concept of God could no longer deny Christ, as it had done with the Jews, but instead appropriated to itself Christ's diminished figure, just as Christ's increased figure had previously appropriated the concept of God. All these things were pure exoteric necessities; if these were not present, there would be no need for religions. Therefore, in order to penetrate the meaning of a religion, one must examine the motives of its dogmas more than the dogmas themselves, at least insofar as the doctrines of secondary import are concerned. It is also noteworthy that Christianity presents itself, not as doctrine, but as history, in whose center is Christ, while the Gospels nevertheless contain a clear, full, and intelligible doctrine, whereas Islam, on the contrary, presents itself as a doctrine, in whose center is the *lā ilāha illā 'Llāh*,[9] while the Koran contains no doctrine, but stories, warnings, prescriptions, descriptions, and maxims. A proof, and an evidence of unity from above, of the fundamental unity of Christianity and Islam is to be found in their highest symbols, the Cross on the one hand and the Kaaba on the other; these are merely different forms of the same geometrical representation, and their equivalence outweighs their difference. Enough of this for the present. Perhaps I shall write on the same subject in *Le Voile d'Isis*.[10]

France has spoken. A policeman knocked at the *zāwiyah* door and fetched me to the police commissariat. In the waiting room an Arab woman sat with her little child, weeping bitterly. I was taken in to the commissar, who bellowed to the policeman to make the woman be quiet, and if this was not possible, to put her in prison. Then this gentleman asked me a series of more or less senseless, hostile questions, with the intention of making my presence with Shaykh Ahmad out to be something extraordinary, inexplicable. As my answers thwarted this procedure, he pounced on my papers, tried to establish that it was a very strange matter to have traveled to Switzerland, Belgium, again to Switzerland, and then again to Belgium in the same year, set up a sort of report about me and my life and at the end kept all my papers, with the remark that I could fetch them before continuing my journey and that he would see to it that I would be known at the Moroccan border and allowed through without difficulties. Then he offered me

[9] The Islamic *Shahādah*, or testification of faith, meaning "there is no god but God".

[10] These reflections resulted in his first published article, "The Ternary Aspect of the Monotheistic Tradition", which he wrote in Mostaghanem and dedicated to the Shaykh al-Alawi.

his hand and had Sidi[11] Adda Ben Tounes, the Shaykh's *muqaddam*,[12] brought to him. In the evening Sidi Adda told me that the commissar had given him dreadful trouble because of me, and that things were going very badly. If the French treat one of their own like this, how would you fare in my place![13]

—·⁞·—

"*Spiritually Joined with Him for Life*"
Mostaghanem, late January, 1933 to Lucy von Dechend

Al-'Īd as-saghīr, the "lesser Feast": on the big mosque the flag with the white half-moon flutters blood-red. Various dervish orders walk through the streets, the Isawiyyas with their silken flags, large hand-drums, and pipes, whose thin, sour tones cut through the muted thunder of the drummers with hypnotic insistency, and other orders that announce themselves with singing, litanies, or intermittent calls.

The preceding night in the *zāwiyah* was indescribable. High-ranking guests, *imāms*, and foreign dervishes from all regions had already been filling the house for two days. On the eve of the Feast, the last prayer of Ramadan was chanted and then about a hundred dervishes danced their captivating and wildly beautiful dance the whole night long, almost without interruption. The frantic noise of their gasping and songs, the incense and perfumed water sprinkled on their garments, the yellowish lighting, all this conferred on that night the character of a drunken dream—until the call for the morning prayer, with the long drawn-out, deathly sad cry: "God is great. There is no god but God." And then again the *wird*, the somber flowing litany on the rosary of a hundred beads.

A few days before the Feast, the *muqaddam*[14] leads me to the half-darkened room of the Shaykh. A breath replies to my softly spoken greeting. No one is in the room other than the Shaykh lying

[11] "My lord" (*Sīdī*), a title of respect used in the Islamic Maghreb.

[12] Adda Ben Tounes (1898–1952) was a representative of the Shaykh al-Alawi during Schuon's first trip to Mostaghanem.

[13] This long letter continues, and includes a lengthy quotation from the *Bhagavad Gītā*.

[14] Sidi Adda.

motionless, the *muqaddam*, and I. The Shaykh slowly turns his head and says something in a weak and broken voice that sounds gentle and almost friendly. Then the *muqaddam* speaks in a whisper with the Shaykh and turns again to me: "Draw near to our Lord so that he may give you the *Tarīqah*." I crouch down very close to the slender, prophet-like figure and kiss his almost inanimate hand; large, dark eyes that are no longer of this world rest their gaze upon me. Then they stare beyond me into the void, and two cool hands with difficulty clasp my hand and hold it enclosed. In the room nothing stirs; only the barely audible words of the Koran, uttered by the Shaykh beside me, vibrate in the semi-darkness. He says prayers; the moments that go by while he prays are holy; something passes over into me from these waxen, other-worldly hands, like a current into the heart. I am spiritually joined with him for life.

Now follow sudden dissonances, but I cannot avoid them because they are the painful truth. It was on the morning of the Feast, after the dervishes and guests had exchanged kisses according to the custom, and many Muslim lips had touched my shoulders and cheeks, that I had to go to the police commissariat. I took off my Arab clothing and left the gathering in a European suit. Then Sidi Tahar called me back and gave me a piece of cake. When I reached the French police cesspit, I was treated with cold hostility and interrogated in the most foolish manner; a file and an alert were laid out before me, as if I were a criminal. The police commissar let me know that I might be forbidden to enter Morocco; he had seen to it that everyone now knows me, I who am a "special case". "I have told everyone that you are with Shaykh al-Alawi", he shouted at me. I asked, "Who is everyone?" "Well, everyone", he answered, "the whole administration! What an affair! What an affair! When one has Christian parents!" "Are you certain of this?" I ask. "Is it in your capacity as a representative of the French government that you are interested in Christianity? Is it therefore better to be a communist than to live in the *zāwiyah*?" "Communist?" he says, "there are no communists in France; there are only malcontents. In case of war all would do their duty in a sublime *élan* of French brotherhood!" In this way he excuses the communists, followers of Lenin; on the other hand, it is a crime to be a follower of the Shaykh. Furthermore, he seems to forget the three hundred thousand Muslims who fell for France, and who certainly did not die in a worse way than the communists. I must have a special reason for having come to Algeria, he surmises finally; my case is extraordinary; quite peculiar, highly suspicious. And so the harassment goes on for two hours or more. Every time I have to go to the commissariat I am called to account in the most brazen way and may not even defend myself properly, lest the oppressors vent their anger on the *zāwiyah*. I was even asked what books I have, where and when I first met a Muslim, what I think about the Arabs, where and why I learned Arabic; and the *muqaddam* is asked the same questions. And for the time being I am still in Mostaghanem.

—·⁝·—

"*Words of Farewell*"
Oran, Algeria, February 21, 1933 to Lucy von Dechend

Dreary day. I am sitting in a low cell; a broken light filters in through a window grille. Here in the *Alawiyyah zāwiyah* in Oran I have again found my old companion, Ali ibn Abd ar-Rahman ad-Damari, the Yemenite, with whom I will set sail tomorrow for Marseilles, probably in storm and cold. A dreary day, as when a few days ago I went down to the shore with Sidi Adda for the last time, over the stony plain, under leaden skies. The *muqaddam* described to me how Sidna Shaykh[15] and his order are subjected to incessant persecutions by the French; the other orders fare little better, but Sidna Shaykh cannot be pardoned for his great influence, even though this influence is purely spiritual, not political. But it is precisely this spiritual influence that is hated by the French, because it hinders them in their work of destruction, because it vivifies Islam instead of undermining it—because for this reason it is "anti-French".

On our last walk to the sea, Sidi Adda was of the opinion that all the dervish orders would in time disappear; several orders already maintain only a semblance of life, not all can undergo the unyielding attacks of the French without accepting their invitations to serve the French influence.

[15] "Our lord Shaykh", i.e. the Shaykh al-Alawi.

Guénon has dared to defend the East from other than a merely innocuous point of view, and to unveil the true face of the West. He, the Frenchman living in Egypt, is faring no better than the dervishes; this is clear enough from his latest letters in which he writes to me of the unbelievable means by which they seek to damage him.

I am writing this so that you can understand me a little when I tell you that I had to state the day and hour of my departure from Oran, then the name of the ship, then the city to which I am going, then the name of the hotel where I will stay! You can imagine what life is like in an atmosphere as suffocating as that of the French-Maghrib, and wonder how spiritual islands can still flourish there!

Dreary day. It was my last afternoon in Mostaghanem; I had strolled down with Sidi Adda to the little *zāwiyah* close by the sea. There the *fuqarā'* sat gathered; *Allāh*, his Envoy, and the latter's representative, the celestial Shaykh Ahmad, were celebrated in song, then the *muqaddam* gave an address on spiritual poverty; his weary, sad voice sounded like the lost tone of a violin in the roaring of the sea. In the evening, along with several visitors, the *imām*, and Shaykh Salah, I was taken to the saint. As I kissed his fingers, he looked up at me with eyes that consume the heart, and asked me, "*Ash hālak*—how are you?"

It was a wonderful morning, and a dervish wandered over the plain; for the last time, he drank in all the darkly glowing colors of this holy ground, looked out over the sea and up into the wide heavens, then walked onwards in the cold north wind. Having reached the deep-yellow ravine of sand, he stopped, knelt down, spread out a white handkerchief, and filled it with sand. Then he knotted it together and was about to return, when a familiar voice called out: "Sidi Isa, what are you doing?" Then followed words of farewell, an embrace, and this, too, was soon over.

I was already prepared for my journey when Sidi Adda called me: "Come and see Sidna Shaykh once more." It was morning; I went into the long room where dark red carpets with silver embroidery hung on the walls and the saint, fading into extinction, lay in half darkness. "Sit down beside him", whispered Sidi Adda as he knelt down at the Shaykh's feet. I sat next to his head, after which he began to speak with difficulty, in a broken voice I did not understand; but still my ears drank in these sounds, these words, whose meaning Sidi Adda explained to me: "He says that he regrets having always been so tired that he could never speak with you." For my part I expressed my regret about the persecutions the Shaykh had been exposed to because of me. Then there was a singing whisper beside me, and Sidi Adda explained: "He says it has always been like this and will always be so; when you have gone, they will persecute him in another way." Then I say how fortunate I have been to receive the *Tarīqah* from the hands of Sidna Shaykh, and I receive his last answer: "He says to you that you can write to him, he will answer you and help you in the Sufi doctrine." I look at Sidi Adda, whose lips intimate a "*bismi 'Llāh*—in the Name of God", at which I kiss the Shaykh's hand for the last time, stand up, then turn around once more: "*As-salāmu 'alaykum, yā Sīdī.*" — "*Salām* . . .".[16] Thus vanished from me this wonderful man, whom the French call "the Mahatma" and of whom they say: "He is Islam's most dangerous fanatic."

Marseilles—a few days later. When people in Europe write about the living East, about the lights of the East, they unfailingly mention the same names: Tagore, Gandhi, Okakura; they do not know the true Easterners. I have never heard anything in Europe about Shaykh Ahmad bin Mustafa al-Alawi despite the feverish search for Eastern miracle men with which many a European author busies himself. And what could a journalist like Romain Rolland make of the Shaykh's life anyway?

The Shaykh is the author of numerous texts, among them a treatise called "*Allāh*", and a diwan[17] whose form is somewhat reminiscent of Angelus Silesius and is sung by the dervishes. It is said that he once brought a train to a standstill with the emergency brake, so as to disembark and pray. Much is told of him, strange and wondrous things; I was shown a high cliff near Mostaghanem from which a dervish is said to have fallen; at the last moment, he called on the Shaykh and fell to the ground unhurt. Such cases belong to the domain of *barakah*; Shaykh Ahmad's *barakah* is invoked by the dervishes, just as the intercession of the Mother of God is by Catholics.

[16] The traditional Islamic greeting, "Peace be upon thee, O my lord", to which the response is, "Peace".

[17] A collection of poems.

I have a dreadful, stormy voyage behind me. I had stayed three more days in Oran, in dervish caves resembling cellars. Then twice more I encountered a mysterious man who before in Mostaghanem had suddenly appeared like a flash of lightning, a prototypical Arab, swathed in black with a sharp aquiline face. In Mostaghanem he was suddenly there; he grasped my hand in a singular fashion and, looking at me piercingly, said in Arabic: "Lead us on the straight path." Then in French he said that he knew me and parted with a "Farewell and thank you!"

—— ·:· ——

"*The Divinity of Christ's Doctrine*"
circa 1933 to Lucy von Dechend

It is not correct to say that among Muslims there is an esoteric doctrine whose adherents consider the words of Christ to be divine revelations, as you explained to your mother; rather *all* Muslims without exception believe in the divinity of Christ's doctrine; they deny only that God Himself became man, for God is Lord of all the worlds and cannot be manifested in a single world only and in that world but once. The recognition of Christ has therefore nothing to do with Islamic esoterism.

God knows the most hidden folds of our hearts. It should not be hard for us to approach Him, all the more so as we must draw near to Him lest we come to ruin. The worse we are at praying, the more we need prayer. We must at all costs have a clear, strong relationship with God. We must find our security in Him, as that mysterious wanderer Ahmad[18] said to me and made me repeat: "Lead us on the straight path." If we do not hear His answers within us, our heart is dead; we must knock, in order that it may be opened unto us. As Sidi Adda said: "To him who takes one step towards *Allāh*, *Allāh* takes a hundred steps towards him."[19]

[18] This is the same mysterious Ahmad who is first described in the letter dated February 21, 1933, titled "Words of Farewell".

[19] Paraphrasing the well-known *hadīth qudsī*, where God speaks in the first person: "To him who takes one step towards Me, I will take a hundred steps towards him."

—·⁝·—

A "Mysterious Stranger"
Paris, June 5, 1934 to René Guénon

When I was in Mostaghanem, I received a letter from you in which you told me that many of the initiatic orders of Islam had become less spiritual, either because of the intrusion of political influences or because of too great a diffusion. Thus I was struck in the *zāwiyah* by the mixture of individuals, which seemed to be a true mixture of castes; next to men of extreme intelligence and distinction, I saw others whose vulgarity and flatness I found disconcerting to the point of sometimes troubling me deeply. In that regard, I recall an incident that I now wish to relate to you.

I was very unfavorably impressed by some of those who lived at the *zāwiyah*, and who spent hours drinking tea and conversing without restraint; their words were puerile, their bearing totally lacking in dignity. They would huddle together thus in the mosque, and when it happened that they would say a word to me it was to express pious banalities. One day their indescribable complacency had sickened me more than ever, so that it was with great disgust that I went to the meal. I would only rarely take this meal with the other *fuqarā'*, but almost always in a room next to the Shaykh's room, in the company of the *tālib* who would read each night in the gatherings and who—along with the Shaykh, the *muqaddam*, the *kātib*, and a few Yemenites—was the only Arab in the *zāwiyah*; the others were Kabyles. Now on this day, I went to that room and saw next to the *tālib* an Arab stranger, very dark-skinned and wrapped in a black burnous; I was struck by the power and majesty of his figure, and a mysterious force seemed to emanate from his whole person. Instinctively, I greeted him first, kissing him on the head according to the custom, and only then did I greet the *tālib*. We ate in silence; I did so hurriedly, as I felt a certain shame in the presence of this stranger. As I stood up to leave, the stranger also stood up, pierced me with his powerful gaze, and kissed me on the forehead; then he said a few words to me—in rapid Arabic—that I did not understand; thereupon I returned to my cell; I was shattered and full of remorse, without knowing why, and I was ashamed of my nothingness. Then, as if impelled by an unknown force, I went outside and remained standing beside the door of the *zāwiyah*, looking out at the plain and the sea. There I began to dream of the future, I felt a great need to purify and renew myself; at this moment, the stranger appeared and stood facing me. His black eyes, tinted with blue, seemed to enter into me, and with a sudden gesture he seized my right hand—I remember the singular way in which he held my hand—and said to me three times in Arabic: "Say: Lead us on the straight path", and I did so each time. Then he said to me in French: "For my part, I do not wish to cause any trouble. I have known you for a long time. Farewell and thank you!" And he left with a light and energetic step. It was then that I noticed his red boots, made in supple leather, as are worn by Algerian horsemen.

This man had impressed me even more than the Shaykh himself; however, I attached no great importance to this meeting and thought no more of it when, obliged to leave Algeria, I was living in the little *zāwiyah* in Oran while awaiting my ship. It was on the night before my departure, while reciting the *wird* after the *maghrib*, when suddenly I heard behind me a raspy voice reciting along with us. I turned around and saw sitting behind me this strange Arab all dressed in black, even his high turban was of a dark color. I embraced his shoulder according to the custom, and he smiled. I was struck by his manner of reciting, for he would suddenly pronounce the syllables in a loud voice, only to continue with a low voice, and sometimes he would be completely silent, while counting the beads of his rosary. He must have entered, without anyone noticing him, during the prayer of the *maghrib*. Once the recitation was over, the *fuqarā'* who had disgusted me with their unrestrained chatter and their vulgar manners, approached the stranger to kiss his head. Standing near to him, I felt as if flooded with trust. He then uttered a few words about solitude in *Allāh*; it was hard for me to understand him because of his strange and guttural pronunciation. I then asked him his name; he smiled and after a short silence said that the name mattered little but that people called him Ahmad. He then stood up and left without greeting; he was so tall that he had to stoop to pass through the door. I asked the others but no one could tell me who this stranger was; he was seen occasionally, I was told, but undoubtedly was not from this region.

I felt an intense desire to see him again; the next morning—the day of my departure—I was in the courtyard of the *zāwiyah* making my ablution for the prayer, when a voice called me, and I saw the tall figure of the stranger standing there in the middle of the courtyard. He smiled at me, without his smile modifying the bronze-like hardness of his face. The expression of his eyes was indescribable. I stood up, streaming with water, to quickly greet him; once again he smiled, then went into the *zāwiyah*. I finished my ablution and followed him in; he had not left me but a few seconds, yet when I entered the *zāwiyah* the room was empty. I looked in the street and saw no one. I never saw this Arab again.

As time takes me away from these events, the meeting with this man of such an extraordinary appearance absorbs my thoughts more and more, so much so that I come to wonder if, during our first meeting in Mostaghanem, the fact of gripping my hand, of piercing me with his gaze, of pronouncing words, and of making me repeat three times the same formula did not constitute a rite. I spoke about it last Saturday with the *fuqarā'* of Billancourt, who told me that it was undoubtedly the Shaykh himself who had changed appearance, and this seemed all the more obvious to them given that this mysterious stranger had told me his name was Ahmad. As for myself, I do not know what to think of this encounter.

—·⁝·—

"*My Shaykh Had Died*"

Paris, July 15, 1934 to Hans Küry

You are receiving from me a sorrowful notice of death. My spiritual father, the eminent Shaykh Ahmad Abu'l Abbas bin Mustafa al-Alawi, passed away last Wednesday, July 11, 1934.

On that day, I was in an unwonted state of inner illumination that overwhelmed me like a sea, so that almost unconsciously I groaned "*Allāh, Allāh*". In the evening I went out into the street and along the Seine, without the holy Name ever leaving my lips. Everything had become transmuted before my eyes. Everything was as if transparent, fluid, infinite. Everything was within me; I was in everything, and I felt myself in the farthest distance and the farthest distance in my heart. Now and then I would stand still and look at the world around me as if at a sight never before seen.

The next day I wrote to Cairo. I thought the Shaykh had conferred on me what is called *tasrīh al-Ism*—authorization for the Name. Yesterday evening I visited the dervishes and learned that my Shaykh had died on that Wednesday. A heavy atmosphere lay over the evening. Four distinguished guests from Algeria were there. Long litanies were sung. The *hadrah* was danced. Some dervishes wept. Outside there was thunder and lightning. One could hear muffled music in the distance, for the Parisians were celebrating their day of independence.

—— ·:· ——

"*My Accounts from Mostaghanem*"
Lausanne, September 13, 1934 to Hans Küry

Regarding a publication of my accounts from Mostaghanem, even with the names changed I must weigh the pros and cons most painstakingly. Apart from this it does not interest me to have people take me for a Muslim. I am a Sufi, and not what a word like "Muslim" means for the masses.[20]

—— ·:· ——

"*The Dignity of* Muqaddam"
Mostaghanem, February 20, 1935 to Hans Küry

I have just now spent seven days and nights in retreat and meditation, confined to a dark cell from which I was allowed to leave only for my ablutions and prayers, with my face covered and without breaking my vow of silence. I received one meal each evening and slept on the floor. I also remained for part of the night in *dhikr*. On the seventh day, Shaykh Adda[21] led me to Shaykh al-Alawi's grave, questioned

[20] Schuon closes this letter with, "From the heart and in the Spirit", an expression he was to use in a number of his letters throughout his life.

[21] That is, Adda Ben Tounes, who was then the presiding Shaykh after the death of Shaykh al-Alawi. During this second trip to Mostaghanem, Shaykh Adda also gave Schuon the additional name of Ahmad, in memory of Shaykh Ahmad al-Alawi.

me about my spiritual experience, congratulated me, and instructed me henceforth to write down what would be revealed to me in my meditations. Then he conferred the dignity of *muqaddam* on me.

4. Truth Must Have Many Forms
Ages 32–57

"In the Center of the Cross"
Postal Sector 390, France,[1] December 22, 1939 to Adrian Paterson

To receive your letters, as well as those of M. Lings and the greetings of R. Guénon, gives me much pleasure in my extreme isolation. For my ten days leave, I am thinking of going to Paris, so as to renew contact with my friends. When the long letter of M. Lings reached me, the farthest things became very near to me. It seems to me that Cairo is even nearer to me than these machine-gun holes.

While passing before Mecca on board the Narkunda,[2] I spontaneously became aware of several things. I found myself in the middle of the vertical axis formed by the Red Sea, and between two continents representing the horizontal axis; I was thus situated in the center of the cross. But I was also situated between the sun and the moon, which I could see simultaneously by turning my gaze westward and eastward. I was also between the East and West, the latter in this instance being represented by Abyssinia and by Abyssinian and Coptic Christianity in general. Being between the sun and the moon, I was also between the Christ and the Prophet, in the sense that the sun corresponds to Christ who is himself the Revelation, whereas the moon corresponds to the Prophet who is the support of the Revelation; Revelation is identified either with Christ or with the Koran; on the other hand Christ is also—as *Jesus Nazarenus* (Nazareth = "flower") (*mani padme* = "jewel in the lotus")—a support of the Revelation, just as solar matter is the support of solar light; and it is this aspect of the *Mleccha Avatāra* that the Islamic perspective has above all in mind. On the other hand, returning now to my voyage, I was struck that the vertical axis—marking my ascent towards the Sinai—was represented

[1] This was Schuon's military address while stationed in France.

[2] During this trip Schuon stopped in Cairo to meet Guénon and then traveled on to India aboard the SS Narkunda. The Second World War began shortly after he arrived in India, and Schuon was thus obliged to return to France to join his regiment.

by the sea and the horizontal axis by the earth, which made me think of the symbolism of the wine and the (eucharistic) bread, and from a more general point of view, of the relationship between esoterism and exoterism, which I have formulated once again in "The Teaching to the Rich Young Man", after having dealt with it in "The Covenant" and other articles.

—— ·:· ——

"*Gaiety*"

Postal Sector 390, May 1, 1940 to Martin Lings

Regarding primordial man, I do not think he either laughed or wept, for his psyche was neither as developed nor therefore as exteriorized as that of fallen man; primordial man was much closer to the state of *prājna*, or rather *samādhi*, which means that everything in him was reabsorbed into a state of beatific non-differentiation; laughter is only a kind of fallen and vulgar fragment of this beatitude, intensified as a result of outwardness; the physical manifestation of laughter stems also from this.

What I mean to say is that there is no primordial laughter, at least not in the sense in which you seem to understand it. It goes without saying that insofar as a thing is positive it has a primordial prototype, but this prototype can be markedly different from what is derived from it. Abd al-Qadir al-Jilani says that the Name *Allāh* dispels all sadness from the heart of man, but he does not say that this Name makes one laugh. I willingly gave up my sadness when God removed it from me. But let no one speak to me of gaiety!

I believe I mentioned to you in my last letter that I have always noticed that vulgar people love above all what makes them laugh, and they flee what is serious; outside of their work they seek things that are gay, abhorring all that is gravity and dignity and all that evokes pain or death. In your article you mentioned several saints who spent the better part of their life laughing and jesting. This is plausible only if their attitude was paradoxical and intentional, as with the *malāmatiyah*; but we are dealing then with an example of asceticism, and this contradicts your interpretation.

I would never think of criticizing spontaneous and unassuming gaiety, provided it is not incompatible with dignity; such gaiety is a question of temperament and thus in itself something neutral. But once gaiety is established as a matter of principle, I do condemn it because it then ceases to be unassuming; it loses its spontaneity and becomes pretentious; it opens the door to foolishness, while including a kind of self-sufficiency that is paralyzing with regard to spirituality, even when it is more or less unconscious. Far be it from me to criticize your gaiety as long as it does not harm your path.

P.S. In Japan, the Noh theater is purely dramatic and hieratic; comedy is reserved for the Kabuki theater, which is bourgeois and in fact much less ancient. In Tibet likewise, the grandly stylized theater is dramatic and distinctly spiritual; comedy is nowhere to be found, except no doubt among street actors. I do not know Chinese theater, but I know that there is a distinction between classical theater and bourgeois theater. In Japan, there are additionally the great epic tragedies, such as the *Chushingura*, which are a kind of intermediary between Noh and Kabuki. As for India, it is also drama that is cultivated above all, for example with Kalidasa.

In modern Europe, I believe there is only one good dramatist, Shakespeare; the French and Germans are quite inferior to him. In the case of Shakespeare, the comic element is always in perfect balance, that is to say, it is offset.

Laughter is the expression of contingency; it is an agreeable and comforting fall into the peripheral; great art can make incidental use of it, but being the expression of equilibrium and the norm, this art cannot have laughter as its basis. Thus, the greatest works, such as the *Divina Commedia*, do not contain laughter.

—— ·:· ——

"*A Higher Significance to Living Spaces*"
Lausanne, January 12, 1942 to Hans Küry

I am glad you have found a good new place to live. I have always given a higher significance to living spaces, and forms in the broadest sense, than is usually done. The body is the first form; dress the second; living space the third; the house the fourth; landscape the fifth. Everything has its respective meaning.

—— ·:· ——

"*The Way of Love as Compared to the Way of Knowledge*"
Lausanne, November 15, 1942 to Leo Schaya

The way of love (*bhakti*) is better suited than the way of knowledge (*jnāna*) for dissemination among the many. In principle, the highest spiritual requirement is directed at everyone, but not in practice. This is why the way of love can be preached, but not the way of knowledge. In the Russian book,[3] certain contradictions become apparent, for the *staretz* orders the pilgrim to recite the formula so-and-so many times—not more and not less—and gives him the initiatic blessing, while the pilgrim transmits this authorization to others without restriction. He may also have added the blessing each time, but the book does not say so. On the other hand, attachment to the religious form is much closer in the way of love as compared to the way of knowledge. In the former, one can remain within the limits of this form, but never in the latter; and many more can participate in the former than in the latter, which is why the way of love is much more prevalent than the way of knowledge among today's initiates; if it has always been so, it is even more so now. Furthermore, the way of knowledge today emphasizes the way of love, and at the same time comes closer to the limitation and exclusivity of the religious form.

—— ·:· ——

"*The Method of the Maharshi*";
"*Ibn Arabi and Traditional Universality*"
Lausanne, May 5, 1945 to Martin Lings

Some people talk about what they call the "method of the Maharshi", but such a method does not exist, for the simple reason that Ramana

[3] This is the first of several references in Schuon's letters to a book detailing the story of an anonymous nineteenth-century Russian peasant's quest for the secret of unceasing prayer of the heart; the book was first published in English as *The Way of a Pilgrim* (London: Phillip Allan, 1931).

Maharshi[4] himself never followed any method. He owes his realization to a sudden enlightenment, and not to spiritual exercises; and since he never followed a method, he cannot teach one; his teaching through the question "Who am I?" is much more the expression of his inner reality, or a principial and symbolic expression of all spiritual paths, than a method that can be imitated in the absence of any other support. This does not at all mean that the Maharshi has no radiance or does not transmit graces, but only that he could not have the mission of forming disciples since he never had to follow a path himself, and this in fact is the reason he refuses to accept disciples; to claim that *mauna-dīkshā* constitutes a complete path in itself, instead of simply representing the essential aspect of every path, amounts to saying that the descent of the Holy Spirit on the Apostles constitutes a spiritual method. Let no one object that the Apostles were therefore unable to form disciples since, like the Companions of the Prophet, they experienced a quasi-sudden realization; the case of the Apostles and Companions is altogether different, for they received not only an initiation, but also a method to be transmitted; this method, which was "simple" and "synthetic" at the beginning, became "differentiated" and more explicit, with the assistance of the Holy Spirit, as the origin and its flood of spiritual graces receded and it became necessary to adapt to more and more precarious conditions; thus the position of a Saint John or *Sayyidnā* Ali is in no way comparable to that of a "later" saint, that is to say, someone who is not the direct disciple of a founder of a traditional form.

As for the Maharshi, he is clearly one of those of whom Shri Ramakrishna says that they obtain realization independently of their will and in a sudden and spontaneous manner; these are the men Sufism knows under the name of *afrād*, and the initiatic meaning of this saying of Christ applies to them: "they that be whole need not a physician."[5] But the existence of such men does not imply that initiatic rites, which exist in Hinduism as in any other tradition, are mere contrivances without meaning, hence stupidities; the fact that these

[4] Ramana Maharshi (1879–1950) was an exponent of *Advaita Vedānta* and one of the greatest sages of the modern era. He experienced the identity of *Ātmā* and *Brahma* while still in his teens, and the fruit of this experience remained with him as a permanent spiritual station throughout his life.

[5] Matt. 9:12.

rites exist means that they must correspond to some kind of reality and necessity. There really should be no problem here: if someone is a *fard*, then the initiatic question does not apply to him, and discussions on this subject are pointless for him; if he is not a *fard*, then he has no choice but that of a normal path transmitted by tradition, which is to say that, with a right intention and the help of *barakah*, he needs to seek for an orthodox *murshid* and receive from him what this *murshid* himself received from his *murshid*.

But returning to the Maharshi: to follow his path is to imitate what he did, or rather what made him what he is, that is to say, to have one's great-grandparents cursed or blessed by a *sannyāsin*, then to be surprised and unexpectedly overcome during adolescence by a spiritual force, then to remain in *samādhi* for weeks and months on end, and finally to enjoy a spiritual realization obtained as a gift, without any inward work; to wish to emulate this "path" would be as absurd as to wish to be crucified by Pontius Pilate and rise on the third day.

I am including here the texts of Muhyi ad-Din Ibn Arabi that you did not have. Concerning Ibn Arabi, I recall that someone once questioned whether Sufism admits traditional universality; Ibn Arabi supposedly would have denied this, having said that Islam is the pivot of the other traditions. Now every traditional form is superior to others in a certain respect, and this is in fact the sufficient reason for such a form; and it is always this respect that a person speaking in the name of his tradition has in mind; what matters in the recognition of other traditional forms is the fact—exoterically astonishing—of this recognition, not its mode or degree. The Koran in fact offers the prototype of this way of seeing: on the one hand it says that all the Prophets are equal, and on the other hand it says that some are superior to others, which means—according to the commentary by Ibn Arabi—that each Prophet is superior to the others owing to a particularity belonging to him alone, thus in a certain respect.

Ibn Arabi belonged to a Muslim civilization and owed his spiritual realization to the Islamic *barakah* and the masters of Sufism, hence to the Islamic form; he was therefore obliged to take a position consistent with this aspect of things, the aspect according to which this form contains a superiority with respect to other forms; if this relative superiority did not exist, Hindus who became Muslims throughout the centuries would never have had any positive reason for doing so; the fact that Islam constitutes the last form of the *Sanātana Dharma* in this *mahāyuga* implies that it possesses a certain contingent superiority over the preceding forms; in the same way, the fact that Hinduism is the most ancient traditional form still living implies that it possesses a certain superiority or "centrality" compared to later forms; there is, quite obviously, no contradiction here since the relationships to be considered are in each case different.

—·⁝·—

"*The Wine of the Supreme Name*"
Lausanne, June 14, 1945 to Martin Lings

I have tasted much of the Wine of the supreme Name, and this Presence in me sometimes prevents me from doing what I wish to do; it is even jealous of my readings, which often I must interrupt to heed this Presence alone. However, my intention is not to speak of myself thus. I wish only to say this, which is that now, "in the middle of the journey of our life",[6] no earthly thought is more pleasant than that of living in a solitary wilderness, alone with the great Name. But my dreams are really without importance.

—·⁝·—

"*The Practice of the Virtues*"
Lausanne, September 11, 1945 to Martin Lings

Did you receive the Buddhist texts on invocation, to which I had appended some quotations dealing with the same subject by Swami Ramdas and Ma Ananda Moyi? At the beginning, I quote one of the most ancient of Buddhist texts, the *Saddharma Pundarīka Sūtra*, then the *Saptashatikā Prajnāpāramitā Sūtra*; then there are some Far-

[6] These words, written in Italian in the original letter, are the opening line of Dante's *Inferno*: "Nel mezzo del cammin di nostra vita" (*La Divina Commmedia*).

Eastern texts. The identical nature of the method with that of other forms of initiation is striking.

The 24th. Some are close to thinking that, by insisting so much on the practice of the virtues, I am being a moralist; however, morality does not have a monopoly on human perfections, for these also exist outside this particular perspective. I deplore the fact that a certain number of those who claim to subscribe to an esoteric science believe that human virtues can be neglected or even scorned, when in fact they form part of the initiatic qualification and of the way itself, as Sufi treatises tirelessly reiterate; my point of view may strike some people as strange, but it is no more moralistic than that of the treatises just mentioned or of the *Yoga Shāstras*, for example, which also set a high value on virtue. If it is true that every perfection has above all a symbolic meaning, this hardly means that perfection itself is superfluous; on the contrary, the symbol is the necessary support for the reality symbolized; in fact, it is a mode of this reality. Every virtue is an eye that sees God.

When I receive a jumble of a letter, for example full of petty, sterile, impotent, and futile concerns, written hastily and in a worried tone, I do not see in it the reflection of a soul that is the receptacle of the Real Presence; the "structure", "style", or "rhythm" of the soul must correspond to the object of its aspirations, and this object is the divine Reality, free from all infirmity. The Divine is Beauty, Grandeur, Solitude; thus the soul must realize these qualities not by imaginative improvisation, which would be fatal, but in conformity with divine truths; thus "greatness" of soul must not be sought by means of a hollow and sentimental attitude, as the Vivekanandists would do, but by hierarchizing the psychic or mental contents and by suppressing what opposes the "one thing needful".[7] Abul Mawahib al-Shadhili says: "Purify thyself of thy vulgar and contemptible traits and adopt His qualities, worthy of praise and full of glory."

There are those who, seemingly unable to understand that esoterism is not anticlericalism, would have much to learn from men such as the Curé d'Ars or a Saint Theresa of the Child Jesus, precisely with regard to a certain perfection or health of the soul. It is in any case impermissible that, upon hearing names such as those I have

[7] Luke 10:42.

just cited, one deems oneself obliged or authorized to take on airs of disdainful superiority; this is foreign to the spirit of Sufism. Whatever the ugliness of soul of those who clothe their esoterism with sectarian prejudices may be, no one will make me believe that esoteric truth is basically petty and undefined, and that nobility and dignity are exoteric prejudices.

I recently had to write to someone: "I will not be a party to any confidential tone"; you can see what this means: one must stay clear of any sentimentality or "sectarian" partiality and never allow oneself an attitude of facile irony because one believes one has the right to speak *pro domo*. For instance, when one is obliged to notice an error or a weakness on the part of a representative of the Church, one must do it with regret, and not with malicious delight; the ills afflicting the Church could make an atheist or a heretic cackle, but never a sage. I could say, to paraphrase what a French prince of our times said, that "all that is traditional is ours".

From a more general point of view, one must be careful to avoid all "dilettantism", for example when interpreting outward facts; arbitrary speculations can easily turn into "mythomania", if not into a "persecution complex"; this is a true usurpation of doctrine, and there is a real risk of compromising it by applying it falsely.

Finally, another form of dilettantism that must be fought is that of collecting in Sufi or even in Hindu writings loose bits of notions and starting to practice them arbitrarily. Now, the initiatic knowledge necessary for a given milieu of *murīdūn* manifests itself through the intervention of the *silsilah*, which transmits this knowledge through inspiration and makes it shine through a chosen instrument. This does not mean that one should not read the treatises of the ancient Masters, but only that one should not adopt a given practice on one's own initiative, at the risk of misinterpreting or misusing a rule valid only in a specific situation or under certain conditions; and this is true even for the texts of the Shaykh al-Akbar,[8] in whom nevertheless Alawism recognizes its doctrinal Master.

—— ⁖ ——

[8] "The great Shaykh", that is, Muhyiddin Ibn al-Arabi.

"*Truth Must Have Many Forms*"
Lausanne, October 7, 1947 to Benjamin Black Elk[14]

In my first letter, which our friend Mr. Brown[15] handed you, I wrote about my brother's and my love for the Indians; now I have learned that you read my letter and explained it to your holy father, and this will make my brother happy. This makes me happy too.

I think Mr. Brown spoke to you about me and my work. Very early in my life I saw the falseness of modern civilization—the "White Man's way"—and I saw it for two reasons: first, I saw with my eyes and my heart the beauty, grandeur, and spirituality of the other civilizations and the ugliness and selfishness, the slave-minded materialism, of the modern civilization in which I grew up; second, I could never believe that one religion alone in the whole world was the true one, and that all the other religions were false. As a boy, when I read about non-western peoples in books my father gave me, I could not believe that so many noble and wise men could have been abandoned by God, and that so many bad western whites could have received the truth; how could God, wishing to save every human soul, have given the saving truth to only one people and thus condemned so many others, who are no worse than these, to remain forever in deathly darkness?

I soon came to feel that this must be false and that the holy Truth must have many forms, just as a light may have many colors; God—the Great Spirit—gave that indispensable Truth to every race in a form suited to its corresponding mentality. Of course there have been people who forgot this Truth, such as the ancient Europeans to whom God sent Christianity, but He did not send Christianity to all the people in the world, for most had not forgotten the meaning of their religion. A heathen is a man who worships idols and ignores or rejects God; as for the Indians, they never worshiped idols nor did they ignore or reject God, the Great Spirit. Consequently, the Indians are not heathens, and their religion, though not fully understood by every

[14] This is the second letter that Schuon sent to Benjamin Black Elk in care of Joseph Brown. The letter is reproduced in more complete form in the Appendix to Harry Oldmeadow, *Black Elk, Lakota Visionary: The Oglala Holy Man & Sioux Tradition* (Bloomington, IN: World Wisdom, 2018), pp. 163–67.

[15] Joseph Epes Brown.

individual Indian, is a true one, and God is working in it and gives His Grace in it. This you know best, of course.

When I was older, I saw that the spiritual and contemplative way I was seeking could not be realized on the basis of the very superficial culture of Europe. I wished to live in God. I wished not only to love God, but to know Him as well, and the Christianity of our time teaches only the love of God, not the knowledge. Moreover, I knew from an early age that God would charge me with a mission. As for the knowledge of God I was seeking—because it is a need of my nature, and God wishes to be worshiped by every man according to the nature He gave him—I found this sacred knowledge through a holy man of the Arab people, whose name was Ahmad al-Alawi. He was a spiritual Master and had many disciples. There I found what I was searching for: the knowledge of God and the means to realize God. This Master told me: "When a man is not like snow in the hands of Truth and does not vanish away in Truth, then Truth is like snow in the man's hand and vanishes away." I was then a young man, and had left Europe for North Africa, where I found this Master. He is dead now, but he is always present in me; he is above life and death and is one with God.

The Great Spirit gave the indispensable Truth to every race: He gave the Indians their manner of praying just as He gave the Christians and Muslims and Hindus and Yellow peoples theirs. Every old and true religion is a necessary form of the eternal Truth and a gift from God, the most-high *Wakan Tanka*. Therefore, nothing in the Indian creed is a mere human invention or a senseless thing; every symbol or rite known and practiced by the Indians finds an analogous form and explanation in the traditions of other peoples—perhaps most directly in the Hindu tradition, for it is as old as that of the Indian one, whereas younger traditions are in a certain sense more simplified expressions of the same eternal Truth. All the "spirits" or "gods" known and invoked by the Indians—the Sun, the Sky, the Earth, the Rock, the Moon, the Winged-One, the Wind, the Mediator, the Four Winds, and the other cosmic Powers—are universal Principles known to every tradition, whatever may be the form of the symbols; the Angels of the Christian, Muslim, and Jewish religions are the same celestial beings as the Indian Powers or Spirits; the Indian "Thunderbird" is none other than the Muslim "Jibrail" and "Israfil" or the Hindu "Shiva". All Indian rites, such as smoking the most Holy Pipe, or the Sweat Lodge, or fasting and calling to the Great Spirit in search of a vision or power or

Friday, October 10. Since Wounded Knee,[17] many Indians could not help thinking that the Great Spirit has been very hard on His red children; many have inferred from the red man's disaster that the white man's way is better than the red man's. They forget that history is not yet ended and that the white man's punishment, at the end of times, must be far more terrible than the red man's punishment has been; even now in the last world war, the sufferings of millions of whites have been beyond every possible description, and all this is nothing else but the necessary result of so-called "progress", the "white man's way". The white men of the west will be punished for their "wickedness"; the Indians were perhaps too proud and sought too much their personal glory instead of the Great Spirit's eternal Glory, but they were not "wicked" like the white man. The whites who see the falseness of the modern civilization do not thereby betray their race; this civilization is false in itself, quite apart from the people, whether Japanese or whites, who accept it; the western whites betray themselves insofar as they identify themselves with the modern civilization. A man who states that his family is sick is not a traitor; truth is never a treason and error never a virtue.

We should realize the truth of Wovoka's vision in ourselves.[18] The ideas of the Ghost Dance were not false, only their too literal interpretation; but Wovoka himself did not understand his visions in this manner. Every religion knows that the "true brother", as the Hopis call the Messiah of the latter days, will come, and every religion gives him a particular name and wishes to possess him for itself; but he will come for all; that is an old and universal prophecy. There must be again holy men among every people; for finally the happy world seen by Wovoka will come even in the outer world, and we must be prepared for it. But before it comes, we are to realize it in ourselves. All this your holy father knows best. He has not waited and suffered

[17] At the Battle of Wounded Knee on December 29, 1890, approximately 300 Lakota men, women, and children were tragically killed by the U.S. Army.

[18] Wovoka (1856–1932) was a Paiute spiritual leader who had a prophetic vision during a solar eclipse on January 1, 1889. The vision entailed the resurrection of the American Indian dead and the removal of whites and their modern civilization from North America. Wovoka taught that in order to bring this vision to pass, the American Indians must live righteously according to the sacred ways of their ancestors and pray while performing a traditional round dance, known as the Ghost Dance.

in vain, nor have his people: the "holy Tree" will not wither, but will bloom again and forever.

—— ·:· ——

"*Love of the Indians Is a Family Tradition*"
Lausanne, October 31, 1947 to Chief Medicine Robe[19]

The ways of the Great Spirit are marvelous. It was a great pleasure for me to hear that our friend Mr. Brown found the way to Chief Medicine Robe and the other wise men of the noble Assiniboine people. We, who belong to a sacred community of the East, are happy to learn that the sacred tree of the Indian religion is still alive, and that it will not wither. In our time, which is approaching the end of times, all spiritual forces of mankind must strengthen one another. Therefore, it is a joy for us to see that the Indians know this, and we do not doubt that the best among the young men of your people will understand the falseness of the White Man's way, which finally abases men to the level of animals; the young men must understand this, as they must understand the grandeur and beauty of the ancient Indian civilization. This Indian civilization gave human life its full meaning, whereas modern civilization kills man's soul; man is no longer a free child of the Great Spirit, but a mere slave of human society, and a slave of a deadly materialism; in such a life, man has no longer time to think of God. We should realize within ourselves what gave the ancient times their grandeur, beauty, and happiness. Every good thing begins in the secret of the heart; outer works mean nothing in themselves, they must be expressions of our inner light. No human soul may encounter the Great Spirit with empty hands. The Great Spirit gave His Red Children their religion at the beginning of the world, and when He appears at the end, He will ask His Red Children what they have done with the religion He bestowed on them; and He will ask the same question of every people He has created. Of course not all Indians will return to the sacred tree of wisdom and virtue they

[19] Joseph Brown served as an interlocutor between Schuon and several American Indian leaders during his 1947 trip to the American West, including Chief Medicine Robe.

inherited from their fathers; but when in every Indian nation there will be a community of men who pray in the manner of their fathers, and whose hearts are steadily turned towards the Great Spirit, and who maintain the holy tradition in its inner and outer forms—for the outer forms are very important too—these men will represent before their Creator the whole nation. In our time the ignorant and wicked govern nearly everywhere, and their loud voices smother the soft voice of truth; but God's is the last word, as after every night the sun comes back again.

November 2. Love of the Indians is a family tradition with us—my brother and myself—and this is why: as a young girl, our paternal grandmother lived in Washington where she became acquainted with an Indian chief who loved her and made a marriage proposal to her. He was called "Singing Swan", and he had come with many other chiefs to Washington for a congress. Unfortunately, my grandmother had to go to Europe with her family and could not marry Singing Swan. He sent her letters in which he called her "my little child"; he also sent her dried flowers from the prairie. The recollection of Singing Swan was so vividly impressed on my grandmother's mind that at the age of eighty she still remembered her friend as if she had seen him the day before, and shortly before she died she still spoke of him. When my brother and I were children, she used to talk to us about Singing Swan; she pictured to us his beautiful long hair and his buckskin dress of light blue tinge. Thus, we were brought up with the love of the Indian peoples, and this was a providential disposition in the plan of the Great Spirit.

I have been very happy to hear that Chief Medicine Robe has given Mr. Brown several strands of braided sweet grass for me; I pray every day for him and his wife and their work, and I have told my community to do the same. Now I would be very grateful if you would be so kind as to translate these lines to Chief Medicine Robe and his followers, and also the enclosed letter that I sent to Chief Black Elk's son before Mr. Brown reached the Assiniboine nation.[20]

[20] This is a reference to Schuon's letter to Benjamin Black Elk, dated October 7, 1947, titled "Truth Must Have Many Forms".

—·⁝·—

"*The Tibetans and the North American Indians*"
Lausanne, May 20, 1948 to Marco Pallis

First of all, I want to thank you for the initiative you took concerning the precious robe of the holy Lama of Lachen; this gift is highly symbolic, all the more since I have received, as you may already know, similar gifts from other saints, these being from the Indians: an eagle plume blessed by Black Elk, a bow that once belonged to Fast Thunder, and incense from the prairies sent by Medicine Robe; the first two are Oglala Sioux, the last is Assiniboine. You are no doubt aware of the affinities existing between the Tibetans and the North American Indians. There are surely profound reasons for our works being known to both of them.

I believe you are right in persevering in the way you have undertaken;[21] Guénon thinks likewise. This does not prevent the inward bond that unites you to me from corresponding to a reality; there are things that go beyond forms.

Do you know whether there is to be found in Tibet a way of *buddhānusmriti* (the Chinese *nien-fo* and Japanese *nembutsu*), namely a way that consists solely in the invocation of the saving Name of the Buddha? If you have received my book, you will find references to this method. The "Original Vow of Amida" cannot be unknown to Tibetan Buddhists, and must have been mentioned at least in some books;[22] but what I would like to know above all is whether there exists a *guru* practicing the incantational method; this is the method that would suit Westerners the best. I regret that no one from our community is in Japan where this method became very well developed.

—·⁝·—

[21] Pallis chose to become a Tibetan Buddhist.

[22] See Georgios Halkias, *Luminous Bliss: A Religious History of Pure Land Literature in Tibet* (Honolulu: University of Hawaii Press, 2013) for a survey of Pure Land Buddhist literature in Tibet.

The "*Meaning of This Earthly Life*"

Lausanne, November 7, 1949 to a reader[23]

What makes your position difficult is the mingling of two quite distinct spheres of desire: you wish, like everyone, to be happy, but you wish also, like every spiritual person, not to miss the sufficient reason or meaning of this earthly life. Now these desires sometimes contradict one another, at least for a while, but the desire for happiness must not diminish the desire for salvation. Understand me! What God asks of us in the first place—for this concerns all men—is to save our souls; whether this salvation is tied to metaphysical knowledge and esoteric practices is quite another question. And here man has three possibilities: either he has no inner relation with ultimate truth, understands nothing of the wisdom of God, and does not wish to know anything about it; or he understands and loves this wisdom to some degree, but for some reason cannot follow a corresponding path; or—and this is the third possibility—he understands and loves this wisdom and can seek to realize it methodically.

Now what you say in your letter about your psychological difficulties leads me to suppose that yours is the second possibility. You have read about initiatic qualifications: a disposition to neurosis is not compatible with strictly and methodically practiced spiritual exercises. What I say here opens up to you the following perspectives: since God asks only *one* thing of you with certainty, because He asks it of every man—namely to save your soul and consequently to incorporate yourself into a tradition that offers you the means to do this—the criterion of the path for you does not lie primarily in esoterism, but simply in orthodoxy. Thus, from a purely principial point of view, your path could be found in either Latin or Greek Christianity, or also in Islam; none of these forms would exclude your need for a metaphysical deepening. But the most favorable would be Greek Christianity or Islam, because in them the spiritually harmful flattening that is peculiar to the Roman Church does not predominate; through philosophy, exclusive moralism, and excessive sentimentality, the Roman Church has become incapable of living spirituality, and its inner nationalization inevitably engages all believers in "public" spirituality—or non-spirituality. Not so in the Greek Church, which has

[23] The recipient was the wife of one of Schuon's disciples.

always defended itself against inner nationalization and egalitarianism, and still possesses a living esoterism, at least on Mount Athos. Be this as it may, Islam has for its part the advantage that every man in it is his own priest; however, for us Western and Northern Europeans it has the disadvantage that it cuts us off to a certain degree from society and condemns us to a certain inner loneliness; but this, from a spiritual point of view, is an advantage, inasmuch as every spiritual man is somehow lonely and indeed our present-day environment is explicitly non-spiritual. In this connection I should like to make plain to you the following: first, that the spiritual rule to which your husband submits does not demand that you follow the same rule; secondly, that it does not require of you any outward isolation from profane people around you; thus if you follow the same tradition as your husband, you can continue to cultivate all your former relationships and activities.

What you should do above all is to practice free prayer, in which you must tell God, as you would tell a person, all your troubles. Someone once said to me: "But I cannot pray", and I answered: "Then say to God, 'I cannot pray.' But express it! Then the spell will soon be broken."

—— ·:· ——

"*The Role of a* Murshid"
Lausanne, December 21, 1949 to Hans Küry

The question has recently been raised, what is a *murshid*'s role and to what extent do present-day circumstances in the West oppose its exercise? I would like to start by recalling a symbol that should always be kept in view: unless a man be like melting snow in the hand of God, the worship of God shall melt away like snow in his own hand. Now, there are two means by which to melt the hardened heart, these being described by Christ with the words "prayer and fasting" (*oratio et jejunium*).[24] One finds this again in Sufism as invocation and fasting. Shaykh Ahmad once sent a disciple for nine months into *khalwah*, to fast and invoke. Who in the West could be sent into *khalwah* for even half of that time? Who could accomplish even eight days of fasting in

[24] See Matt. 17:20; Mark 9:29.

khalwah? For there is one's professional work, one's need for rest due to fatigue from this work, one's family, one's health. Who manages to fast often and, above all, according to the Koran, to invoke much? Far be it from me to reprimand anyone for this, but one should then not reproach me if I show some understanding for these difficulties. And then, what can I do about the fact that the friends live so far apart, when strictly speaking a *khalwah* should take place under the supervision of the *murshid*? And finally, who can be ordered to change his profession in order to avoid a dissipating activity? All told, whoever is not content with his spiritual life or with my role in it, should first remember that in Sufism the basis for the spiritual life is much rigorous invocation together with fasting, and that the role of the *murshid* rests on this basis.

Someone might ask me, how is a *Tarīqah* possible under such circumstances? To which I answer, do Westerners have another choice? And is that which, despite everything, may still be accomplished not better than nothing? Is this little not full of blessings? These are questions that each must answer for himself. It cannot be denied that a spirituality practiced only by halves is a double-edged sword, given the nature of the soul. There is nothing I can do about this. In the East, these dangers are at least much smaller. And they are also so with people who are highly gifted spiritually.

I do not wish to discourage anyone, but in these lines lies a salutary warning for all. For each person can do more than he does. Of this, at least, I can remind the friends from time to time.

—— ·:· ——

"*Offer Your Sufferings to God*"
Lausanne, May 13, 1949 to Valentine de Saint-Point

The facts you relate in your second letter are indeed miraculous. They highlight the spiritual and providential meaning of the trials that followed them. Such trials have a twofold cause: the exhausting of our past errors—which may come from a former existence—and the cosmic reaction against our current ignorance; there are also sufferings that have the meaning of a martyrdom and that a saintly man can assume for others. In your case there is no need to worry about your incapacity to concentrate or meditate; it would have sufficed to offer your sufferings to God and to invoke His Name without concentration. In a great suffering as in a great joy, it is the experience of it that serves as meditation; and it is the acceptance of a suffering—in view of God—that serves as concentration. I know this myself, for I have suffered horribly in my life.

In the lives of certain saints, such as St. Theresa of the Child Jesus, suffering due to an almost total lack of physical well-being, above all cold and illness, plays an important role. Assuming that St. Theresa had followed a way requiring intellectual concentration, her attitude towards suffering would have been the same. Suffering is—by a direct "vision"—a meditation on death.

To understand and accept the cosmic and spiritual meaning of pain is the temporary equivalent of concentration. It could be said in such a case, solely on condition of the attitude I have just defined, that the Angels concentrate for us—just as it is said that the Angels pray in place of the person whom illness prevents from praying, on condition that he have the intention to do so.

—·:·—

"*The Character of a Tradition*"
Lausanne, July 12, 1950 to a reader[25]

To speak of tradition is to speak of continuity. In this continuity there is something absolute, as in tradition itself. In order to grasp what the character of a tradition is, there is no need to seek for inaccessible or unverifiable criteria; the essential elements—the constants—of the tradition are sufficient. The integral understanding—the rediscovery—of a tradition could never depend on historical researches; it depends by definition on the constants of the tradition on the one hand, and on the metaphysical and mystical knowledge of the person seeking to rediscover its spirit on the other. Thus, there are three things that matter: the nature or form of the symbol or the means of grace; its doctrinal and hence traditional definition; the metaphysical knowledge and the spirituality of the person examining them. This

[25] The recipient was a Catholic.

applies to all symbols and all revealed forms, whether sacraments or scriptural formulas. To affirm the contrary is to destroy the very idea of tradition by emptying it of the absolute character that defines it in an essential way.

One must practice the *Ave* because it alone is practiced in the Catholic Church. However, it is possible, while being Catholic, to obtain the Jesus Prayer from an Orthodox priest; permission can be obtained, apparently, from some Benedictines who are in contact with the Orthodox Church.

One must also practice individual, inward prayer, and tell God everything, that He may enlighten us even in our certitudes. Towards God, it is necessary always to start over from the beginning, to submit all our problems to Him, the doctrinal as well as human ones.

There is no spiritual method that does not wound our soul. Spirituality is both the easiest and the hardest thing. The easiest: because it is enough to think of God. The hardest: because fallen nature is forgetfulness of God.

Sanctity is a tree that grows between the impossible and the miracle.

—— ·:· ——

"*God Is Neither a Muslim Nor a Christian*"
Lausanne, October 22, 1950 to Martin Lings

God is neither a Muslim nor a Christian. He knows our exceptional situation: He knows that the great majority of the brethren are not by origin Muslims who have grown up under Koranic Law and in the fear of God, but Christians who have grown up in lukewarmness and base their thought—after the fact—on Hindu doctrine! Most of them have never passed through the "religious experience" that all Muslims grow up in; they have never had the experience of an integral traditional ambience; they do not know that there are virtues—we can read Al-Qushayri and Ibn Arabi on this subject—that Western dilettantism could never improvise. Man, so long as he cannot move a mountain or the moon, must fear God, and he must manifest this fear, as the Prophet manifested it. Every act must derive from a withdrawal to the Eternal.

—·:·—

"*The Grace of a Divine Name*"
Lausanne, March 28, 1951 to Hans Küry

The blessing and wisdom that lie in the Name *Allāh* can be compared to a snowy field: an endless, white, pure, fresh peacefulness. The Jesus Prayer corresponds more to a glowing center—to a burning rose, one could say. When one has experienced the grace of a divine Name directly, that is to say, with one's whole being, one can no longer feel desire for another Name and another grace. A lifetime is not too long to attain the grace that lies in the Name of God. The Name must break something in us; hence a man may sometimes wish to flee from it as from an enemy. How much passion, discouragement, distraction, hardening, how much pettiness, narrowness, and ugliness must yield in a man before his soul, penetrated by the Name of God, becomes a white expanse, like a snow-covered plain where all is clear. Then time stands still and space lies within us.

In every man's life there are dangers seeking to devour him: he then becomes discouraged, melancholic, bitter, skeptical. But all of this is nothing. The Name of God is a ship that cuts through every danger. This knowledge is essential when weakness, bitterness, and doubt say: "Now you are ours"—this knowledge that tells us: "All of this is not you."

Man has but a single life; unfortunate is he who trusts in his wavering soul. How can that save which itself must be saved? How can that bless which itself must be blessed? Truth does not lie in our feeble thinking, but in God's means of grace, which we cannot understand *a priori*. When man is reduced to nothing, when he thinks he can no longer see anything, then the Name of God sees in him and for him—until the two become one.

—·:·—

"*God, World, I, Thou*"
Lausanne, July 23, 1951 to Leo Schaya

There are for man as it were four fields of experience or four realities with which he must come to terms: God, the world, the "I", the neighbor. God speaks within each of these realities in a particular way: in the world as destiny; in the I as pure Spirit; in the neighbor as need. How does one encounter God in the world? In destiny, which one accepts precisely because one submits to God. How does one encounter God in one's own soul? In pure knowledge, which indeed is pure and suprahuman Truth. How does one encounter God in the neighbor? In the love of the neighbor, in good deeds, on whatever plane our talent may lie. One cannot serve God if one does not also see Him in destiny, in knowledge, and in the neighbor. When destiny comes, God says: "Here, too, am I." When man acts on the basis of truth, God says: "Here, too, am I." When the neighbor comes in need, God says: "Here, too, am I." To serve God in the world means to thank Him for every aspect of destiny; to serve Him in one's own soul means to know and will the True, to fulfill the law, and to invoke the supreme Name; to serve God in the neighbor means to provide him with what we have and what he needs, whether with food or the Spirit. All these things are inseparable.

Expressed differently: we must always give something to our neighbor, for "Inasmuch as ye have done it unto one of the least of these my brethren, ye have done it unto me."[26] But in order to give our neighbor the best that we have, it is not enough to draw from out of the doctrine as if writing a book; rather we owe our neighbor in a certain sense what we owe God: for what we fulfill for Him in secret we can also then give our neighbor. What we do spiritually also benefits our neighbor. He who out of carelessness neglects spiritual duties should tell himself that he also owes their fulfillment to his neighbor; what we do not wish to do for ourselves, we should at least do for others. We therefore owe our fellow men in a twofold way: first the intention to give something, and secondly the gift. The first is not enough if one does not have the second, and the second is not enough if one does not have the first.

[26] Matt. 25:40.

Or stated differently yet: our fellow brother also stands before us in a twofold way, first as the one who receives in God, and secondly as the one who teaches us on God's behalf; in the first case, the thanks comes from God, and in the second case the teaching is from God. For every man, even the most ignorant, can teach us in some way; this is what the Hindus call an *upaguru*. Animals and plants are our neighbors also, and as such have a claim to our confraternity and can teach us something.

Thus is God in our neighbor. God is also in our own soul in a twofold way: first in the center of our being, in the pure Spirit that is one with Truth, and secondly in worship, in the fulfillment of duty, in good deeds and, above all, in the invocation of the supreme Name. Man must repose in the Spirit, and he must perform good deeds.

God is also in our environment in a twofold way: on the one hand in the destiny we experience every day, and on the other hand in the symbols, the "signs", that we see and hear every day. In both of these we must think of God: in experience and in what we see; in destiny and symbols. Our environment reminds us of God, and this is its spiritual function, its mystical significance.

God, world, I, thou; fundamentally, however, there are only two things, God and the soul, everything else being for us in some way either God or the soul. And fundamentally there is only God.

—— ·:· ——

"*Marvelous Siena*"[27]

Florence, Italy, September 25, 1951 to Ruth Michon

Picture to yourself a city where many of its streets are made up of tall, gloomy, ostentatious palaces, where one finds churches like mosques, built of white and black stone, where there are streets with names such as "Via delle Belle Donne", and where so much reminds one of Dante, Savonarola, and Fra Angelico—such is Florence, where we have been for the past week. But we have also visited Pisa with its leaning tower, Pistoria[28] with its splendid churches, and

[27] See *Frithjof Schuon: Messenger of the Perennial Philosophy*, chap. 14, "Travels".

[28] The Latin form of Pistoia, the medieval Italian city located northwest of Florence.

marvelous Siena, in whose museums one finds early Italian images of the Madonna that are among the most beautiful I have ever seen. I think the world's best painters are the early medieval Christians, particularly the Italians and Russians, and the Buddhists, particularly the Tibetans and Japanese.

—— ·:· ——

"*The Special Nature of Our Vocation*"
Lausanne, December 20, 1951 to Hans Küry

One should not confuse vocations; there are vocations that mutually exclude one another. As a Muslim initiate, one has two duties in the West, one that is purely inward and another that is directed outward. The first concerns our soul and God, the second the world in which we live; in our case, however, this second duty results automatically from the first, through the mere fact of our spiritual presence. This kind of spiritual influence through mere presence, mere existence, excludes an outward influence from person to person, in the same way that one cannot be both a hermit and preacher; and yet the world needs the hermit as much as the preacher. It is said in Islam that the equilibrium of the world depends largely on the existence—partly hidden—of saints, or also on the invocation of God's Name. If man is not holy, the Name nevertheless is holy, and man is made so by the invocation.

The *Tarīqah* corresponds, therefore, not only to a spiritual path comparable to others, but also to a specific vocation. Should one find oneself in the position of having to express oneself on spiritual matters—a position one must indeed avoid, precisely because of this vocation—then one should do so, not in the name of traditional orthodoxy, but in the name of a faith encompassing all forms. There are Protestants who also accept Catholicism and find it right that Catholics remain Catholic, and who even think the same about believers of other religions. "There must be religion", these people say. We need not give any other appearance than this.

To profess to be a Catholic could result in very painful situations, for example if one were led by circumstances to have to take a position openly against Islam or Hinduism.

To express myself concretely: if one feels the inclination to correct someone's opinion, one can put this inclination into effect by praying for the person concerned, while remaining outwardly silent as far as possible. One must be thoroughly imbued right from the start with the special nature of our vocation. It is somehow comparable to the "function of spiritual presence" of the Maharshi, who indeed never expressed himself doctrinally.

—— ⁘ ——

"*A Minority in a Hostile World*"
Lausanne, September 18, 1953 to Walter Mautner

I regret that you must live so far away, but you are not the only one in this situation. I would like to take this opportunity to say a word about the idea of "the *Ṭarīqah*". In our circumstances, "the *Ṭarīqah*" is not composed of people, rather it is a principle; it is impossible to hold a spiritual community accountable for individuals who perforce are not well integrated. For the West is chaotic, and its people are chaotic. I can do nothing *a priori* to change this. In the Islamic world, all the *fuqarā'* grew up on the soil of Islam; psychic possibilities and spiritual criteria are transparent, everything is to be found in a certain way in the air one breathes; in the West, one must take men as the West delivers them, with all the inscrutable, disparate tendencies of the most varied milieus and cultural backgrounds. Before one accepts a person, one would almost have to create him. There are of course a few *fuqarā'* who represent "the *Ṭarīqah*" just as well—and sometimes even better—than native Muslims do on average, but there are also others who, without lacking in spiritual gifts, mar their good traits with chaotically individualistic tendencies; and "the *Ṭarīqah*" really cannot be held responsible for this. Moreover, there is the fact that each one lives his life in his own corner, purely due to outward necessity and to the limitations of time.

It is in the nature of esoterism to require much from the free will of each person; that the appropriate cultural atmosphere for this free will is absent in the West is neither the fault of the *Ṭarīqah* nor that of the master. Thus if we are not to wonder pointlessly about the inevitability of these circumstances, we must hold to the following notion: the *Tarīqah* is first of all the doctrine, the initiation, the path, the master, the community in the narrowest and best sense of the term—by way of criteria, the three cardinal virtues are indispensable here—but it is not the totality of all the Westerners who are initiated. The Westerner must not only rid himself of his faults, but he must also overcome a whole series of unconscious attachments and inherited or acquired bad habits, and do so in an environment in which he is exposed to very particular types of perils—in Eastern or in Medieval circumstances things would not have gone so far.

Since the *Tarīqah* gives of itself—since it gives the doctrine, the initiation, the means of grace, and a master—the individual owes it his own sanctity. Instead of making demands based on false expectations and wanting to be the judge of the community, the individual should quietly endeavor to become sanctified, for one owes it to the means of grace to make effective use of them. What would have happened to the decaying monastic orders had the saints of those times turned their backs on them? No, they gradually purified and saved their communities through their own sanctity. What African *Tarīqah* could subsist were one to measure it by the quality of the majority of its members? I know whereof I speak, for I lived there. If I mention all of this here, it is because I have had several discussions about this recently; thus, I wanted to repeat these important explanations to you as well. I want to add this also: wherever there is something sacred, antagonistic forces will work all the more harshly. I have experienced things—disappointments if you wish—whose unspeakable ugliness and almost inconceivable absurdity can only be explained by the presence of the sacred.

I return to your letter. The Hassidim did live as a minority in a hostile world, but this world was still one of faith—it was not today's world, it was old Catholic Poland and Orthodox Russia—and the Hassidim themselves came from a closed cultural circle, for the Jews of that time had *a priori* their tradition and customs. This is the only way an intimate community existence is conceivable: on the basis of a preexisting culture that regulates everything from the outset and hence from the outset excludes a thousand evils. In a true culture, the channels for the spiritual are already there, and if a vocation emerges already in childhood, one can pursue it and need not waste any time, as we ourselves all had to do; we had to squander a spiritual thirst for decades without being able to make hardly any use of it. Moreover, in a healthy culture, one works much less—and differently—than nowadays. In our world, the friends simply have no time to meet socially outside of the regular weekend gatherings, and it would be a mistake if they were to do so. There would be no time left for what is essential. Moreover, the sheer outward agitation of human affairs in our world is much more senseless and intrusive than in ancient cultures, where everything is much simpler and where the customs prevent in advance many dissonances and mishaps. Also, Hassidism has a more popular character than our Shadhilism, which originally was more or less aristocratic and inclined towards solitude.

—·:·—

"*A Legal Minimum*"
Lausanne, October 15, 1953 to Hans Küry

In Judaism, the *sharī'ah* is indivisible and absolute; Jewish esoterism makes a precondition of this indivisibility and absoluteness, and it allows for no compromise. Either one submits to hundreds of prescriptions, or one is no longer a Jew; as a result, the majority of today's Jews no longer belong to orthodox Judaism. The Islamic *sharī'ah*, in contrast, is characterized by its flexibility: it takes into account a legal minimum—what is indispensable, *fard*—and to claim that this is not the whole of Islam is a false belief, it is pharisaism. Of course—and this is something that my opponents consider to be a valid objection—a born Muslim living in *dār al-islām* will hardly be satisfied with the legal minimum, for he has little reason to be so: he has been raised in Islam and masters its forms with ease, and in fact has learned hardly anything other than those forms; in addition, he is backed by the rhythms of the entire social life. In our case, we must also take into consideration our rootedness *a priori* in metaphysics and esoterism, the uniqueness of our cyclically determined situation, our spiritual connection with Hinduism and Christianity, and the nature of our environment; all of this must be placed on the scales and gives our community a special style, without releasing it from orthodoxy. For Islam is truth, and consequently it can incorporate anything into itself that lies in the nature of things. The fact that our point of departure is the validity of all revelations (the transcendent unity of religions) and that our foundation is *a priori* metaphysical, creates precisely a completely new spiritual landscape, which God—obviously!—is the first to take into account.

—·:·—

"*Worldliness*"
Pully, Switzerland, November 21, 1953 to Hans Küry

This evening we held the first gathering in our new house.[29] It is still not yet completely furnished, but this should not prevent you and other friends from visiting us. During the gathering, I said the following:[30] worldliness, which is a danger for some, is based primarily on a lack of fear of God and love of God. To fear God is to see, in the domain of action, the effects of causes; to love God is to choose, between the spiritual and non-spiritual, what is spiritual.

Secondly, the outer world will be dangerous for one who has no direct knowledge—but only bookish notions—with respect to the following: the spiritual particularity of Islam, the value and beauty of tradition in general, the value and beauty of God's virgin nature, and the worthlessness and ugliness of the modern world.

To this I wish to add the following: in the spiritual life, equilibrium and perseverance are everything. The fruits of perseverance are always good. Boredom, oppression, dissipation, hardening, and the like only reveal to a person the ugliness of his own soul; were there no such ugliness, he would not have to make an effort. When spiritual masters say that one should hate one's soul, or look at it as something contemptible before God, this means that one should experience one's soul, one's ego, as a bundle of tendencies opposed to God; to love one's ego as such, hence to consider it to be good, means to affirm man's fallen nature, to deny the fall of Adam. The danger of pleasures lies in this, that man may forget God when enjoying the pleasure, not

[29] Schuon moved to Pully, near Lausanne, in 1953. See *Frithjof Schuon: Messenger of the Perennial Philosophy*, chap. 12, "Marriage and a New Home".

[30] This letter refers to a commentary given by Schuon at a prayer gathering of his disciples. In later years these commentaries on the spiritual life were memorialized in written texts.

that God will begrudge us the pleasure. For the fallen soul, pleasure becomes a false god; this does not lie in the nature of pleasure, but in the soul's estrangement from God. When the masters speak of the soul's contemptibleness, they have in mind its weaknesses, its vanity, greed, and hardening.

The meaning of the love of one's neighbor can be expressed thus: the rift between man and God will be bridged when the rift between "I" and "thou" is bridged. He who cannot see himself in others and others in himself—he who does not experience others as himself and himself as a stranger—cannot then place his existence in God, nor receive God in existence. To exchange one's own being with the divine Being can only be done by one who has exchanged his self for the self of others.

—— ·:· ——

"*Dances of the Pow-Wow Troupe*"; "*Yellow Tail*"
Pully, January 1, 1954 to Hans Küry

We were in Paris a few days ago to see the Indian dances of the pow-wow troupe; on seeing an Indian woman on the street, we followed her and took a room at the Hotel West-End where she and the other Indians were staying. Titus Burkhardt and his wife were also there and spoke, as we did, with the Indians. I expected nothing more than traditional dances and was prepared to see only unremarkable people; but already on the journey there I had the distinct impression that I would experience something important. And as it happened, I met one of the noblest men I have ever met: Yellow Tail, the younger brother of the Crow Indian chief of the same name.[31] Burckhardt spoke to him about me and about our perspective; the next day, after Burckhardt had left, Yellow Tail invited me and my wife into his room, where he smoked the peace pipe with Deer Nose[32] and me; after we had smoked, he gave it to me as a gift—a small pipe out of sacred red clay from Minnesota; he also gave me sacred tobacco from the mountains in Montana. On the same day, around midnight, Young

[31] Schuon is referring to Thomas Yellowtail and his older brother, Robert Yellowtail.

[32] Donald Deer Nose.

Hawk came to take us to a Sun Dance ceremony;[33] this experience was unforgettable in its spiritual authenticity. Yellow Tail stood there for a long time and prayed in the Absaroka language to the Great Spirit; then I had to take eagle feathers in my hand while he prayed for me; he also asked me to pray for him and for his people. We parted late in the night.

—·:·—

"*The Visit of Shaykh Al-Mahdi*"
Pully, July 28, 1954 to Martin Lings

We have had the visit of Shaykh al-Mahdi from Mostaghanem, the son and successor of Shaykh Adda; he is leaving for Cardiff today and wants to visit you afterwards. He should be told that you alone are officially Muslim, and that the situation of the others is similar to ours, that is to say, we must surround ourselves with the utmost discretion, for social, political, and other reasons. They should also be told how difficult our situation is politically, and that therefore all publicity should be avoided; you can tell them that you can go from time to time to Cardiff, but that it is impossible for you to maintain regular contacts with these *fuqarā'*, to receive visits, etc., and that above all you must be careful about English Muslims, the frequentation of whom could destroy your private life. Also, that if one were sociable like them, there would be no more time to invoke, and that frequenting certain people brings much more dissipation than spiritual advantages; I also had to tell them why it is impossible for us to make propaganda, and that it is God who sends us those who are qualified for our milieu.

The Shaykh al-Mahdi is, moreover, an intelligent and refined man who understands our need for isolation and discretion. He should be told that the means of action we use is the invocation, and that we address our message to qualified intellectuals, not to coarse men whose psychological presence would destroy our community. I have

[33] That is, to a monthly prayer ceremony associated with the Sun Dance religion. See *Yellowtail: Crow Medicine Man and Sun Dance Chief*, edited by Michael Oren Fitzgerald (Norman: University of Oklahoma Press, 1991), pp. 129–35.

already spoken to the Shaykh in these terms, but it would be good if you could remind him of this, so that he sees that our mission cannot coincide outwardly in every respect with that of the Arab Alawites.[34]

—— ⁘ ——

"*Southern Spain*"
Seville, Spain, August 15, 1954 to Titus Burckhardt

Granada was a precious experience. The Alhambra is like a reddish flower in the desert. Its dreamlike surfaces, filled with arabesques, transpose the green profusion of the gardens into the realm of the spirit; it is as our Spanish guide said: the Muslim contemplates the beauty of nature, the better to know the beauty of God.

Before we came to Granada—it was at the seaside, near Tossa de Mar—I had a vivid experience regarding the *Shahādah*; I saw suddenly and quite clearly how everything we have ever sought is present in the *Shahādah*, namely metaphysical doctrine and spiritual realization: doctrine because the *Shahādah* is a discernment between the Real and the illusory, and realization because the *Shahādah* is an invocation, like every divine Name; metaphysics and invocation are everything for us, and both are to be found in the *Shahādah*. In this connection, the names *Rahmān* and *Rahīm* have the sense of an *a priori* non-metaphysical invocation of the divine Person, whereas the Name *Allāh* corresponds to an existential and entirely non-mental invocation; God is the Invoker, we are but the substance.

After looking at the Alhambra for hours, it became clearer than ever to me that Islamic art is contemplative, whereas Gothic art is volitive; not to speak of the Renaissance, in which the volitive becomes worldly, hypocritical, sensual, and ostentatious. For Charles

[34] Subsequently, it became clear that the young Shaykh al-Mahdi (1928–1975) had ambitions to expand his influence and prestige over larger parts of the Islamic world and Europe, establishing a journal called *Les Amis de l'Islam*, whose propagandist content supported this aim. Schuon and Titus Burckhardt both refused to contribute to the journal, which meant that relations with Mostaghanem became distant and to a certain extent strained. See *Frithjof Schuon: Life and Teachings*, p. 37 for further details. See also the letter to Michel Vâlsan, dated May 24, 1973, titled "A Spiritual Heritage".

V, the Alhambra was worldly because it is beautiful and joyful, and to this apparent worldliness he opposed the dull, oppressive, and completely unspiritual ostentatiousness of his palace. Here ugliness and stupidity wish to pass themselves off as virtues, namely as seriousness, strength, and otherworldliness. The otherworldly is seen purely in volitive fashion, as something negative, and not as something spiritual that reveals itself here below.

In the Alhambra and its gardens, I experienced something similar to what I have known in the solitude of the Alps, namely that the divine Name lay in the air, that it invoked itself. Indeed, a spiritual perfume pervades the whole landscape of southern Spain, with its olive and palm groves interspersed with desert areas, and everywhere its altogether Arab-looking villages; and even amidst the deafening noise of dancing and singing gypsy women, this perfume does not leave me. There is a certain goodness and a certain presence of God in the air.

Yesterday evening in Seville's narrow streets, we heard medieval trumpet music, then heavy, powerful drumming. We followed the sounds and came upon a procession that, slow and dreamlike, made its way along the street; a statue of the Madonna—tall, rigid, resplendent with silver and gold, and surrounded by many candles—was being borne along through the dark, half-Arab city. We thought at first it was the Macarena, but a woman told us it was the Virgin of Snows. A huge silver triangle, surrounded by many heavy candelabras, which appeared to be pushed along on a heavy silver- and gold-ornamented carriage—in reality, there were men beneath the metal pedestal to carry it—thus did the divine image move slowly forward through the night, to the accompaniment of a now shrill, now melancholic funeral music. Sometimes the procession would make a long halt, until a jolt and a shudder would go through the Madonna and the *barakah*-laden image would move further along the street, scraping against the houses on its way. At length, we stood still and watched as the glittering and resounding enchantment slowly passed out of sight.

—— ·⁝· ——

"*Christianity Is a Total Tradition*"
Pully, May 31, 1955 to a reader[35]

It is not possible to make a systematic distinction between the supernatural and the spiritual, because the former necessarily intervenes in the latter in diverse ways. The intellect, too, has a supernatural aspect, but this is beyond the ordinary theological perspective, for which there is in man only the will and reason.

In Christianity, it is baptism, confirmation, and communion that constitute what can be termed initiation: the "total" character of these sacraments excludes the existence, alongside them, of more or less secret initiatic rites that would be superimposed on them, as is found in Orphism, in Sufism, etc. The particularity of Christianity is precisely the open character of the initiatic means; it is a particularity, at least, in the Semitic and Western world. On this point there is disagreement between Guénon's thesis and mine. Indeed, one cannot conceive that there could be, in Christianity, a more profound and more precious source of graces than the blood of Christ, or that there could be souls or intelligences for which this source would not be good enough. The difference between exoterism and esoterism is here uniquely a question of perspective and method. There is of course a purely exoteric participation in the sacraments, so that it would be an abuse of language to qualify the bulk of Christians as "initiates", but monks and nuns are initiates by the fact that they follow a spiritual path; the same applies to priests who are saints, such as the Curé d'Ars. As for the intellective way, *gnosis*, it is represented above all by Clement of Alexandria, Meister Eckhart, and Angelus Silesius; but it is always a specifically Christian *gnosis*, that is to say, one that stays very close to the perspective of love.

Consequently, the two strange occurrences you allude to in your letter cannot be initiations in the strict and technical sense of the term, for Heaven never acts without sufficient reason; on the other hand, such occurrences can be "accidental"—and at the same time "providential"—contacts with the world of Essences, whether this world is envisaged in a subjective manner or in an objective and cosmic manner. What could the practical value be of such "encounters" with "higher states"? They are summons, or callings, to undertake a con-

[35] The recipient was a Catholic.

templative life. One should, after having experienced such "fissures" in the individual hardening, make of life a continuous and secret prayer. But this is only possible with the help of the Name of God, that is to say, with the invocation of Christ, of the "Jesus Prayer". In order to enter into such a way, one must have above all the indispensable theoretical knowledge, and a purity of intention that excludes all conscious or unconscious individualism; one must be centered on God, not on the ego. There are multiple illusions on this plane. But with God, all things are possible.

The impossibility of having an esoteric ritual superimposed on the sacraments results from their total character, notably the character of the Eucharist. The revelation, in Christianity, is Christ himself; now the Eucharist is Christ, all of Christ. Since Revelation must contain by definition all spiritual modes, and since Christ unifies in his divinity all these modes, including of course those that can be rightly qualified as "esoteric" or "universal", the same applies to the Eucharist, which is the Word incarnate and not only a "part"—an exoteric part—of the God-Man. Thus, it is the central and total character of the Christian dogmas and sacraments that is opposed to the Guénonian thesis.

In order to invoke the Name of Jesus without risk—and in the absence of a spiritual master—it is necessary first of all to know the doctrine contained in the *Philokalia* or, what amounts to the same, in *The Russian Pilgrim*[36]—an essentially Patristic doctrine—then to call upon the Holy Spirit and place oneself under the protection of the Virgin; one must realize in oneself the virtues of humility and charity, that is to say, one must be conscious of personal as well as existential limitations, and consider oneself as a stranger while considering the neighbor as oneself. It is better at the beginning not to invoke too much at one time, so as not to produce tensions or "outbursts"; one must speak to God in inward prayer, as if He were our visible master, and describe to Him our difficulties with resignation, gratitude, and trust. One must not speak to anyone of one's spiritual experiences. In the case of grave difficulties, one must cease all invocation and take refuge in ordinary prayer, in the Lord's Prayer, and in the rosary. The invocation of the Name of Jesus is not recommended or is even forbidden to people with stubborn, pretentious, or eccentric characters. An objective intelligence must be combined with childlike simplicity.

[36] That is, *The Way of a Pilgrim*.

As for language, I am opposed to invoking in French or in some other modern language, because these languages bear the imprint of the modern deviation; they are "worn-out" by "literature", etc. A liturgical language must be chosen. Regarding the choice of a formula, this is a matter of vocation.

The soul is complex and it has need of diversity; there are thus various means to overcome our nature and to obtain transforming and sanctifying fervor and concentration. What I mean is that there are different modes of prayer: the Name of Jesus, the Lord's Prayer, the rosary, the Psalms, personal prayer; it is above all the latter that, next to the invocation, must not be neglected. In the Name of Jesus, it is as it were God Himself who pronounces His Name; there is a great mystery in this. In canonical prayers, it is man who prays, man as such and not this or that man; whence the use of the plural "we" in the Lord's Prayer. The prayer of man as such is necessarily revealed, it is the prayer God wishes to hear. In the case of personal prayer, however, performed in a vernacular language and not in a liturgical one, it is a specific person who prays; it is a specific soul that channels its powers towards God. One must tell God everything in this prayer, even of our boredom, even of our incapacity to pray, if such is the case. Invocation, canonical prayer, personal prayer: these are the three necessary modes of the way of prayer.

The connection between invocation and eucharistic communion is admirably captured in the following liturgical formulas: "I will take the bread of heaven and call upon the name of the Lord", and "I will take the chalice of salvation and call upon the name of the Lord".[37] There can be no initiation superior to the Eucharist, for the simple reason that the blood of Christ contains all of the divinity of the Word made flesh; the Eucharist perpetuates the Word incarnate, in totality and not in part.

Christianity is founded—in its general form, not in all of its possibilities—on the volitive, hence passional, aspect of man: man is will, then reason, without which the will would not be free. Christianity is a *bhakti* by its form, but *jnāna* has its place in it too, thanks to the universality of the Christic symbolism; this is necessarily so since Christi-

[37] Both formulas are written in Latin, and taken from the Latin liturgy of the Communion.

anity is a total tradition. Before the Council of Nicaea, the boundaries between the perspectives were not definitively set; the Council of Nicaea marks the crystallization of Christianity into a bhaktic perspective, one which officially excludes *jnāna*, that is to say, a way based on intellective factors and therefore on the axiom that man is the intellect. Christianity has a voluntaristic, individualistic, and sentimental character; these words have here no pejorative connotation, but express outward traits that Christianity necessarily has inasmuch as it must suit the Western mentality. In keeping with this mentality, Christian exoterism lends an absolute value to a historical fact, and conversely attributes a relative character to the Absolute; it takes no account of the degrees of Reality, exactly as Hindu *bhakti* does, for which the world is real. The result of this is that Christianity attributes, in fact, an immense importance to intermediary relativities; the cult of the Virgin, prayers for the souls in purgatory, masses for this or that purpose, etc. Being individualist, Christianity is overly focused on sin and underestimates positive means, based on concentration and aesthetic intuition, of spirituality; its mysticism overlooks in general both intellection and concentration, and admits in practice only individualist asceticism and sentimentalities; intellectual and technical—or "yogic"—means strike it as being "easy", as if this were a criterion and as if things that are easy in theory could not be difficult in practice.

Christianity contains a certain hostility towards intelligence, for it is neither indispensable to *bhakti*, nor accessible to all men; *bhakti*'s exclusively ascetic and sentimental point of view leads—in fact if not in principle, and due to popularization—to a kind of cult of stupidity and ugliness, and also of the disagreeable. Therefore, intelligence readily appears as "pride", and is always reduced to reason, which is something individual; beauty for its part appears under the aspects of seduction, sensuality, sin, or at least as that which is agreeable and easy. Nature is "of this world", and one always dreads a "pagan" naturalism. Such a perspective admits nothing "supernatural" in man, save grace, but this is not something that man can bring about; it is fundamentally dualist, due to the very fact of its theological anthropomorphism. What is serious is that, upon contact with intellectual or jnanic perspectives, a "personalist" mysticism is substituted for suprapersonal metaphysics, and this constitutes an inversion of metaphysical relationships; to save the lower perspective—that of *bhakti*, which needless to say is in no way threatened by *jnāna*, since *jnāna* situates everything in its correct place—one seeks to belittle the higher perspective, and once again an absolute character is attributed to the relative and conversely

—— ·:· ——

"*The Question of Reincarnation*"
circa 1955 to Martin Lings[38]

You know that the question of reincarnation holds no special interest for me, given that it is no doubt difficult to define the exact boundary between facts and symbolism. Nevertheless, in order to clarify Guénon's thoughts on the matter, I would say this: if Guénon does not accept, among an indefinite number of other possibilities, the possibility of "that which returns" to return to the bodily human state, this is because he accepts the return to the same possibility only within a limited system, the sensible world for instance, and of that only within certain "dimensions", such as space; now the criterion of our exit from such a system is the objective destruction of the empirical subject. In sleep, the subject is subjectively eliminated, but not objectively destroyed; but upon death, one cannot—since one is leaving a limited possibility—but fall under the rule of All-Possibility, the illimitation of which excludes any repetition. Be that as it may, if reincarnation were something as banal as it is in the minds of the average Easterner—who believes that the fish in a pond are reincarnated lamas (there is no point of being a lama if one is to be reborn as a fish!) or that a particular goat is a recently deceased English Lady (in the Maharshi's entourage)—if things actually were like this, there would be no explanation as to why beings such as Christ, Muhammad, Moses, and Abraham never said a word about it. Generally speaking, I think that in every tradition there are some "solidified", hence crude, concepts, and this may be why an Asiatic sage said that only error is transmitted, not truth; for instance, the Muslim denial of the fact of the crucifixion is as astonishing as the Christian denial of the salvation of pre-Christian saints, not to mention the denial of the "paganisms", and so on and so forth. I would add that

[38] Schuon's letter to Marco Pallis, dated November 8, 1959, titled "The Problem of Transmigration", also deals with reincarnation and transmigration.

the ease with which Tibetans believe that a given European genius is a reincarnated Tibetan saint—there have been instances of this—or the manner in which Ramakrishna wanted to make of Vivekananda the reincarnation of a *jīvan-mukta jnāna*, is hardly reassuring for me.

—·:·—

"*We Are All One*"[39]
Pully, September 1955 to Hari Prasad Shastri

I feel that when I am invoking the Name of God, wherever I may be, I am with you; for in this state there are no longer spatial distances, and in the holy Names of the Infinite we are all one.

—·:·—

"*A Transcendence of Forms*"
Pully, January 28, 1956 to Donald Matheson

Many failures can be explained, all told, by a lack of faith and lack of fear, within a general milieu in which faith as well as fear appear ludicrous; it suffices for passion, inexperience, and unintelligence to become involved, and then the devil too—who cannot but take advantage of a golden opportunity, he who always takes advantage of the weaknesses of men. In a traditional world, in which everything is homogeneous and shares a solidarity of purpose, there are temptations that are inconceivable; "traditional forms" are not presented as merchandise in a store window, and daily life is not a struggle in a bog of trivialities. Now we must recognize that we do not live in a world governed by tradition, and awareness of this fact spares us from being surprised at certain things.

In any case, our situation is very peculiar, even from a spiritual standpoint, given that we are of non-Muslim origin and that our immovable point of departure is Hindu doctrine. We have "contents

[39] See *Frithjof Schuon: Messenger of the Perennial Philosophy*, chap. 15, "Noteworthy Encounters".

of consciousness" (in German: *Bewusstseinsinhalte*) that Muslim-born individuals do not have, which gives us some sense of perspective with regard to the most particular aspects of Islam. It would be quite wrong to base ourselves in this case on the example of Hindus who become Muslims in spite of their "contents of consciousness" or their "imagination", for in this case there is, precisely, conversion, which means that one has "burnt what one had worshipped" and that one has started anew from nothing; such is obviously not the case of the *Tarīqah*. The fact that Sufis from India may understand Hinduism *a posteriori* is quite another question, for they have grown up within Islam; their Islamic perspective is congenital, initial, spontaneous; their intellectuality develops out of forms, instead of relativizing them *a priori*. As for ourselves, I will say that it would be quite abnormal, according to the nature of things and therefore "in the eyes of God", that men finding themselves objectively and subjectively in our situation be Muslims in exactly the same way as Muslim-born people, including esoterists; this is what explains in part that it is normal for the *sharī'ah* to be reduced, among us, to a strict minimum, a justification that results from a hostile ambience on the one hand and the graces of the divine Name on the other. Since we have not "burnt what we had worshipped"—quite to the contrary, since we understand Christianity better than before—we cannot pretend not to know what we know, nor to forget what we remember; we cannot feign a "selective lack of imagination", which in our case does not correspond to any reality. I will add that life is too short for an extensive study of formal or "terrestrial" Islam, unless one sacrifices the "one thing needful",[40] namely the one thing that is the sufficient reason for our traditional attachment.

So, what distinguishes us above all from Muslim-born or converted individuals—"psychologically", one could say—is that our mind is *a priori* centered upon universal metaphysics (*Advaita Vedānta, Shahādah, Risālat al-Ahadīyah*) and the universal path of the divine Name (*japa-yoga, nembutsu, dhikr*, prayer of the heart); it is because of these two factors that we are in a traditional form, which in fact—though not in principle—is Islam. The universal orthodoxy emanating from these two sources of authority determines our interpretation of the *sharī'ah* and Islam in general, somewhat as the moon

[40] Luke 10:42.

the first instance even includes, esoterically and at the extreme limit, a circumstantial aspect of abrogation (*naskh*), a little like the verses that abolish given enunciations of primordiality or universality—for example with respect to the *qiblah*—but in a reverse sense, that is to say, going from the particular to the universal. I also want to mention in this order of ideas—although this takes us out of the domain of Islam—the Buddhist doctrine according to which the entire Law of the Buddha will be lost, except the invocation, which will last until the end; and I want to mention in an analogous sense that among the "offenses against the divine Name" (*nāma-aparādhas*) that *japa-yoga* enumerates, there is the fact of granting other virtues or practices such as fasting, charity, sacrifices the same rank as the Name as if the Name alone were insufficient. This is related to a very important aspect of *japa-yoga*: the trust placed in the Name alone; and this aspect, which has been taken to its ultimate conclusion in Japanese Buddhism, also highlights the legitimate basis for our attitude, which draws its inspiration from the principle that the divine Name is better than the whole *sharī'ah*, and that it would suffice in principle to save us.

Concerning the question of the "formal" and the "informal", or the "letter" (which may kill) and the "spirit" (which vivifies), I would like to note that there is always, or almost always, an intermediary region between exoterism and esoterism, a *barzakh*, which appears both as an esoterized exoterism and an exoterized esoterism; Christianity is nothing else, whence its paradoxical character, and with regard to Islam we find this *barzakh* in the ritualism of a Ghazzali and in popular Sufism, but also throughout the collective forms of *Tasawwuf*. Between exoterism and esoterism there always exists a ritualistic and moral *karma-yoga*; now this *yoga*, by the very fact of its individualistic nature—for action and merit necessarily belong to the individual—is opposed to the metaphysical perspective as well as to the way of the saving Name. The rationalizing individualism of Muslim piety is as non-metaphysical as the sentimental individualism of the Christians. There is also in any esoterism—inasmuch as this point of view is affirmed in a direct manner—a marked tendency towards a transcendence of forms, on the doctrinal plane (where every formulation becomes an *upāya*, an "unavoidable artifice") as well as on the methodical plane (where concentration and its direct supports absorb most of the exterior rites); to deny this tendency is to go against the nature of things.

The whole emphasis must be placed on metaphysical truth and the divine Name; this is a "religion" that runs through all traditional forms just as the thread runs through the cloth. Starting from a source of doctrinal, hence intellectual, evidence, one must realize faith and find—in and by the Name—the inner certitude that is our very being.

—— ·:· ——

"*Simple but Consequential Attitudes*"
Pully, February 7, 1956 to a reader[43]

I am glad to learn that you have finally found a setting that suits your aspirations, that is to say, one arranged in view of the "one thing needful".[44] "Easy solutions"—since you bring up this moral problem and this typically modern way of looking at things—are always legitimate if God is the aim, for "my yoke is easy, and my burden light";[45] worldly people make a cult out of difficulty, which is merely a form—and a fairly hypocritical form at that—of individualism; it is to forget that greatness comes from God and not from man. The greatness of divine qualities reveals itself in one who opens himself to them, if one may express oneself thus.

In the spiritual life, difficulties often reside in apparently simple things; victory belongs to him who, in secret, knows how to persevere in little things. To think of God, to empty oneself for Him, to escape from that habitual dream in which the ego mirrors and repeats itself—this seems simple *a priori*; what could be easier than to repeat an ejaculatory orison? But to do this always, to renounce our dream always anew, to acquire the habit of keeping ourselves in God's presence, thus to go against the congenital tendencies of our soul—tendencies towards dissipation as well as laziness—this is a great thing, the "dimensions" of which cannot be measured from the outside. If you read the lives of saints, you will see that they were great above all through simple but consequential attitudes; the more visible glories were somehow superimposed upon these.

[43] The recipient was a young Catholic monk.

[44] Luke 10:42.

[45] Matt. 11:30.

Worldly people like to appease their conscience by musing about sublime realities, as if by thinking about them they participated in them; it is of course good to think about such realities, and one cannot even help doing so, but it is important not to let this habit take the place of real virtues. One must dedicate oneself to a discipline that is not above our strength—that may even appear to be beneath it—but one must dedicate oneself to it totally. And one will then see over time that it is above our strength, but that everything is possible with God's help; nothing is possible without it. There are things that are little in themselves but that, when practiced with perseverance, lead to great things; this is what is forgotten by those who constantly bring up the reproach of "easiness".

People often speak to me of concentration, and complain they are lacking in it; this is above all a lack of imagination, for one who knows that God is infinitely lovable and that there is nothing to fear when with Him, has little difficulty in maintaining himself in a certain state of recollectedness. A man sentenced to death has no trouble remembering death, and likewise a man parched with thirst effortlessly remembers water; it is not difficult for the young man to think of his betrothed. So should every man think of God; if he does not do so, it is because he lacks "imagination". And this is the great surprise of death: the soul, once it is wrested out of the body and this earthly world, is confronted with God, and it sees the fulgurating and infinite Essence of all that it loved—or could have loved—on earth. In a word, to "concentrate" on God is to know right now that all that we love, and all we could love, is to be found infinitely in God, and that all we love here below we love, though without being aware of it, only because of God. We attach ourselves to the fleeting reflections on water as if the water were luminous; but at death we see the sun with immense regret—unless we became aware of the sun in time.

I claim no merit in being able to speak in this way, for God "forced matters", if I may say so, by placing me in a destiny that made me appreciate very early my helplessness and the marvels of His grace.

—— ·:· ——

"*Death Is Not a Real Separation*"
February 28, 1956 to Hari Prasad Shastri's widow

We know that death is not a real separation, that it is but an illusory and fleeting veil, and that in God souls meet, even here-below. We cannot be closer to those whom we love than by clinging to God, and in losing ourselves in Him. It is in losing ourselves in Him that we find ourselves in Him again, along with those whom we love.

—·⁝·—

"*Heaven Placed the Function on Me*"
Pully, March 7, 1956 to Martin Lings

Given the terrible disappointments I had to face, I sometimes asked myself if I have the right to be Shaykh. I had forgotten in those moments that this function did not depend at all on my choice, that it had been placed on me at a given moment and completely unexpectedly. I became Shaykh at a providential time when I was in doubt about any spiritual possibility in the West, and when I was ready to give up everything. Heaven placed the function on me suddenly, without transition, as a ray of light falls in a dark room; it was totally contrary to my state of mind, but it was irresistible. Likewise in the case of the daily invocation and the themes of meditation: these came upon me from one day to the next, with violence, at a time when I was neglecting almost everything, when I was overcome with unspeakable weariness. When I ask myself the question of knowing whether I am worthy of my function, the problem is unsolvable for me; but when I remember that this function was placed on me by Heaven, as also our method, there is no longer room for any uncertainty; praise be to God.

—·⁝·—

"An Essence Rather Than a Form"
Pully, April 4, 1956 to Martin Lings

To return to the questions discussed in my preceding letters, I will say this: the great religious happiness of a Muslim as such is Islam in all its extension; it is not *a priori* the Prophet or the Koran, but Islam; it is the happiness of plunging the individual will into all the ramifications of the Law—*sharī'ah* and *sunnah*—which is itself the crystallization of the divine Will, and of accumulating supererogatory practices and merits. In an analogous way, the happiness of a Christian is Christ; the Church with the sacraments is the extension of Christ, who is everything. For a Muslim, it is not the Prophet but Islam—and all it comprises—that is everything, for here what matters is totality, not the center; the Prophet is the personification of totality just as Christ is the center of the cosmos; the totality—the Koran—comes "before" the Prophet just as Christ comes "before" the cosmos. But here is the point I wish to make: the properly religious side of Islam—or the formal aspect—is something that encompasses the whole individual; now it is impossible to conceal something that encompasses us totally. We must therefore reduce the *sharī'ah* to its simplest expression. I am basing myself here on the argument of *dār al-harb*, not on that of the *haqīqah*. One must choose: if one does not want to simplify the *sharī'ah*, then one must become a missionary. An essence can be concealed, but not a form. Another point to be made in this vein of ideas is that the *sharī'ah* is much harder in the conditions of our life than it is in the East; things that are simple in themselves can become complicated. Now the general tendency of the *sharī'ah* is to avoid complications.

If the happiness of an ordinary Muslim is zeal in the accomplishment of the *sharī'ah* and the *sunnah*, and if the happiness of a Christian is in the attachment to the saving divinity of Christ, where then is ours? It lies in what is common to all traditional forms: metaphysical truth and the divine Name. Our "Islam" is conformity to the nature of things and to the divine Will manifested in it; our "Christ" is the saving Name of God. Islam contains this Name since it contains everything that is for us in conformity to the divine Reality. Islam is surrendering oneself to the Name, and it is this Islam that encompasses our whole being. But this Islam is an essence rather than a form.

Christianity is like a dot that is red and warm, and Islam is like a surface that is green and fresh. From the point of view of *gnosis* and *tasawwuf* and *ma'rifah*, the color becomes white. But Islam also contains an element of warmth, which is *mahabbah*, and Christianity an element of freshness, which is *gnosis*.

P.S. Marco Pallis wrote me two letters; in one of them, he asks if I want to read *Time and Eternity* by Coomaraswamy.[46] Yes, I would like to read this book, and would you be so kind as to mention this to him and to greet him on my behalf? Coomaraswamy is an extremely precious author.

—— ⁘ ——

"*A Special Wisdom Connected with Traveling*"[47]

Athens, Greece, April 5, 1957 to Titus Burckhardt

We arrived in Athens six days ago, after spending two days in Venice and two more days at sea. During the voyage among the Greek islands, I found myself reminded of my childhood and the Greek legends, Odysseus and Aeneas suddenly coming to life.

The summit—and also the very center—of Christian art belongs to the icons, and I must say that even if one is familiar with the best books on the subject, one cannot form a sufficient idea of this art without having seen its masterpieces. Several of the most important masterpieces, which I have seen here in Athens either in the Byzantine or Benaki museum, have never to my knowledge been reproduced. Certain images, strongly reminiscent of Buddhist mandalas, may not be considered to be "art", but are true jewels, even in a purely artistic sense.

[46] Ananda Coomaraswamy (1877–1947), for many years curator of Indian art in the Boston Museum of Fine Arts and one of the founding figures of the perennialist school, was the author of numerous books and articles on art, religion, and metaphysics from the point of view of the primordial and universal tradition.

[47] For more information about Schuon's travels see *Frithjof Schuon: Messenger of the Perennial Philosophy*, chap. 14, "Travels".

From the spiritual point of view, a journey is always something of a double-edged sword, because the distraction that results from contact with so much that is new—one cannot simply shut oneself off from this newness or one might just as well stay at home, for if one is going to travel, one naturally wishes to learn something—this distraction has as its reaction an acute exposing of the ego, so that one suffers from its insignificance until this impulse has been mastered. It is beneficial also to perceive how we are always the same person—or always the same—in the supreme Name; we feel at home where the Name is with us and where we find ourselves in the Name; wherever the Name is, there we seem somehow always to have lived; when we experience the Name on the sea, perhaps, or in some Greek garden, it is as if this place is the home where we grew up, and as if our actual home were in some foreign land. Thus we realize that God is everywhere, that He is everywhere the same Bestower and Deliverer, and that we are happy and secure—indeed we are born—in those places where we meet God. I might almost add that we are with God wherever we breathe with the remembrance of God, and since we are always breathing, we are always with God, in the Center, in the golden Now.

April 6. Kaisariani is a deserted monastery in the neighborhood of Athens. Picture it to yourself: walls of which it is hard to say whether they are made of stone or earth, and on top of them roofs that look like mounds of earth; everything yellowish or reddish with rose-colored flowering trees about; then pines and cypresses and a dry landscape all reds and olive greens, bathed in an intensely clear, crystalline light. The building is early Christian and the church painted inside; add to this icons and lighted candles. Then a wild garden with the dwellings of the monks around it, tiny cells such as there must be on Sinai and Athos. This place has something paradisal and one-with-nature about it; something spring-like and blissful. One sees at once that it cannot be only the Catholics who are right. But for the Turks, a Baroque church would now be standing here and there would be no more long-bearded priests.

Sparta, April 9. Today we spent the day with Sherrard,[48] who went with us to Mistra: a place like Kaisariani, but ten times the size, lying

[48] Philip Sherrard (1922–1995), the Orthodox author and translator of the *Philokalia*.

on the slopes of the snow-covered Taygetos. Everything in reddish and golden colors, with asphodels strewn like a veil of pearls, and deep red anemones, and orange trees and aloes. We visited the nunnery and were asked to write our names in a visitors' book; then we were permitted to visit the ancient churches scattered over the mountainside. The region is reminiscent of the Valais, with snowy mountains rising from the blossoming plain.

What is the world around us but a magic fan, which God is ever opening anew? There is no before and no after—nothing is good or bad because it came before or after; rather, everything comes from God and we must receive it as such. We are most ourselves when we are most with God. Nothing is foreign where God's Name is.

There is a special wisdom connected with traveling. The world seeks to distract us and thus to harden the ego—one notices that it is not only unpleasant things that test us, but pleasant things as well, the latter of course in a more esoteric sense. At the same time, however, the world is all the more easily seen through—as a result, that is to say, of the continual changes in the outward scene—and it is the world that loses the wager. I understand how it is that perpetual wandering can be a spiritual vocation, as with pilgrims and *sannyāsins*.

—·⁝·—

"*Three Great Crises in Life*"
Pully, June, 1958 to Aristide Messinesi

There are three great crises in life: the first is when the child becomes an adult, the second when the adult enters into the second half of his life, around fifty years of age, and the third when he enters old age, at around seventy years. Just as at fifty, this third transition requires a readjustment and demands a great deal of voluntary sacrifice, resignation, and serenity. One must accept, through an energetic spiritual act, all the risks and servitudes of the new condition; this is what is called detachment. One must free oneself absolutely from all regret, all sadness, all bitterness. There are many men who do not age well because they drag behind them the psychology of a bygone time. If one must bury oneself somewhat at fifty, one must do so even more at seventy. It is as if one were to conclude, on a personal basis, a new pact with God. What is absolutely imperative is to be content with one's condition.

Every age has its advantages: from a certain point of view, old people are to be envied; their state simplifies many things; all they need to do is to live in God until the end; they can be sure that God does not ask more of them. Traditionally, old age is a blessing.

Often, in prayer, grace comes at the moment when one resigns oneself happily to dryness. If something is painful for you, give thanks to God, this is the best way to come out of it.

—— ·:· ——

"*At the Crossroads of Traditional Worlds*"
Pully, November 20, 1958 to Martin Lings

I recently made a painting depicting the White Buffalo Woman bringing the Sacred Pipe to the Indians. Someone might ask me why I made this painting, or others, and why I take such an interest in the American Indians. In a related vein, it appears that many readers of *Études traditionnelles* have been critical of me, given my function within Sufism, for having written a long article on Shinto; it would be more normal, they say, if I restricted myself to writing on Islam; such absurd opinions obviously do not preoccupy me.

But to return to my paintings, or their contents, what accounts for them is my position at the crossroads of traditional worlds, and this position in turn is explained by the cyclical moment in which we live; as for the Indians, they present a "neutral" possibility in the traditional universe, and at the same time they also exhibit something relatively "primordial". It is worth noting, moreover, that there is a relationship between them and the Japanese: in the last century, the Japanese were the only non-"decadent" Eastern people, whereas the Indians seem to be the only true "primitives" among all the "savages"; this amounts to two "miracles", one could say. Both peoples have something fascinating about them, for the *kshatriya* spirit, which is very pure in each case, is at the same time penetrated with a *brāhmana* spirit: the warrior spirit is "complete" but it is not "worldly", allowing Heaven to shine through.

—— ⁘ ——

"The Difference between the Religions"
Pully, April 20, 1959 to Keshavram Iyengar

In the West, esoterically speaking, the difference between the religions corresponds to the difference between the *darshanas* or *yogas* in India. A Westerner who, for esoteric reasons and on an esoteric basis, attaches himself to a foreign spiritual form does not forsake his *dharma* any more than a Hindu who adopts a *darshana* he had previously not understood. This has nothing to do with "conversion". It might of course be asked why the same possibilities do not exist in Christianity as in Islam or elsewhere. But by its very form, Christianity is a *bhakti* that rejects all other spiritual forms. In retrospect, I was able to perceive, thanks to the *Vedānta* and Sufism, that orthodox Christianity (Western and Eastern) contains at least in principle a kind of *Vedānta*; but from within Christianity, I would never have been able to make this discovery. This I owe to Brahmanic metaphysics and to several years of Islamic esoterism, with its spiritual practices that are unknown to modern Christianity.

—— ⁘ ——

A "Critical Age"
Pully, April 28, 1959 to Marco Pallis

You make allusion to this "critical age"—between forty-five and sixty years old—of which I have sometimes spoken. It is a time when a veil seems to come between the world and ourselves, as if everything were put into question and as if we would have to start from the very beginning again. One must then find a new *modus vivendi* with regard to what is relative as well as with regard to the Absolute; one must, through meditation, arrive at a definitive position with regard to life and its contents; this is obvious. One must above all not sacrifice concentration to our uncertainties, for certitude comes precisely from concentration. If you want to know what you must change in your existence, how you ought to simplify it, which things are appropriate to renounce—because they become too invasive—you must start by reposing in the *mantra* as if you had no worries; this is what the Hindus call *prapatti* and the Muslims *tawakkul*; then clarity will certainly come; problems resolve themselves to the extent that we detach ourselves inwardly.

There is also the question of one's willpower with regard to the *mantra*, how to strengthen it or determine it. The answer is simple: by the imagination, for the will obeys the imagination, the "subconscious" if one may say; it is our spiritualized imagination, our fundamental conviction, that makes concrete for us what we must will in an absolute manner. The themes of meditation play no other role, on the plane of the will, than to allow us to really will what we have to do; they provide us with the arguments, as they do on all planes, moreover. When we base ourselves solely on the will as such, we are incapable of willing what surpasses us; but imagine a man in the face of a danger or seduction: in both cases it is easy for him to act, that is to say, to obey the determination that comes from the object; it is easy to love beauty and to flee death. So, if we have the impression that our will is weak—our willpower for concentration on the *mantra*—it is because we do not see sufficiently, not "concretely" enough, the necessity of the *mantra*, nor its infinite beauty, nor our misery; and this also proves that we concern ourselves with things we should not concern ourselves with, things outside our *dharma*. At the time of death, one may regret many things, but one will never regret having omitted something in order to "think of the Buddha".

What we do in the morning is very important for the whole day; it is good not to leave the morning's invocation before having the certitude that it has determined our whole being and therefore our whole day. The brain is a sponge that absorbs the river of appearances; it is not enough to empty it of the images from which it lives, one must also satisfy its need for absorption and its habitual movements; this is what psalmodies do, the reading of sacred texts, meditations, invocations. One must infuse into the mind, to the extent it can carry it, the consciousness of the Real and the unreal; this consciousness will be the framework for everything else. The world is a multiplicity that disperses and divides, at least *a priori*; the celestial Word—true "manifestation of the Void" (*shūnyamūrti*)—is on the contrary a multiplicity that brings together and leads to Unity, whence the importance of ritual recitations. The celestial Word absorbs the soul, and transposes it imperceptibly through a kind of "divine ruse"—in the sense of the term *upāya*—into the serene and immutable climate of the Absolute; the fish of the soul enter into the divine net without distrust. In this sense, psalmodies of sacred texts are very efficacious; they show us in a way what we should think and what we should be.

To fight sadness, we have no other means than to fix the gaze of the intelligence and the soul on the Infinite, which contains all that is perfect and lovable. This point of view is easily realizable, it seems to me, in a perspective like that of the Amidists, but in principle it is present everywhere; it is up to us to discover it. It is in this sense that Lord Northbourne told me recently: "Fundamentally, we should dance with joy". To overcome the temptation of sadness, one should use the appropriate meditations and practice the invocation with the desired intention, for one or two hours, in a sanctuary or in virgin nature, depending on the circumstances. One must cut off sadness at its root and not allow it to accumulate; if it arises one day, it should disappear the same day; one must strive, with all the means, to overcome it—with ritual recitations, with the *mantra*, with meditation.

—— ⁘ ——

"*The Essentials of Indian Religion*"[49]

Wyola, Montana, July 24, 1959 to Benjamin Black Elk

Our visit to Keystone is unforgettable even though it was so short. I should now like to write down for you some considerations about the Indian problem, because it is easier for me to write than to speak English. The fact that the "white man" will never understand the Indian's soul nor the Indian's religion is not of course a question of race, but a question of civilization. I am a white man by race, and I understand you as well as a traditional minded Japanese or Persian would understand you; but I am not a "white man" in the sense of "modern civilization", as I do not accept its fundamental ideas of "civilization" and "progress".

[49] Written during the Schuons' first trip to the American West after meeting Benjamin Black Elk in Keystone, South Dakota.

What is a civilization in the true sense? It is a spiritual and social order revealed by the Great Spirit. In this true sense, the Indians had—and still have in principle—a real civilization. No civilization is unique, for the Truth has many forms, and men are different too.

What was wrong with the Indians? Not of course their civilization as such, but a partial forgetfulness of the deep meaning of their religion. The Indians must not be converted to a foreign religion; they must turn back to the ideal of their forefathers. As there is no progress, it follows that ancient man was more perfect than man of today. I think the Indians of historical times were too much concerned with looking for their own glory and were too often forgetful of the Great Mystery; this may partly be the key of their calamities. The white man does the same in a much worse way, and his end will come too.

There are several true civilizations in the world. The European civilization was also a normal one up to six hundred years ago; this was the Christian civilization. But the modern world is no longer Christian; there may have been some true Christians among the American whites who came to the West, but the civilization they brought with them, and which they represented often quite unconsciously, was not Christian at all; it was anti-Christian. As a Sioux writer, Ohiyesa (Charles Eastman), has pointed out, the modern white civilization has nothing to do with Christianity.

What is the meaning of this modern civilization? To make all people forget God and thus prepare the end of the world.

The Indians are not alone in their struggle to maintain their tradition; throughout the world there are traditional peoples or minorities defending the inheritance of their fathers.

Every old and God-revealed religion is true and beneficial. I never quarrel about religion. The essential teaching of every true religion is that this world of vanishing phenomena is unreal and that the unseen world of the Great Spirit is real. There are many degrees in the Unseen, but I just want to say that there is more reality in the Unseen above than in this visible world, and that God is the absolute Reality.

With this essential Truth of every religion comes the essential Path: this is prayer; everlasting prayer within the heart, if possible; at every hour, and perhaps much more often, the invocation of a Name of God, the Great Spirit.

But there must be Tradition; nothing can be realized without it. After having read your venerable father's book and some other reports, it seems to me that the essentials of Indian religion are: 1. the Sacred Pipe; 2. the Sweat Lodge; 3. the Solitary Invocation ("Lamenting"); 4. the Sun Dance. The Ghost Dance is also good if performed with the intention of union with God and without false interpretation. It always existed among some Indians and Wovoka only renewed it.

Old man Little Warrior said once to Joseph Brown that he was very often performing some inner and secret invocation, like the following: "*Wakan Tanka onshimala ye*",[50] or just "*Wakan Tanka*" or "*Tunkashila*". This is very important. The Catholic and Greek Christians also know such invocations, to be performed as often as possible. The Hindus and Buddhists say—following their holy Scriptures—that the almost uninterrupted invocation of a revealed Name of the Divinity is the best means of salvation in the last times, the period before the end of the world; this implies the practice of the virtues and submission to God's Will.

So, this has become a long letter. I hope some Indians at least may become—or remain—conscious of their tradition and its deep meaning. This is the aim of your father's work and also of Little Warrior's teaching. I wish the Indians to understand that they are not alone.[51]

—— ·:· ——

"*When I Was in America*"

Pully, September 30, 1959 to Hans Küry

The travel journal I wrote in America contains two kinds of texts, namely descriptions of events and occurrences and doctrinal reflections.[52] After the All Indian Days,[53] in which we were adopted into the Sioux tribe, we visited also the Mandans and Assiniboines, made new

[50] "*Wakan Tanka*, pity me."

[51] This letter is signed "F. Schuon (*Wambali Ohítika*)", "Brave Eagle" (*Wambali Ohítika*) being the name Schuon was given when he was adopted into the Sioux tribe.

[52] Excerpts from this travel journal and a later journal written in 1963 were published in an Appendix to *The Feathered Sun: Plains Indians in Art and Philosophy* (Bloomington, IN: World Wisdom, 1990), and as "Travel Meditations" in *Studies in Comparative Religion*, Vol. 12, Nos. 1 and 2 (Winter-Spring, 1978):64–75.

[53] In Sheridan, Wyoming.

acquaintances, and finally returned to Pine Ridge where we paid still two more visits to the ailing Chief Red Cloud.[54] Then I received from another chief an eagle-feather headdress—in the name of the Sioux tribe—which had a symbolic meaning for me.

What this journey signified for me can be seen in my written reflections. When I was in America, I felt—against all expectation—no longing at all for my home far away, so strong was my sense that all lies in the supreme Name and that there is neither here nor there, neither close nor far, neither now nor then.

In the wonderful, paradisal landscape of the Rocky Mountains—the Bighorns—I had to think of this inscription of the Taj Mahal: "If there is a paradise on earth, it is here; it is here; it is here!" But those mountains are only a symbol, and the saying refers in reality to the supreme Name; in it all beauty is contained.

—— ·:· ——

"*The Problem of Transmigration*"
Pully, November 8, 1959 to Marco Pallis

Concerning the problem of transmigration, it seems to me that one does not take sufficiently into account the fact that there are between incarnations intermediary states—either celestial or infernal—whose length is described in sacred Texts as being very long. The Bible and the Koran speak of the resurrection of the flesh, which is indeed a "re-incarnation"; but at that moment the present earth will have ceased to exist. In any case, the facile reincarnationism of most Easterners does not conform to their own Scriptures. Obviously, there are widely diverse theories and symbolisms to be considered here, which indicates just how complex the problem is; perhaps it cannot be expressed in human language, since this language is terrestrial, at least in a certain way. In this sense, it is easier to speak of metaphysics than of cosmology; from a certain point of view, the Absolute is closer to us than are the other worlds.

[54] James Red Cloud, grandson of the famous Red Cloud (1822–1909) known to history.

—·:·—

Recommended "Hindu Books"
Pully, February 14, 1960 to Martin Lings

Hindu books that all of our friends should possess and read are the following: the *Bhagavad Gītā*, the *Yoga Vasishtha*, also called the *Mahārāmāyana*; the *Srīmad Bhāgavatam*. These books, which have exceptionally the value of an *Upanishad*, contain the very essence of the Doctrine, which is expounded by Shri Krishna and—through the intermediary of Vasishtha—by Shri Rama.

—·:·—

"*Reading the* Bhagavad Gītā"
Pully, March 11, 1960 to Martin Lings

The *Bhagavad Gītā* played a certain role in my life; I read it already in my childhood and it greatly impressed me. When the Shaykh al-Alawi died, may God sanctify his secret, I was in Paris in my garret room reading the *Bhagavad Gītā*; suddenly, I was overwhelmed by the supreme Name and could no longer read; I was as if drunk and went out into the street and walked along the Seine, unable to think or utter anything else other than the supreme Name; I felt wholly light. There was no direct relationship here between this and my reading, yet finally these things are not due to chance.

—·:·—

"*His Holiness the Jagadguru*"
Pully, July 5, 1960 to Keshavram Iyengar

I have received both of your letters, along with the beautiful Sanskrit manuscript, the booklet by Shri Shankaracharya, and the image of Dakshinamurti. You have taken tremendous trouble with all these things, far too much trouble for me. Until now, I had only a few Chinese inscriptions; this is the first time I have received a piece of calligraphy in Sanskrit.[55] The blessing of all this will return upon you. I thank you, and also His Holiness.[56]

Mr. Burckhardt tells me that you have received the American Indian paintings, and thus also my letter. I hope that His Holiness the Jagadguru will have a chance to see these pictures, as he had inquired about Last Bull, a priest of the Cheyenne, of whom there is unfortunately no picture.[57]

But these are all little things. I am happy for you, and with you, for the spiritual gift that you have received from His Holiness; this means a new life for you. Now you need have no more cares; you must simply devote yourself to the sacred *japa*—as it were immersing yourself in it—so that it may guide you to the other shore.

You are fortunate that you can visit so many holy places. Last year, with the American Indians, we visited a holy place in the mountains: an enormous wheel of stones, set in the ground perhaps several thousand years ago.[58]

—— ⁘ ——

"*Why Is There Evil in the World?*"
circa 1960 to a reader

You ask me, in substance, why is there evil in the world? Here is the reason: God, being infinite, created the world, that is to say, the creation of the world is a necessary manifestation of His infinitude and absoluteness. Now the world is not God; not being God, it cannot be perfect; were it perfect, it would be God Himself. And the world

[55] The Sanskrit calligraphy is of a Vedantic maxim ascribed to Shankara: "God is real, the world is appearance; the soul is not other than God" (*Brahma satyam, jagan mithyā; jīvo brahmaiva nāparah*). A reproduction of this calligraphy still hangs in the Schuon home.

[56] His Holiness Sri Chandrasekharendra Saraswati Swamigal, the 68th Jagadguru of Kanchipuram, to whom Schuon had dedicated his book *Language of the Self* (Madras: Ganesh, 1959).

[57] This meeting is the subject of Schuon's article titled "His Holiness and the Medicine Man", which subsequently appeared in *The Feathered Sun*.

[58] The Medicine Wheel, located in the Bighorn Mountains in Wyoming.

unfolds in duration; towards the end, imperfection predominates, whereas at the beginning of humanity, it is perfection that prevails. I have spoken of this in my books, and better than I can do here in a few words.

To be alone with God—without bitterness towards anyone, this is a formal condition—is a wonderful thing; this solitude that lives from the invocation of the divine Name. Our life is there before us, and we must live it; we cannot escape it. I know where the difficulty lies: it is easier—or less difficult—to be alone on a desert island, than to be among men who do not understand us. But if we have no choice, then we are forced to accept the destiny God has given us and do the best we can with it. Through prayer we can transmute lead into gold, alchemically speaking; we can even transform, in a certain measure, those who are part of our life.

Your life cannot be without meaning in the eyes of God, for you exist and you have intelligence and free will. We must start with what is certain, and not waste time fretting about and evaluating what is uncertain; now what is absolutely certain is *death, the meeting with God, eternity*; then *the present moment*, the one that we experience at this very instant and that we experience always, and *in which we are free to choose God*, by remembering Him. Things that are uncertain must be subordinated to those that are certain—that are spiritual—and not conversely.

—— ·⁝· ——

"*Guénon's Particularity*"
Pully, October 9, 1960 to Michel Vâlsan

You never knew the Shaykh al-Alawi and you cannot have a concrete sense of what he means for me. Nor did you know René Guénon; you venerate him through his books without ever having been his *murīd*; moreover, he did not have any *murīdūn*. In your life, Guénon appeared in fact as a *murshid*; not in mine, for I knew the Shaykh al-Alawi and was subjected twice to the mark of his influence. Guénon was for me a master in doctrine who might have lived several centuries before me; his books marveled me from my youth onwards—starting around 1924, the year *East and West* first came out—and there is no need for me to describe all that they brought me; but the Shaykh al-Alawi bequeathed treasures to me of another order, and certainly not of lesser value. I could say that Guénon's personality is of no concern to me, and this in fact would be in perfect agreement with his own point of view; it nevertheless concerns me in that his work bears its imprint. I was troubled early on by certain things, but I forced myself at first to accept them; the thesis on Buddhism[59] was all the more disappointing for me in that encountering the image of the Buddha, together with its nirvanic doctrine, was one of the spiritual events of my childhood. Later, I dissociated myself from certain traits of the Guénonian work, and my attitude did not change for many long years and is the same today.

From the point of view of traditional habits and customs, my opposition to certain aspects—not essential, but very disturbing—of the Guénonian work is hardly unusual; doctrinal masters of the East did not hesitate to contradict one another; Al-Jili contradicted Ibn Arabi. "Disputes among the wise are a mercy."[60] Now I have received gifts or graces that allow me—and that oblige me—to be what I am and to think what I think.

If you feel a particularly direct and profound bond with the very person of Guénon—somewhat like I feel for the Shaykh al-Alawi—I would be the last to reproach you for this; and likewise if, from a doctrinal point of view, you intend to follow as closely as possible the path set by Guénon; what I have in mind are certain particularities about which a choice can be made, not the great principles that apply to everyone. Your group must have a sufficient reason for being, and this reason can only be Guénon's particularity, and your affinities with it, or your natural desire not to follow another particularity of character. For this, I bless you; but do not ask me to follow you in this; I would not even have the right to do so.

I could someday explain to you point-by-point what disturbs me in the Guénonian work; but even were it not to disturb me, I would be the disciple and heir of the Shaykh al-Alawi; my mission, if I may

[59] Guénon had followed Shankara in condemning Buddhism as a heresy, but was later convinced by Ananda Coomaraswamy, Marco Pallis, and Schuon to change his views. See *Frithjof Schuon: Messenger of the Perennial Philosophy*, chap. 11, "At Variance with Guénon".

[60] A *hadīth* of the Prophet Muhammad.

say, would be determined by his *barakah* as much as by Guénonian "Vedantism". This indispensable—and, in the West, incomparable—message of Guénon's work is something that I defend everywhere the opportunity presents itself.

For Guénon, our *Tarīqah*—and you will note that I went to Africa on my own initiative and without yet knowing Guénon's traditional affiliation—could only be an extension of Shadhilism implanted in the West; for myself, on the contrary, the new branch must realize both a synthesis and a quintessence determined on the one hand by the awareness of the metaphysical significance of forms, and on the other hand by the contingencies of the modern world, with the simplifications and compensations this implies.

October 10. For many well-gifted readers, the Guénonian work is discouraging because of the disproportion between the knowledge of principles and the weakness of their application to human matters; it is as if there were here intrusions of the "mathematical" element in domains where this element ceases to be infallible.

I am not saying that I am better than René Guénon; I affirm only that I complete him, and even necessarily so, and that I neutralize the "weak points" of his work. This in a certain sense is why I write books; but I also write them so that there can be no confusion for seekers; finally, I write them for the sake of the truth and for no other motive.

I am writing all of this, not to change you, but to explain myself and to give you a sense of why on a certain plane I could not submit to a "control" that is impossible. I am not asking for others to become like me, but I do not want to become like them.

The *barakah* of the Shaykh al-Alawi in particular and of *Tasawwuf* in general are unrelated to the Guénonian work. That Guénon had a different conception of a Western *Tarīqah*, a conception different from mine, is not something that bothers me; that was his right, and his point of view in this matter is respectable, quite clearly. And it is your right to perpetuate it,[61] with God's help; "there is no assistance save that of God".[62]

[61] Vâlsan's independent branch of the *Shādhilīyyah-Darqawiyyah Tarīqah* exists to this day and traces its lineage to the Prophet Muhammad through Schuon, who had initiated Vâlsan and many of his followers into Sufism.

[62] See Koran, *Sūrah* "Hud" [11]:88.

—·⁝·—

"*A Question of Imagination*"
Pully, December 17, 1960 to a disciple

Your difficulties stem from the fact that you are not aware of the full gravity of the human condition, and you are not aware of this because nothing in your habitual surroundings—the world in which we live—suggests it, to say the least. It is finally a question of imagination; I am not saying that you are directly responsible for this, but you are in any case its victim, and you are not alone in being so. The articles I am presently writing—"Man in the Universe" and "The Cross of Space and Time in Koranic Onomatology"[63]—can give you many answers.

The infinite divine Mercy, which is miraculously contained in the Name of God, saves us to the degree of our trust, and our trust springs from the depth of our distress; without an awareness of our distress, no trust is possible, and without trust, no Mercy. We must therefore know that we are fallen from original perfection, that we are incapable of saving ourselves, and that God alone can save us; knowing this, we could despair, logically speaking; but it is here that trust comes into play, for we know through Revelation that God wants to save us and that His Mercy is infinite. Trust—or what amounts to the same, faith—is thus determined "above" by our knowledge of divine Mercy and "below" by our awareness of human wretchedness.

Most people believe that a person goes to Paradise because he follows the rites of a religion and has neither killed nor stolen, and so on and so forth; but in fact only the saints and sages go straight to Paradise, and even they do so only because Mercy dissolves their imperfections, not because they are perfect. When you are walking along the street, you believe that "I"—Mrs. H.—"am here", "on this street", "now"; you do not see, I assume, the metaphysical and eschatological abysses surrounding you. In the Middle Ages, the whole civilization was structured in such a way as to give a person at least some sense of his cosmic situation; today, we live in a kind of misleading "extraterritoriality", in opaque back rooms that hide reality. Nevertheless, God

[63] See *Light on the Ancient Worlds* (London: Perennial Books, 1965; Bloomington, IN: World Wisdom, 1984, 2006) and *Form and Substance in the Religions* respectively.

touches us everywhere, for there is no empty space and no respite. He is "the First" and "the Last", "the Outward" and "the Inward"; man is like the point of intersection of the "divine dimensions".

You must detach your life from the awareness of the multiple and reduce it to a "geometrical point" before God. You have but one life, and it is not just anything; this life is everything for you, and it owes its greatness to its divine origin and goal. The human condition is something great because its foundation is God; the modern error is to believe that we are small, that we are biological accidents, that we are entitled to lukewarmness—that we are free to be small, lukewarm, mediocre. In reality, we are condemned to greatness, if I may express it this way, and we find this greatness in spiritual smallness before the divine Greatness. It is God who is Great, but we must open ourselves up to this Greatness, knowing that there is only He, that we are bound to Him, that we cannot escape Him; knowing this, we must resign ourselves to our human and personal condition—to the fact that the sacred is everywhere—and we must repose in trust.

—— ·:· ——

"*Errors of the Mahesh Yogi Movement*"
Pully, March 15, 1961 to Marco Pallis

The errors of the Mahesh Yogi[64] movement are patently obvious. In reality, the goal of meditation is not to have access to "limitless energy, heightened efficiency of thought and action, and release from tensions and anxiety [leading] to peace of mind and happiness"! None of these advantages has any spiritual value, for it is not happiness that matters, it the motive of happiness and the nature of happiness. The Sadhu says nothing of this, the sole important question, and this is what condemns him.

But there are also extrinsic criteria: the complete lack of intelligence and *barakah*, the propagandist triviality, the modernist and

64 Mahesh Prasad Varma Yogi (1917–2008) founded the "Spiritual Regeneration Movement", more widely known as the Transcendental Meditation movement, in 1958 with a view to the "spiritual regeneration of the world"; the author here quotes in English from a promotional pamphlet.

void. Finally, one must unite to the divine Name as if we were but one substance with it; we then have no more ego, and it is the Name that takes the place of our heart; it is neither our body nor our soul, but rather the Name, that is "us"; and we are "ourselves" neither in this or that thought, nor in this or that act, but uniquely in the divine Name, which is mysteriously identical to the Named, or in the sacred invocation, which unites us mysteriously to the Invoked.

Life is precious, for it allows us to attach ourselves to *Ātmā*; this is why we must be happy to live, and full of gratitude for our human condition.

—— ·⁝· ——

"*My Interest in Indians*"
Pully, July 9, 1961 to Thomas & Susie Yellowtail

I learned from the long letter you wrote to Jean-Louis [Michon][66] that you were holding these last days a Sun Dance at Wyola. We pitched our tipi in our garden and we smoked every day praying for you and for other Indian friends; we smoked with an old Sioux pipe. We hope this Sun Dance gave you much spiritual strength and light.

We were very glad to learn from your previous letter about the eagle who was waiting for you on the road. This makes me remember that I had a talk with you about Indian religion, some years ago in Paris; you said to me: "I pray that you may know what you wish to know of our religion, or that it be revealed to you, maybe in a dream." Two days later I dreamt in the morning: I had an eagle bone whistle in my mouth and was looking at the sun, and from every side there were thousands of buffalos running towards me, and I heard thousands of voices singing in every direction of the sky: "They say: a herd of buffalos is coming. . . ." This they sang in an Indian language—Absaroka or Lakota—but I could understand it in my dream. Catherine[67] told me afterwards that these words are the beginning of the Sioux Sun Dance song: "They say: a herd of buffalos is coming; here it is! Its

[66] Jean-Louis Michon (1924–2013) was a French perennialist writer, editor, translator, Arabist, and artistic consultant who specialized in Islam.

[67] That is, Schuon's wife.

blessing will reach us; now it is upon us!" As the buffalo symbolizes the Sun—who manifests in a certain manner the Great Spirit—all these running buffalos were like the rays of the sun, or in other words, they were the blessings which emanate from the Great Spirit, whose veil is the visible sun.

A little later I dreamt I was an eagle flying towards the sun, and I had an eagle bone whistle. At another moment, I dreamt I smoked an Indian pipe, and the name of God was written with the smoke, with Arabic letters: *Allāh*.

I never speak about these things with ordinary white people; I do so only with my closest friends. Some people may have supposed that my interest in Indians and their holy traditions is a "scientific" one, but this is absolutely not the case; I did not come to America with the intention to write a superficial book about the Indian religion. I am interested in spiritual truth and spiritual life, not in external classifications.

Religion is basically: first, to distinguish between what belongs to the Great Spirit and what belongs to this world of shadows, that is to say: to tell the vanishing from the Everlasting, or the illusory from the Real, or the finite from the Infinite; secondly, to remember always the Everlasting and to live with it and in it, that is to say: to have the mind always fixed on the divine Sun, which no eye can see, except the eye of the heart.

Old man Little Warrior once said to my friend Joseph Brown that some of the old Sioux were pronouncing very often or almost without interruption within the heart a name of the Great Spirit, such as *Tunkashila* or *Wakan Tanka* or some other name in Lakota; and old man Black Elk told my friend that the deep meaning of the Sun Dance is union with the Godhead. Man must always look at the divine Sun in his heart, and the call of the secret eagle bone whistle of the heart must never cease.

I was very happy to see the holy ceremony of the Tobacco Society,[68] and I hope that many young people among the Crow understand not only the depth and beauty of their tradition, but also its absolute necessity. I think the whole Plains Indian tradition is found in the Pipe and the Sweat Lodge and the Sun Dance, and also in the spiritual retreat in the mountains. There may have been many other

[68] During the Schuons' 1959 visit to the Crow.

practices, but it seems to me that these four are the most important, and that they must be kept under all circumstances. But all this you know better than I do.

—·⁝·—

"*Within the Framework of Judaism*"
Pully, July 15, 1962 to Leo Schaya

S. T., who is here for a while, told me of a Russian Jew who heard about me and read some things of mine and wants to follow our path within the framework of Judaism. He is observing a tolerable minimum of the prescriptions. Given that he is the intellectual center of other Jews and can exert a good influence, he wants to remain in Judaism.

Could you inscribe in Hebrew and in Latin the Schema Israel and the Names Adonai and Yahweh?

—·⁝·—

"*Some Indian Guests*"; "*Regarding the Piano*"
Pully, Summer, 1962 to Leo Schaya

I have received your three letters, and also the beautiful page with the holy formulas in Hebrew. I am glad that the tipi was able to convey some of the prairie atmosphere to your home, that is to say, that you were able to experience its spiritual message so appreciatively. As I am writing this, there are once again some Indian guests in our house: the Real Bird couple, whom we know from Lodge Grass,[69] thus two Crows. I hear the man drumming quietly, while she—a beautiful young woman—is helping my wife with household tasks. Both of them are here for a few days; sometimes they spend the night in the tipi that is in the garden.

[69] Lodge Grass, Montana.

Regarding the piano, I must once again emphasize—we already spoke about this earlier—that it is a wholly outward manifestation of the individualist and sentimental bourgeois culture of the nineteenth century and—as an object and in tone—its significance is that of the bourgeois and "civilizationist" credo; in a word, it is the epitome of what is *wasichu*, as the Lakotas say. There are three aspects here: object, sound, and content. One could tolerate the practice of Western music up to Bach—including him—and the playing of the spinet and harpsichord, or also of the zither, lute, or guitar; before Bach, instruments and melodies are still noble and connected to the spiritual, after him everything becomes chaotic, individualistic, bourgeois; the man marked by this culture will dramatize the unspiritual life of his soul. It is absolutely impossible to bring the work of spiritual realization in harmony with this musical background. Were your child to dwell in this bourgeois, pseudo-religious opium, then the prospects of a truly spiritual life in the future would be drastically reduced. All the grace that God might send would be taken away in advance by the individualistic ambience of the piano music, that is to say, it would be made impossible due to a psychic *shirk*. And what endlessly enormous efforts and how much of the soul's substance this stifling cult requires! I would like to note in passing that Beethoven was a thoroughly honorable man and true genius—and, moreover, a believing Catholic too—but he was a victim of his times and of his own torn soul and melancholy, and we certainly do not want to be like him; I say this only because I cannot bear that one misjudge men like that. But let us leave men aside and return to what is principial: our existential atmosphere is God's free nature, then the sacred, that is to say, traditional forms, but never the "civilized" chamber-culture of the nineteenth century! One cannot conceive of a piano, this bourgeois sentiment machine, either in God's free nature or in a golden sanctuary, but one can conceive of a koto, or zither, or flute, or anything else that comes from the world of tradition. One must have the correct measures for things, measures that are found in the Eternal.

—— ⁘ ——

"*The Sense of Sin*"
Pully, November 28, 1963 to a disciple

In the case of a disciple who breaches sacred laws, one can do no more than draw this person's attention to the grievous consequences of such a way of acting; people have forgotten that "the fear of God is the beginning of wisdom".[70] In a *Ṭarīqah*—thanks to the constant practice of the remembrance of God—one ought to be able to avoid the fire of hell after death; it is the *dhikr* itself, tradition says, that wards off the flames, for it has entered into our substance. But it is impossible to avoid a painful passage through the flames when the *dhikr* is neglected and when one has, next to it or in some way in its place, a disordered passion. Such a passion cannot benefit from the consecration of the *Basmalah*; one cannot, for instance, go straight to Heaven while smoking passionately or taking drugs because it goes without saying that such things cannot be done in God's name. Even an inclination that is in itself *makrūh* and not *harām* becomes *harām* if it becomes a kind of *shirk*. One must know that there can be *barakah* in some earthly pleasures, but not in others; everything that is naturally useful for an individual or for society can be done in the Name of God.

What is pernicious, I repeat, is that people lack sufficient imagination to conceive of what happens after death; the sense of sin has been completely lost in our times. Who on earth would want to hold his hand in the fire for a quarter of an hour? No one. But then why do believers sin? Perhaps it could be explained to this person that any inveterate and passional habit leads to suffering.

November 29. In the case I alluded to yesterday, there are two different sins that should not be confused: first, the fact of violating a traditional prescription, even if it is not done out of passion; secondly, pursuing a passion even without violating the prescription formally, by taking advantage of the fact that the Law did not explicitly foresee such cases, or that it does not indicate the point at which what is *makrūh* becomes *harām*. The person concerned should be told, if possible, that such faults jeopardize the initiatic oath and the validity of the *dhikr*, but at the same time, one does not want to discourage anyone; one does not want to take away from the weak the last

[70] Prov. 1:7.

thread holding them to God. We live in a world where such questions become terribly complex.

—— ·:· ——

"*The Inner Unity of Religions*"
Pully, May 29, 1964 to a reader

I must call your attention to an important aspect of universality or unity: the divergence between religions is not only due to the incomprehension of men, it is also in the Revelations, hence in the divine Will, and this is why there is a difference between exoterism and esoterism; the diverse dogmas contradict one another, not only in the minds of theologians, but also—and *a priori*—in the sacred Scriptures; in giving these Scriptures, however, God at the same time gives the keys for understanding their underlying unity. If all men were metaphysicians and contemplatives, a single Revelation might be enough; but since this is not how things are, the Absolute must reveal itself in different ways, and the metaphysical viewpoints from which these Revelations are derived—according to different logical needs and different spiritual temperaments—cannot but contradict one another on the plane of forms, somewhat as geometrical figures contradict one another as long as one has not grasped their spatial and symbolic homogeneity.

God could not wish for all men to understand Unity since this understanding is contrary to the nature of man in the "dark age". This is why I am against ecumenism, which is an impossibility and absurdity pure and simple. The great evil is not that men of different religions do not understand one another, but that too many men—due to the influence of the modern spirit—are no longer believers. If religious divergences are particularly painful in our times, this is only because the divisions between believers, in the face of an unbelief that has become more and more menacing, have become all the more acute and also all the more dangerous. It is therefore urgent that: 1. men return to faith, whatever their religion may be, on condition that it is intrinsically orthodox, and in spite of dogmatic ostracisms; 2. that those who are capable of understanding pure metaphysics, esoterism, and the inner unity of religions discover these truths and draw the necessary inward and outward conclusions. And this is why I write books.

There is, moreover, a fatuous universalism, that of a Vivekananda and other pseudo-Hindu dreamers. Better to believe intelligently in one's own religion—while believing it to be the only true one—than to believe stupidly in the validity of the other doctrines and traditions; stupidly, that is to say, on a sentimental basis devoid of any intellectual quality. The dreamers I have in mind, moreover, never understand anything of metaphysics or of spiritual life, so that their universalism amounts to nothing.

—— ·:· ——

"*Modern Science*"

Pully, June 22, 1964 to Lord Northbourne

One cannot reproach any science for not being what it does not want to be or for not providing what it does not want to provide. In this respect, one cannot reproach modern chemistry insofar as it studies the phenomena it intends to study, for on its limited plane it remains within appropriateness and does not exceed its strengths; nor can one blame it for remaining within the strictly human perspective of matter, for it need not go beyond this, and no physical science need do so.

This last point is of capital importance, and it allows me to mention the following: the universe of an insect does not interest us, for this perspective is peripheral, whereas ours is central, so that all we need to know is that lower perspectives exist; our perspective must contain that of the insect and even that of the plant in a certain manner. As for the world of an angel, this perspective differs from ours only insofar as the angel does not intervene in human affairs; in itself, it is derived from the universal essences—which no sensible man will attempt to "imagine"—but when it is correlated with the human world, the angelic perspective makes itself human; the angel sees us as we see one another, when he has a reason to look at us; and on the same level he sees the universe as we see it.

Since "limitation" does not mean "falsehood", the specific limitation of the human state is completely separate from the question of scientific errors. For one of two things: either we are God, and then we are aware of pure and total Reality, or else we are not God, and then our vision of things is limited, as is the object of our vision; a cosmic science "at the level of God" would be an absurdity. Nevertheless, the possibility of adequation exists at our level: if we say that two plus two equals four, this is true; if we say that two plus two equals five, this is false, and the abyss between the two assertions is absolute. Either I know what is behind me, or I do not; if I know there is a tree five meters behind me, my science is adequate for what it intends to include; the question of the metaphysical meaning of the tree or the "horizontal" limitation of all knowledge is irrelevant; and if I believe my tree is the only tree there is or if I deny that it can flower when in fact it can, then it is not my momentary and concrete science of the tree that is false but the hypothesis I pinned onto it; this is more or less what happens with modern science. Therefore, when it comes to determining the value of a given opinion of this science, there is no need at all to resort to the argument of the ontological limitation of the human mind, for traditional men also give their sciences an objective scope; all we need to know is whether in fact modern science is wrong on the plane it is studying or whether any of its claims are unwarranted.

As I said in my remarks sent previously, modern science is only partially wrong on the plane of physical facts; on the other hand, it is totally wrong on higher planes and in its principles. It is wrong in its negations and in the false principles derived from them, then in the false hypotheses deriving from these principles, and finally in the monstrous effects this science produces as a result of its initial prometheanism. But it is right about many physical points and even about certain psychological points, and indeed it is impossible for this not to be so, given the law of compensations; in other words, it is impossible for modern men not to be right on certain points where ancient men were wrong; this is even part of the mechanism of degeneration. What is decisive in favor of the ancients or traditional men in general, however, is that they are right about all the spiritually essential points.

The 23rd. Most of the remarks I have just made will no doubt seem obvious to you, but what prompted me to talk at length about them was a sentence in your letter concerning the limitation of the human state. I would like to add yet another remark: traditionally, astronomical questions have no importance whatsoever, except for the data necessary for astrology, though this data is neutral as regards the measures of astronomy. The heliocentric system is not exclusively modern; I will not be telling you anything new in recalling here that Aristarchus of Samos and Hipparchus—and later al-Battani—taught it; nevertheless, one understands why the ancients finally preferred the geocentric system: because this system corresponds to immediate experience, hence to sacred symbolisms, whereas the opposite system is beyond most men's capacity for assimilation and entails serious dangers—it "troubles the repose of the Gods", as the opponents of Aristarchus said—which does not mean it is astronomically incorrect. In any case, pushing scientific curiosity too far—to the detriment of contemplation and the inward knowledge of appearances—is imprudence and luciferianism, and it is partly for this reason that the ancients instinctively retained the geocentric doctrine.

Notwithstanding that an inopportune piece of knowledge can occur accidentally, it goes without saying that the knowledge of realities that are normally unknown and contrary to current experience is a matter of indifference from the point of view of pure intellectuality and esoterism; if I bring this up here, it is simply because the context more or less requires it.

—— ⁘ ——

"*The Animal State*"

Pully, January 3, 1965 to Hans Küry

It is well known that the three monotheistic theologies teach that at Judgment Day animals and plants return to "the void"; I have written somewhere that this "void" stands for the transmigration of souls, because for the Semitic monotheisms everything that is not part of the human state is as if inexistent, hence the transmigration of souls is the "void", if it is not limbo or hell. And yet in Islam it is generally accepted that certain animals enter into the human paradise—without however becoming men—namely animals that have been filled with a powerful *barakah*, such as the cat of Jalal ad-Din Rumi or the dog of the Seven Sleepers from Ephesus; if other equally lovable animals are not reborn in our paradise, but in the *Krita-Yuga* of some other world or as brahmins, they are certainly not to be pitied. The sufficient reason for the human state is in fact the possibility of exiting the

Samsāra; the animal state cannot embody this possibility as well, but it can, as I said, be a direct way to an extraterrestrial state that corresponds to the human one; or else it may happen that an individual animal, owing to its hidden *karma* and through close connection with the spiritual or the holy, will as it were be drawn into a human paradise. And God knows best!

—— ·:· ——

"*A Choice of Professions*"
Pully, March 14, 1965 to Keshavram Iyengar

Regarding the choice of professions in today's world, it is difficult to establish general guidelines; a number of our friends have frankly disagreeable professions. There are only two things that can be of help, and these are reason and prayer; it is impossible that God will not over time help a man who loyally and fervently—and with full patience and trust—practices *japa-yoga* and at the same time beseeches the Divinity that it might help him find a bearable type of work. With reason, we must seek and evaluate professional possibilities, but with prayer we must set Heaven into motion, if I may put it this way. For many years, I was a textile designer, until finally God gave me a way out; the profession in itself would not have been so terrible, but the human ambience was unbearable; it was anything but *satsangha*. There are no fixed rules on the plane of a choice of professions, any more than there are on the plane of a spiritual vocation; whether or not we are called to fight for a truth depends on our inner relationship with God; when this relationship is correct, we will also then know what we must or must not do.

All that you say against Picasso and Le Corbusier is absolutely correct; they are destroyers of all true art. It is a great pity that these and other people of this sort are taken seriously in India; the Indians could still continue with their ancient arts and, wherever necessary, adjust to new circumstances.

What your *dharma* may be in this connection is a totally different question. First of all, hold to what is certain, then you will also realize what for the time being is still uncertain; certain is our relationship to God, and uncertain is the question of what we must do with respect to the world; this uncertainty can only become a certitude through our relationship with God. I do not know whether you are supposed to combat the modern world in word and writing; but if things are well for you in your spiritual life, in your *japa-yoga*, then things will also be well for you in everything else. Certitude about what you should or should not do outwardly will come to you over time from your *japa*.

5. It Is She Who Chose Me
Ages 57–60

"*Immense Graces*"
Fez, Morocco, March 29, 1965 to Titus Burckhardt

Morocco is a kind of healing for me; now that we have the right situation here—thanks to the Moroccan friends—we should really come here more often. At the beginning of my journey, I felt very ill in body and soul; all kinds of tensions and bitternesses that had accumulated within me suddenly burst forth, so that I felt like a drowning man and could keep above water only through the supreme Name. During the journey to Marseilles, I even feared I would die, and only became better on the ship; there I suddenly experienced such immense graces that I wondered whether it was not for their sake that I had had to suffer so.[1] I had thought I would never again be happy in my life, and this same thought rose up in me again on Moroccan soil, until I found myself alone for a few hours in my room in Tétouan; there the unexpected grace came to me anew—it was one of the most powerful things I had ever experienced; and suddenly I also saw clear portents of this in my past. In time, God willing, I will be able to put some of it into words, without thereby betraying Heaven's secrets.

—— ·⁞· ——

"*It Is She Who Chose Me*"
Pully, March 20, 1967 to Martin Lings

There are two ways of following the Prophet, one that is general and the other particular. The first is that of any man practicing Islam at one

[1] This is the first written reference to Schuon's visionary experience of the Virgin Mary while on a ship docked at Port Vendres, France. This spiritual grace was to change the remainder of his life. See *Frithjof Schuon: Messenger of the Perennial Philosophy*, chap. 17, "A Spiritual Patroness".

degree or another, if this practice is sincere: he who is in Islam follows the Prophet and cannot be situated outside of him. The second way is that of *fuqarā'* who have a very particular devotion to the person of the Prophet: they know even the least incident in Muhammad's life and scrupulously follow the *Sunnah* while studying the *ahādīth* continuously; they are as if possessed by the avataric person of the Prophet. It is a kind of exclusive *bhakti* found in certain *turuq*.

Now in order to be able to follow the Prophet in this way, it must be possible for one to follow the integral *Sunnah* in addition to having a providential vocation; and this is technically impossible for us, even vocationally so. But there is something else to consider: we are marked first by our intimate knowledge of other *Avatāras* and their Laws and Wisdom, and secondly by our awareness of the *Religio perennis*. Next, we are of Christian origin, and our point of departure is the *Vedānta*, and finally we live in an unbelieving world. And given the world and times to which we belong, we are in any case under the regimen of Mercy. All these factors, and others still, enable us to understand better the significance *Sayyidatnā* Maryam holds for us. And this cannot but please the Prophet, who knows our situation and our needs and who in any case envelops us with his Presence.

The Holy Virgin is not only the link between Islam and Christianity—the summer and winter caravans in the *Sūrah* "Quraysh", according to a certain interpretation that came to my mind—but also the personification of the *Religio perennis*, which is rooted in the Names *Rahmān* and *Rahīm* and in the *Basmalah*; there has never been a woman superior nor even equal to her in the Semitic world, and thus she alone has the plenary right to embody Layla for us.

According to her "earthly body" (*nirmānakāya*), she was the Israelite princess we know through the Gospel; according to her "heavenly body" (*sambhogakāya*), she can take on all forms and she also appears, and integrally so, in the Paradise of Islam; and according to her "divine body" (*dharmakāya*)—this is the supreme meaning of the "Coronation of the Virgin"—she is the *Shakti*, that is to say, she is identified by ineffable integration with divine "Femininity" and therefore with the Names representing it; in this sense, *Sayyidatnā* Maryam is also—in a divinely underlying manner—Maya, the mother of the Buddha, and Pte San Win, the revealer of the Sacred Pipe, or Kwan Yin in her feminine aspect.

In one of her apparitions, the Virgin said that one must pray "with recollectedness and love". She is not situated "next to God", but "in front of God"—like the Prophet and like *Ar-Rūh* or any other Intermediary—and also "next to man" and "in man", in the sense that she puts her perfection in place of our imperfection, or her strength in place of our weakness. She is no more "next to God" than the Arabic Name "*Allāh*", and the letters graphically expressing it, is an "association"; and an analogous remark could be made with respect to the Koran and even of any Scripture, of any Prophet.

March 23. It is not I who chose the Virgin, it is she who chose me. Several years ago, I was in my prayer room invoking the two Names of Mercy; and as I was doing so, I felt something totally unexpected penetrate my whole being, and it was the blessed Presence of *Sayyidatnā* Maryam. From this blessed moment onwards, I recommended the recitation of both Names, but I drew no other conclusions from this event.

Later, while on my way to Morocco, she saved me from the deepest distress: I had thought I could never again be happy and had even thought I would die. The miracle occurred on the ship at the midpoint of the journey, then at Tétouan and again at Fez, as if by reverberation. And yet, I had in no way been thinking of the Holy Virgin when she intervened on the open sea; *Stella Maris*!

I write these things not without some reluctance; what brings me to do so is the desire to make understood that it is the Virgin who chose us and that I have nothing to do with this. I thought for a moment that the divine Name alone could have saved me, but I quickly understood that this is exactly what it did, in the way pleasing to it—in saying this, I am identifying the Name with the Named—and in the form He wished to take. God comes to our aid as He wishes. "And there is no assistance save that of God."[2]

—— ·⁝· ——

[2] See Koran, *Sūrah* "Hud" [11]:88.

"*My Marian Prayer*"
Pully, April 4, 1967 to Hans Küry

Here is a Marian prayer I have written, together with the German translation and some explanations. This prayer and its explanations mean that *Sayyidatnā* Maryam is a supreme incarnation of spiritual realities; they do not necessarily mean that the disciple should add something new to his spiritual way, unless he wishes to read the prayer sometimes—not as a poem, but really as a prayer.

Everything we do spiritually occurs in the framework of Islam and thus in the spirit of the Prophet: nothing that belongs to Islam can go outside the domain of the Prophet; he is Islam in human form. And in this framework *Sayyidatnā* Maryam is for me the celestial Layla in human form, thus *gnosis* or *haqīqah* made manifest; hence my Marian prayer.

It goes without saying that Muhammad, like every *Avatāra*, incarnates in his way the same heavenly realities as Maryam—the third and fourth verses of my prayer are influenced by Ibn Mashish's prayer on the Prophet—but Maryam is divine Femininity, thus she incarnates the *Basmalah* and signifies beauty, love, and holiness.

May 5. The soul of the Holy Virgin is the remembrance of God, and she can love nothing in us more than the remembrance of God and the virtues.

—·:·—

"*The Holy Virgin Allowed Us to Continue*"
Fez, May 10, 1967 to Titus Burckhardt

On the day before our planned departure,[3] we learned that our ship could only leave four days later, so we decided to wait in Arles until then. From Arles, we visited three times Saint Sarah of the Gypsies in Les Saintes-Maries-de-la-Mer, a renowned and richly-clad image that the gypsies on their yearly pilgrimage carry into the sea; in Sarah are combined a legendary queen and the Virgin Mary. She stood in the

[3] From France to Morocco.

crypt of an ancient church; illuminated by many candles, she stood there like the image of a Hindu goddess, and her dress sparkled like the star-filled heavens.

When we arrived in Marseilles, we learned that our ship had unexpectedly left the day before; and no message informing us of this had been sent because the clerk in charge had fallen ill and forgotten us. After some back and forth, we finally decided to travel through Spain, since the next ship they could offer us was also delayed—likewise because of a strike—and no one could say with certainty when it would leave.

All this was indeed arranged by Heaven, if I may put it so, for the land journey took us to Saragossa where we visited the famous Nuestra Señora del Pilar. Following this, we spent the night in Santa Maria de Huerta, and then our journey took us to Seville, after we had in vain sought accommodation in Córdoba; Providence had once again arranged this well, for in Seville we could visit the Alcázar and then the famous Virgen de la Esperanza, also called the Macarena—our third statue of the Madonna recalling India and Ramakrishna, resplendent in gold and lit up by many candles. After we had prayed in her presence, the Holy Virgin allowed us to continue our journey to Morocco.

May 12. In Seville, where the Virgin had led us, Islam and Christianity shone before us in all their respective beauties: the Alcázar represented Islam's aspect of expansion and liberation, and the Macarena Christianity's contractive aspect, opening onto a glowing center. The Macarena—like other deified images of the Virgin—is deep-golden center, it is inebriation and wine; the Alcázar—like all Islamic buildings or sanctuaries—is appeasing, dissolving, and liberating expansion, in a certain sense it is divine space.

The Prophet is an absolute in Islam inasmuch as he summarizes and manifests all values or virtues, and this is also why he is the last of the Prophets; then also inasmuch as his message—the *Shahādah*—is pure *gnosis*, in the sense of *jnāna*. The Holy Virgin is an absolute in Islam inasmuch as she is in fact the only feminine *Avatāra* in the Semitic cosmos; hers is the only feminine name in the Koran, and not only is this name mentioned more than thirty times, it is even the title of a *sūrah*. You know all of this, but I did not want to leave it unmentioned here.

May 14. There is a special connection between Maryam and me, but there is not a special connection between her and every disciple of our *Tarīqah*. On the other hand, there is a special connection between the Virgin and the *Tarīqah* as such. The Virgin requires nothing of us but to remember God in the invocation; if she wanted an individual disciple to turn towards her, she would give him a longing for this. No one need ask himself questions about this matter; say *Allāh*; therein lie all answers and all certitude.

Just as the world seduces man and leads him away from God, so conversely does the Virgin, through her beauty, draw towards God the man who is called thereto. "The Buddhas also save through their supernatural beauty." The beauty of the Virgin touches us first of all through the virtues, which belong to faith; but it can touch us in other ways too, if this is Heaven's will.

P.S. I am told that Shaykh Hassan[4] of Chaouen said, quite spontaneously: "This (our times) is the age of *Sayyidatnā* Maryam". He also said that the Virgin is *Rahmah*, Mercy.

"*Maryam Is the Fount*"

Chaouen, Morocco, May 21, 1967 to Titus Burckhardt

We were twice with Shaykh Hassan. When I greeted the old Shaykh for the first time, he sat down for a while beside me, and tears ran down his cheeks; he was happy like a child.

Before my two visits to him, the old Shaykh had said to our friends: once *Sayyidatnā* Maryam has cast a glance on someone, this suffices. And it was reported to me by one of Shaykh Ahmad's disciples that he said: Maryam is the fount of the *Tarīqah*.

This old disciple, moreover, remembered me and said that the Shaykh al-Alawi had loved me very much. I write this to you simply because it was said. What I knew before was that Shaykh Ahmad had awaited my arrival.

[4] Shaykh Hassan ben Abd al-Wahhab was a Sufi master from Chaouen, Morocco, whom Schuon visited several times.

—·:·—

"*Venice*"; "*The Hagia Sophia*"
On board the San Giorgio, May 4, 1968 to Titus Burckhardt

Venice is one of the few places I always like to come back to, for I experience it as spiritual center; here this center is San Marco, the incomparable city being simply its outward radiation. San Marco is a direct expression of the sacred that manifests God; here the golden sacred presents itself to us in a most beautiful display, but people do not see it nor do they understand it; for them, it is a "period" or a "psychology"; and this psycho-spiritual decay is unforgivable. In San Marco, one finds oneself beyond time, in the eternal, golden "Now" and the inwardly infinite Center. And the Holy Virgin looks down upon us from the mosaics; San Marco is obviously a shrine of the Virgin, and throughout the whole city one feels the imprint of this destiny and of this presence.

What I wish to say is this: Venice is one of the few places where I feel that I am really altogether in the center, in the sense that the surroundings are like a direct expression of myself; not that elsewhere I do not feel myself to be in the center. If I am center, then whatever I see of God's creation becomes also in a certain way center; but this is a general truth, and I am thinking now, in connection with Venice, of a particular truth, one that is conditioned rather from without.

The center is everywhere, but in holy places—as for example in Chaouen or Fez—one experiences the center also in the outward; it comes to meet us and takes us in. In such places, the remembrance of God is as it were in the air. Wherever the center is already present in the outward, there is our true home, it is there that we were born; what is so tremendous about such an experience is to meet oneself—one's best self—in the outer world, as if a most intimate, a most holy dream had by some miracle become reality.

May 8. The Hagia Sophia is a San Marco enlarged into gigantic dimensions and blended with Islam. The fact that the Muslims have prayed for centuries here under the great mosaic images of the Holy Virgin is both moving and revealing; only in the course of the past century did it occur to a Sultan to cover the mosaics. One the images of Mary is located over the prayer niche in the apse and the other farther forward, just inside the entrance. But you have already seen all this. Over the prayer niche, and then on one of the windows above it, I read the Koranic verse that speaks of Maryam in the prayer niche.[5]

A complement in terms of spirit and soul to the shining, golden Hagia Sophia is to be found in the Blue Mosque; in both sanctuaries one is as it were drawn upwards into the splendid arabesque-ornamented cupola, only in one case the *barakah* is golden and in the other it is blue like the sky.

What makes San Marco seem so familiar to me is its Oriental, timeless, and all-embracing quality. Now that I have seen the Hagia Sophia, I can say that I had an intimation of its wonder in San Marco—not indeed of its exclusively Christian wonder, but rather of the one that is Islamic or Gnostic-Platonic; I might say that I felt at home in Venice on account of the Hagia Sophia; I hope this too figurative manner of expression is understandable. In another respect, these two sanctuaries are incomparable, without any question of a "more" or "less", and there is no temptation to think of the one in terms of the other.

Quite independently of what has just been said, I might add that I feel a particular affinity with the mosques of the Maghreb, because here an austere and crystalline richness is combined with a marvelous simplicity always near to nature.

—— ·:· ——

"*In the House of the Holy Virgin*"
Ephesus, Turkey, May 12, 1968 to Titus Burckhardt

Here in Ephesus—or more precisely in Kusadasi—we are staying in a bare, white room with a splendid view overlooking a blooming hillside garden and the sea; add to this bright sunshine and singing birds; it

[5] The Arabic inscription from this verse still hangs in the Schuons' home; this Koranic phrase is an excerpt from *Sūrah* "The Family of Imran" [3]:37: "And her Lord accepted her with full acceptance and vouchsafed to her a goodly growth; and made Zachariah her guardian. *Whenever Zachariah went into the sanctuary where she was*, he found that she had food. He said: O Mary! Whence cometh unto thee this (food)? She answered: It is from God. God giveth without stint to whom He will."

could not be more beautiful. Every day we visit the house of the Holy Virgin on the mountain—the "Meryemana Evi"—and let ourselves be penetrated by this *barakah*; there is also a spring here that was flowing in the time of the Virgin. It had been blocked up for hundreds of years; only in the last century when the house was discovered did it gush forth again. It was here, in this region of the great Ionic Artemis, that *Sayyidatnā* Maryam lived—she who was herself Artemis; she lived hidden—"I am black but beautiful"[6]—while ecstatic feasts were celebrated in honor of the stone Artemis.

The supreme Name is not represented by the Arabic inscription only; it manifests itself—according to the *Religio perennis*—in the human body, above all in the avataric body, which is both norm and synthesis. In another sense, the supreme Name is represented by the sun—so to speak as a complementary pole to man. Not without reason is it said that the Holy Virgin is "clothed with the sun";[7] her body itself is the sun. In yet another respect, the supreme Name manifests itself through the heart; here Name and invocation are one. The body, moreover, is nothing other than the unfolding of the heart. Name-Inscription, body, sun, and heart are one and the same. The primordial sound, the human voice, the primordial word—such as the *Pranava Om*—are of the same order.

Every word of the *Avatāra* is a form of the primordial word. When the Holy Virgin says: "They have no wine", this is not merely a statement of fact, but a spiritual teaching; it is a characterization of fallen, profane man. When Christ replies: "Mine hour is not yet come", he means: "The hour when I shall pour the true wine, which I myself am; for the present, I give a symbol of it." And when the Virgin then says: "Whatever he saith unto you, do it",[8] this saying has an altogether comprehensive meaning.

Wilāyah—sanctity as such—is the wine. So it is that Christ is the "Seal of Sanctity"—he who is the wine, and who pours the wine; and Mary is inseparably connected with him. Perhaps I could say that he gives the dry wine and she the sweet. This is the wisdom of Jesus and Mary in Islam; thus do they radiate into Islam, or more precisely, into Sufism. Solomon's "Song of Songs" and Umar ibn al-Farid's *Khamri-*

6 Song of Sol. 1:5.

7 Rev. 12:1.

8 John 2:3–5.

yyah bear witness to this *Haqīqah 'Īsāwīyyah*, and *Maryamīyyah*. This radiation of earlier prophets in Islam lies in the very nature of Islam; it is in a sense demanded by this nature; it is not a poverty, but a richness of the Islamic reality; not the religions, but the prophets themselves radiate into Islam, and they do so as it were out of their own *islām*, if I may express myself thus.

In the house of the Holy Virgin there are two adjoining rooms, the larger of which faces east and the smaller south. In the larger room, through which one has to pass first, Mass is recited toward the east; the smaller room is empty, but there are prayer rugs for Muslims. In the larger, hang Christian *ex-voto* objects recalling miraculous healings or other graces, and there are also many lighted candles; in the smaller, hang the colored silk ribbons of the Turks, with the same *ex-voto* meaning. There where the prayer niche would be, on the south wall of the smaller room, was the resting place of the Holy Virgin; we stood or sat in front of this spot for a while and invoked the supreme Name inwardly. "God nourishes whom He will without measure."[9]

[9] Koran, *Sūrah* "The Family of Imran" [3]:37.

6. Above All the *Religio Perennis* Ages 62–72

"*From One Religious Form to Another*"[1]
Pully, November 16, 1969 to Martin Lings

In principle, it is obviously possible to go from one religious form to another; this presupposes that one be keenly aware of the pillars of the *Religio perennis*—discernment, concentration, virtue, symbolism—and also that one have a valid motive for making this passage. Formerly, I would never have dreamt of encouraging anyone to go from one orthodox religion to another orthodox religion, quite to the contrary; but now the situation of the Catholic Church is such that I will not undertake anything to prevent such a change, if leaving Catholicism is the issue. From my point of view, the author of the letter is free to consider the change he has in mind, if this is God's Will; he must therefore pray with this intention, so that Heaven may guide him.

November 17. The change from the invocation of Jesus to that of *Allāh* cannot give rise to any difficulty, for Christ cannot be opposed to our invoking God. And I have often said that *Sayyidatnā* Maryam is like a link between the two religions; in her Essence (*Dharmakāya*), she is the Mother of all the Prophets; her message is the *Religio perennis*; she is the *Sophia* that was at the beginning.

—— ·:· ——

"*Those Who Have Passed*"
Pully, June 10, 1970 to Hans Küry

We on earth feel somehow separated from those who have passed away, however for them this is not so: they are nearer to us than we

[1] This letter is in response to questions about leaving the Catholic Church after the modernist innovations imposed by the Second Vatican Council of 1962–65.

can know. We can help them through prayer, insofar as they still need such help—this being in God's hand—while they, the departed, can in turn help us.

There is no spiritual way without death. The passing of your wife is a kind of death for you too, and I can say this because I myself have experienced such things, indeed more than others can imagine. In a certain sense, your wife has taken something of you with her, and out of this a spiritual blessing can and must grow; you can no longer be completely of this earth. It is as if your wife has opened a door for you; you must now enter this new land, with her and in God.

—·⁞·—

"*Metaphysical Truth, Unitive Concentration, and Heavenly Beauty*"
Pully, September 6, 1970 to a reader

Man is distinguished from the animals by 1. a total intelligence, capable of conceiving of the Absolute; 2. a free will, capable of choosing the Absolute; 3. a heavenly soul, happy only with the Infinite. As a result, man is only truly human in virtue of contents proportioned to his intelligence, his will, and his soul; namely spiritual contents, which by definition converge on God, or are God, the Absolute, the Infinite. It is thus our human nature itself that proves religion; it is only through spirituality, I repeat, that man is truly man.

All religion or all spirituality comes down to these three factors: 1. discernment between the world and God, or between the contingent and the Absolute, or between the illusory and the Real; 2. permanent concentration on this Real; 3. happiness in this Real.

Christianity's originality is to place the accent on the divine Manifestation: it is therefore Christ who represents and embodies the Real; Christ and in a certain way also the Holy Virgin. Christ corresponds more particularly to the elements "Absolute" and "Truth", and the Virgin to the elements "Infinite" and "Mercy" or "Beauty". We thus must know that in Christ and in the Virgin we are oriented towards the divine Reality.

And what does permanent concentration on the Real mean in practice? It is essentially ejaculatory orison, such as practiced by the Desert Fathers. This prayer consists in either the Name of *Jesu* (in the vocative, in Latin), or in the double (Latin) invocation *Jesu Maria*, or sometimes in the single Name of *Maria*, or yet in the Greek invocation (the "Jesus Prayer" of the Hesychasts) Κύριε Ἰησοῦ Χριστέ ἐλέησόν με.[2]

And what does finding our happiness in the Real alone mean in practice? It obviously means: to put all of our joy in the invocation of God.

Oratio et jejunium, Christ said.[3] That is to say, it is impossible to do what leads to God without abstaining from what removes from God, namely not just sins as such, but also profane distractions, trivial things, reading things that are useless and unworthy, in short just about everything that the modern world offers.

And it is impossible and, moreover, illogical, to practice permanent prayer—the invocation of Christ—without practicing the fundamental virtues, for no spiritual activity is possible without beauty of soul. The soul thus must realize an attitude of poverty or of childlikeness; of vigilance; of contentment or of patience; of generosity or of trust, in short, of fervor; of self-effacement; of inwardness.

That is all; I could end here. But I want to reread your letter, Reverend Sister,[4] in order to answer some possible questions. You allude, in referring to certain readings, to a concentration that, in becoming more inward, would pierce through to the "determining cause of the inner phenomena" of man. In order to reach this, it is enough to concentrate on the divine Name that one is invoking, by eliminating all imagination, and also any intention that is too contingent. There is much discussion nowadays about concentration, but it is done in a manner that is extra-traditional, hence in a purely profane and uniquely psychological way. These kinds of pseudo-*yogas* lead to nothing, if only because nothing can be done without grace, and grace acts only within methods that are intrinsically orthodox, that is to say, within religions.

Hence: the quintessential path is concentration by means of the invocation of God; this path proceeds on the basis of the metaphysical discernment between the illusory and the Real; and it is carried on with the help of the virtues of patience and trust, or

[2] "Lord Jesus Christ, have mercy on me."

[3] See Matt. 17:21; Mark 9:29.

[4] The recipient was a Christian nun.

with resignation and joy. The fact that your religious ambience is sentimental and therefore individualist does not concern your spiritual life. What concerns you truly is your ejaculatory orison, your invocation of God.

Alongside this invocation, you have the sacraments; the Eucharist will be of great help to you, this is obvious, though the invocation of the divine Names is also a kind of Eucharist. You also have your personal prayer, addressed to Mary or to Christ, in which you speak to those celestial personages by describing your state of soul, freely and without constraint. When one thinks that one cannot pray, one must say so; but one must pray.

If you deem that you cannot pursue your invocatory path within a religious community that, for various reasons, is an obstacle rather than an aid, you could obviously return to the world, despite your vows, given that those vows were not taken in full awareness of the situation. I do not know Anglican monasteries and I do not know if a strictly contemplative path can be practiced there without hindrance.

I said that religion should be reduced to what is metaphysically essential, which finally is identified with the *Sophia perennis*. And we must choose the conditions of life or ambience that offer us the greatest chance of harmoniously following our path of discernment, invocation, and virtue; I could also say: of metaphysical truth, unitive concentration, and heavenly beauty.

—·:·—

"*Why I Write Articles*"
Hamburg, September 9, 1970 to Martin Lings

One of the reasons why I write articles is that I hope to influence not only the intelligence, but also the soul or sensibility of readers, and to teach them how to think.

—·:·—

"*Some Extraordinary Graces*"; "*Situated Beyond Forms*"
Pully, December 5, 1970 to Rama Coomaraswamy

It is true that I received on the part of the Holy Virgin some extraordinary graces, the nature of which I have described to no one. The authenticity of such graces is proven by the fact that they leave durable traces in the soul, to the point that we are no longer the same person as before; they remove from the world and draw towards Heaven. And there is a kind of vision or inward presence that remains.

If the spiritual master belongs directly and consciously to the *Religio perennis* and is therefore concretely situated beyond forms—which implies that he accepts them in practice and in knowing their value—and if the aspirant, whatever his formal religion, is situated within the same perspective, in this case there is nothing to prevent the aspirant from becoming the disciple of a master belonging formally to another religion.

—·⁝·—

"*Poetry Is the 'Language of the Gods'*"[5]
Pully, January 12, 1971 to Martin Lings

Poetry is the "language of the gods", and *noblesse oblige*; what I mean by this is that the poet has certain responsibilities. In poetry, the musicality of things, or their cosmic essentiality, erupts onto the plane of language; and this process requires the grandeur, hence also the authenticity, of both image and sentiment. The poet spontaneously intuits the underlying musicality of phenomena; under the pressure of an image or emotion—the emotion, moreover, being naturally combined with concordant images—he expresses an archetypal beauty; without this pressure there is no poetry, which implies that true poetry always has an aspect of inward necessity, whence its irreplaceable perfume. Therefore, we must have the subjective and objective

[5] Schuon wrote poetry at different points in his life, starting at the age of fourteen and continuing until fewer than two months before his death. See *Frithjof Schuon: Messenger of the Perennial Philosophy*, chap. 23, "A Profusion of Songs".

grandeur of the point of departure or of the content, then the profound musicality of the soul and the language; now the grandeur of language must be drawn from its own resources, and this is the whole formal art of poetry. Dante not only had grandeur, he also knew how on the one hand to infuse this grandeur into language, and on the other hand to wield language so as to render it adequate to his inward vision. When Shakespeare describes, following the strains of a popular song, some situation or other, he usually succeeds in presenting its quintessence and thereby brings appearances back to their cosmic musicality, whence the liberating feeling characteristic of all true poetry.

Translations of Oriental poems provide only the meaning, not the cladding; thus, an essential element of musicality is lost, so that literal translations—the English for instance—of Attar or Rumi cannot be said to be paradigms of poetic art. This brings to mind—since the form is nearly the same—"rhythmic prose" or "poetry in prose"; in most cases, this is not poetry at all, but imaginative chattering punctuated by stops intended to be "poetic"; in fact this type of literature is always too gratuitous, too "philosophical" also, and certainly too small-minded. It is the style of Whitman and Eliot, which is really conversational; with Tagore there is a truly poetic element that intervenes—he does not stoop to chat with the reader.

There is the beauty of content and that of language; in the Bible—the Books of David and Solomon notably—the beauty of the content is such that it remains intact when translated; but when Dante takes advantage of the musical resources of the Italian language to make some kind of description, the beauty, or musicality, is obviously lost in translation, unless an Italian linguistic quality can be incidentally replaced by an analogous quality in the translator's tongue.

I am rather hostile to poetry because hardly anyone knows how to write it—spiritual motives notwithstanding—and also because most true poets are the dupes of their talent and get lost in prolixity instead of letting the muse take over, for the muse is sometimes very parsimonious, which is saying something! This implies that there is an inward pressure that tolerates no vagueness or chitchat, and this pressure must be the result of a certain order of grandeur, whence the "musical crystallinity" of poetry, the convincing power of its inward necessity. There is no beauty without grandeur; these two qualities must be in the soul of the poet as well as in the form that he knows how to impart to language. Gem of perfection and vibration of infinitude!

There are not only gemlike poems, there are also stream-like poems, epic poems; the rigor of the form in this genre is in the structural element, whether it is classical hexameter or the *terza rima* of the *Divine Comedy*. One can put an indefinite quantity of images, thoughts, and feelings in this stream, but even in this case there are architectural limits, as is proven precisely by the subdivisions in Dante's poem. I would add that epic poetry has rights that cannot be attributed to lyric poetry.

Eloquence is not prolixity; the Psalms are eloquent, but the inward necessity that manifests them is rigorous, and this is something that is always felt; it is a condition of their beauty, which is at once rich and lapidary.

—— ·:· ——

"*The Crucial Question of Traditional Orthodoxy*"

Pully, March 1, 1971 to a reader

Finally, I have a moment to answer you. There is no need for you to apologize in advance for an appearance of "banality", or for a lack of education; there is no such thing for me, all that matters is the distinction between the true and false, the good and bad, the noble and base. The only fault in your letter is that you do not always express yourself with the simplicity allowed—or required—by the subject matter at hand.

You mention your readings: Ramakrishna, the Maharshi, Swami Ramdas; this is very good. But you also mention Gurdjieff, Krishnamurti; this is horrible. This has nothing to do with spirituality, either from the point of view of truth or the path.

There is first of all the crucial question of traditional orthodoxy; there is nothing valid outside of this orthodoxy. In other words, metaphysical truth and the spiritual method can only be found within intrinsically orthodox traditions: Latin and Greek Christianity, Islam, Hinduism, Northern and Southern Buddhism. Hinduism is excluded for Westerners because in order to be able to practice a Hindu method, one has to be born a Hindu, and thus belong to a caste; and certain methods are accessible only to brahmins.

It is true that metaphysical truth by definition transcends all forms, hence all religions; but man is a form, and he cannot attain to the non-formal except in a form; otherwise the religions would not exist. The religious form must be transcended within the religion itself, in its esoterism. "Without me ye can do nothing," Christ said,[6] and he knew whereof he spoke. And Muhammad said, "None shall meet *Allāh* who hath not first met His Prophet"; now the Prophet is the sacred Form. Nothing can be done outside of form except vain philosophy and pseudo-spirituality.

Spiritual seeking must start with the following truths or principles. First of all, metaphysical truth is essentially the discernment between the Real and illusory: *Ātmā* and *Māyā*, *Nirvāna* and *Samsāra*, God and the world; all relative truths are derived from this fundamental discernment, which is to be found in the esoterism of every intrinsically orthodox religion. Secondly, this truth requires quasi-perpetual concentration on the Real. In Hesychasm, this is the role of the "Jesus Prayer" or "Prayer of the Heart"; it is the "remembrance of *Allāh*", *japa-yoga*, the *nembutsu*. Thirdly, there is the practice of the virtues, which are essential, for "vertical" realization requires "horizontal" perfection; it also requires, apart from the moral virtues, the qualities of dignity and nobility. Fourthly, all of this is situated in the framework of a traditional orthodoxy, with all of its liturgical conditions; and sacred art, in the broadest sense, is part of those conditions.

This is what matters. You have read far too much and without discernment, as shown by the philosophical and psychological reflections in your letter; you think too much, and any which way. For instance, you say, like Kant, that we can never see things the way they are due to the limitations of our senses, and so on and so forth; you are wasting your time. I have in fact responded to this error in my book *Logic and Transcendence*; this book dismantles the whole notion of relativism.

—— ·:· ——

[6] John 15:5.

"*Above All the* Religio Perennis"[7]
Pully, August 21, 1971 to Martin Lings

The fact that my spiritual function—expressed by my Arabic name—is known by a number of people in the outer world is obviously not a reason to make it known on our own initiative. If it happens that someone asks you who is this Shaykh Isa whose name ends with Ahmad al-Alawi, you will invariably be obliged to answer more or less the following: "He is a disciple of the Shaykh al-Alawi; as he told me afterwards, he absolutely does not want to be known, which I did not realize when writing the dedication . . .". Moreover, I dread the curiosity of Westerners much less than that of Muslim Easterners, for whom a Shaykh in Islam embodies not only the side that is lofty and mysterious, but also the side that is narrow and sentimental, in fact diminished and conventional, whereas in reality I want to represent above all the *Religio perennis*; that is the meaning of my Lakota name Wichahpi Wiyakpa,[8] which evokes the *kawkab durrī*[9] as well as the *Stella Matutina* or the *Stella Maris*. I am writing all of this to you because it occurs to me, though I know you are aware of this.

—·⁝·—

"*Misunderstanding Between Spiritual Men*"
Pully, July 10, 1972 to a disciple

I come now finally to the question of the sign or the inspiration. I will simply say it is totally unacceptable regarding a brother, a friend, a lucid and disinterested man that one refer to occult sources in order to know how to behave. In a misunderstanding between spiritual men, let us have the simplicity—and the humility—to remain on the plane of the human, the reasonable, and of what is in our power to control.

[7] This letter is in response to the dedication in Martin Lings' book *A Moslem Saint of the Twentieth Century: Shaykh Ahmad al-Alawi* (London: George Allen & Unwin, 1961), which was dedicated to Schuon using his Islamic name.

[8] "Bright Star".

[9] "Shining star", from the famous Verse of Light in the Koran, *Sūrah* "Light" [24]:35.

There are gifts—or realizations—lacking a sufficient foundation from the point of view of moral breadth, and this is highly dangerous, for one proceeds without any guarantee of equilibrium into a transcendent dimension where one has tasted too soon, if not of the wine, at least of its perfume. In other words, the human receptacle must be proportioned to its supernatural content; this is the crux of the matter. A saint once said that humility is to the virtues what the string is to the rosary: remove the string and all the beads escape; remove humility and all the virtues disappear.[10]

There is no sanctity without a great victory over the soul. It is not enough to live by the spirit, one must also have died by it. One must know how to "jump over one's own shadow"; very few succeed in doing this perfectly. And yet our natural gifts and our supernatural gifts are nothing without this.

There is a great teaching to be found in this criterion well known to mystical theology: if a man has a celestial vision, and if this vision is authentic, the man will have become noticeably better; if he has not become noticeably better, according to objective criteria, it is because the vision was false. Sanctity not only has intrinsic characteristics that are possibly unverifiable, but it also—and by the same token—includes extrinsic signs. And this has absolutely nothing to do with *adab*, which does not necessarily interest me. For without those signs or those criteria, *adab* is nothing.

July 11. The humble man is not sensitive to a slight humiliation from a brother—from an elder brother especially—and he is even prepared to humble himself in order to approach another person. "When the servant takes ten steps to meet his Lord, He will arise from His Throne and takes one hundred steps to meet His servant"; it even may be that the servant will take but one step, and the Lord will take one thousand; now if this is how God acts, how much more should we be ready to sacrifice a bit of our pride! And the humble man is less concerned with his little claims to preeminence, and more careful not to forget his smallness before God; would he want God to manifest Himself to him only according to incommensurability and under the aspect of Majesty?

[10] Schuon is referring to the Cure d'Ars.

—— ⁖ ——

"*A Spiritual Heritage*"
Rabat, Morocco, May 24, 1973 to Michel Vâlsan

Your two letters reached me here in Morocco. I will start by answering the first. Here is the chronological succession of the events in question:

January 1933: initiation by the Shaykh al-Alawi.

July 1934: death of the Shaykh al-Alawi. Spiritual heritage, reception of the supreme Name. I know that I am spiritually independent, but I hesitate to consider myself as administratively independent from Mostaghanem, or more precisely I put the problem aside.

Summer 1935: Sidi Adda ben Tounes, as *khalīfah* of the deceased Shaykh, confers upon me the function of *muqaddam.* I am not comfortable with some pressure placed on me—people want to make a "missionary" out of me, and there is talk of a "society of French Muslims" and of the "Friends of Islam"—and I aspire to independence, but without taking any measures in that direction.

The year 1936: after having affiliated a certain number of people, and having run into all kinds of unforeseen difficulties, I consider giving up everything; I fear that a *Tarīqah* is something that cannot be realized in the West: one morning, I awaken with the certitude of being *Shaykh al-barakah,* and this certitude—entirely unexpected in that moment—is corroborated by various sacred dreams in my entourage; I know that I am independent from Mostaghanem, and that I am obliged to maintain and extend the *Tarīqah.*

But let us return to the year 1935: very mindful of formal orthodoxy, I went into *khalwah* in Mostaghanem while knowing that I did not need this, at least not under Sidi Adda's direction.

Starting in 1934, René Guénon favored my independence, while cautioning me to be prudent. In any case, there were no difficulties with Mostaghanem while Sidi Adda was alive. Those difficulties began in fact only after Shaykh Mahdi's visit.

According to Guénon, I was entitled starting in the summer of 1934 to consider myself as attached only to the Shaykh al-Alawi; this implies that in principle the functions to be considered—*muqaddam, murshid, Shaykh al-barakah*—were given at the outset, though in fact they were actualized successively. By *muqaddam* I mean: the capacity to initiate; by *murshid*: the capacity to give the *dhikr*, to point out faults, and to indicate remedies; and by *Shaykh al-barakah*: the mandate to direct an independent *Tarīqah* connected to a spiritual heritage. I will add that in some cases the beginning of a function—or rather of its being exercised—cannot be strictly determined or fixed: if one does not begin too soon, then one will begin too late; there is no other choice.

Inspiration and experience: these elements are combined, but each can also replace the other, depending on the case, and on the basis of an overall aptitude. You know all of this, but I am writing it because it occurs to me.

—— ⁘ ——

"*Sacramental Sexuality*"

Pully, August 4, 1973 to a reader

Certainly, the priest's thesis has something appealing given that it evokes a certain symbolism that is plausible; but in the end it is false because it goes against the nature of things and therefore the total and essential symbolism. First of all, sexual union is in itself a positive reality, I will even say a divine one; Genesis says nothing to suggest the contrary, and Hinduism attributes this union to the Divinities themselves. Secondly, the cause of the Fall is not in a given aspect of nature, but uniquely in the fact of separating all natural aspects from their divine Source, in experiencing them outside of God and attributing their glory and enjoyment to ourselves.

The priest in question is therefore not completely wrong if he says that God alone has the right to ravish virginity; but he overlooks the fact that in sacramental sexuality it is precisely God who is operating, whereas man participates in the divine operation. And, moreover, this principle of union with God applies to all the aspects of normal eroticism—the Church is metaphysically mistaken in bringing back everything to the concern for procreation, which implies a certain hypocrisy on the one hand and a partial falsification on the other—and this union with God applies also, and even above all, to our intelligence and our will in an altogether general way. The sin of Adam was not a specific outward action; this sin was fundamentally the fact of being, thinking, willing, acting, and enjoying outside God; in the act of knowledge or of will, it was to isolate both the subject and object; it was to separate them illusorily from God, "sole Subject and sole Object" as the Sufis would say.

The sexual behavior of the human couple in the earthly Paradise, or in the Golden Age, was the same as that in men of other Ages; proof of this is that a Rama, a Krishna, a Muhammad were married as ordinary men are, but with the notable difference that sexual pleasure, far from being locked in an individualistic passion at once compressive and centrifugal, was on the contrary a participation in divine Beatitude, on the very basis of the extinction entailed by sexual union, as Ibn Arabi notes.

P.S. "The tree of the knowledge of good and evil":[11] this is the separative distinction of the Substance from the accidents seen in themselves. The disturbing aspects that sexuality *de facto* may contain do not come from the thing in itself, they stem from the degeneration of matter or the flesh, and also from that of man in general; for one degeneracy leads to another. It is also noteworthy that most Westerners—unlike Hindus—do not have the innate sense of what I term "the metaphysical transparency of phenomena".

If the priest that you speak to me of were right, Christ and the Holy Virgin would not have attended the wedding at Cana; and Christ would not have said: "Wherefore they are no more twain, but one flesh", and he would not have forbidden to put asunder "what therefore God hath joined together".[12]

—·:·—

"*Concupiscence*"; "*Christian Marriage*"
Pully, February 15, 1974 to a reader

Concupiscence is neither the desire for enjoyment in itself, nor enjoyment as such, but both inasmuch as they are situated outside of God and are therefore no longer supports for spiritual contemplation, nor

[11] Gen. 2:17.

[12] Matt. 19:6.

concrete contemplative participations in divine Beatitude; enjoyment separated from God—because of the Fall—takes one away from God, owing to the fact that it appears as an end in itself; it is practically speaking an idol, since it replaces God on the one hand and puffs up gross individuality on the other; there is therefore something luciferian about it. Before the Fall the desire for carnal union coincided with a spiritual desire, that is to say, with the desire for a particular perception of the Infinite or with a desire for extinction in the consciousness of the Divine; this primordial point of view, if one may say, is always accessible in principle on the basis of a certain esoteric sanctity, as is proven above all by examples such as Krishna, David, Solomon, Muhammad.

Regarding women, it is not childbirth that comes from the Fall, it is only the pain. It is absolutely wrong to claim that original sin is the violation of woman's virginity. Original sin is uniquely enjoyment outside of God, hence the desire to see and experience cosmic reality—or illusion—in itself and without God. Primordial copulation was a prayer and not a sin. For Islam, copulation exists in Paradise; if Christ says that in Paradise "they neither marry nor are given in marriage",[13] he means marriage as a social institution, not as a sacrament that is at once natural and supernatural.

Regarding marriage in Christianity, there can be no reference here to an ideal couple; the Christ and the Virgin do not constitute a couple. There remain Joseph and the Virgin, then the Holy Spirit and the Virgin; now Joseph cannot be the model, precisely, of a husband, and as for the Holy Spirit, which husband would dare put himself in its place? And which husband would dare touch—in imagination—the Holy Virgin? The model of the Christian marriage is either the relationship between Christ and his Church, or the soul's love for its Creator or for the divine Infinitude; in this case, the partner—male or female—takes on a mystical symbolism, an example of which is given to us by the troubadours; the case of the *Fedeli d'Amore* is no doubt analogous.

—— ·:· ——

[13] Mark 12:25; Matt. 22:30; Luke 20:35.

"*Whether, for God, You Are Christian or Buddhist*"
Pully, May 31, 1975 to a reader

Eastern masters almost never understand the situation of the Westerners they initiate; they almost always lose sight of two factors, fundamental though these are: on the one hand psychological conditions, and on the other hand conditions of the ambience. One might call these the moral and aesthetic conditions of the path, both of which are difficult to fulfill in an abnormal world such as ours, whereas in the traditional East the question never really arose. This is why the practices of Zen, for instance, grafted onto the mental trivialities engendered by modern life, are in general more harmful than useful; for one must be deeply imbued with the sense of the sacred, and also by a kind of holy childlikeness, in order to be able to benefit from initiatic graces, or spiritual graces as such.

And this obviously concerns Christians as well, who in general live on the margin and not within their religion; to be a true Christian, one must become medieval again, psychologically and aesthetically speaking, though of course without sacrificing any real and spiritually useful knowledge. *The Golden Legend*[14] does not prevent us from understanding the *Bhagavad Gītā*.

Be that as it may, here is what I would say to a Christian seeking an esoteric path, that is to say, a path going beyond basic belief and conventional mediocrity. Every religion is first of all a doctrine; now the fundamental content of this doctrine is discernment between the Absolute and the contingent or between the Real and the illusory; then comes the method, namely—and essentially—continuous or at least frequent concentration on the Absolute or the Real. To doctrinal discernment and methodical concentration, one must add intrinsic virtue as a condition *sine qua non*, and this means beauty of soul; for the truth requires beauty. The Christian seeker should know that the quintessence of his religion is to be found in these elements, for they are the quintessence of all possible religion and all spirituality; the rest is *upāya*, "mythology", formal cladding. 1. Discernment (doctrine); 2. Concentration (method); 3. Virtue (moral beauty).

[14] A collection of hagiographies by Jacobus da Varagine that was widely read in late medieval Europe.

The question for you is that of knowing whether, for God, you are Christian or Buddhist; assuming that your sense of the sacred and your intuition of spiritual forms have enabled you to assimilate the specific atmosphere of the *Mahāyāna* to a sufficient degree, I will tell you that the situation in that case is strictly analogous to what it is in Christianity, the central spiritual means being the *mantra*—the ejaculatory orison—all the more as you have received an initiation referring to Amitabha Buddha, who corresponds metaphysically to Christ. And I would not advise a western Buddhist to follow any path other than that of the invocation of Amitabha—whether in its Japanese or Tibetan form—assuming of course that one have a valid reason in the eyes of God for being a Buddhist and for entering upon a path so foreign to our traditional climate in the West. I suppose that this question is not entirely resolved for you.

If I understand you correctly, you sometimes receive what you call "metaphysical" communion in the Church; but if you are validly affiliated with Buddhism and practice a Buddhist method, all Christian rites are excluded. Moreover, one does not take communion "metaphysically"; one concentrates on God, the Absolute, the Real, or on the radiation of His Mercy, and one lets God act as He will. What you are doing, according to your letter, is doubly dangerous: first because it is a heterogeneous mixture of sacred forms and then because we have no right to impose a doctrinal program on Grace; Grace acts as it wills. Tibetans, not knowing western religions, confuse them with secondary cults and are not competent in these matters. And you most certainly have not "gone beyond both infidelity and religion"!

Ramana Maharshi, being a Hindu, could not give any advice to non-Hindus, and being a kind of *pratyeka-buddha* he could not have disciples in the strict sense of the term. It is not possible under any circumstance to "go beyond doctrines"; moreover, the Maharshi knew Vedantic doctrine very well. Having been born with a lofty spiritual degree—which is exceptionally rare—the Maharshi was a kind of incarnation of the *Vedānta*; but he knew only how to speak "for himself" and his words cannot all be taken literally; his "advice" does not in most cases lend itself to concrete applications.

—·:·—

"*The Modern Cult of Sincerity*"[15]
Pully, August 19, 1975 to a disciple

I would like to draw your attention to the danger of the modern cult of sincerity, which in our social contacts is in the air we breathe; this "sincerism" is obviously nothing more than individualism, more or less cynical and, moreover, democratic in tone. There is always some danger of contamination when one lives in a decadent world, unless one has implacable lucidity and adamantine vigilance.

Cynicism and hypocrisy are two forms of pride: cynicism is the caricature of sincerity or frankness, while hypocrisy is the caricature of virtue or discipline. Cynics believe that to display defects and passions is sincerity, and that to hide them is hypocrisy; they do not dominate themselves and still less do they seek to transcend themselves; and the fact that they take their fault for a virtue is proof of their pride, precisely. Hypocrites on the contrary believe that it is virtuous to display virtuous attitudes; their vice consists, not in manifesting the forms of virtue—which is a rule incumbent upon everyone—but in believing that the manifestation is virtue itself and, above all, in mimicking virtues in the hope of being admired; but this is pride because it is individualism. Pride is to overestimate oneself while underestimating others; and this is what the cynic does just as much as the hypocrite, either crudely or subtly depending on the case.

A virtuous man conceals his faults for the following reasons: first because he does not concede them any right to exist and because, after each lapse, he hopes it will be the last; a man cannot really be reproached for concealing his defects because he is striving not to sin and to behave correctly. Another reason is conformation to the norm: in order to be rid of a fault, one must not only have the intention to rid oneself of it for the sake of God and not just to please men, but one must also enter actively into the mold of perfection; and if it is clear that this must not be done just to please men, it is no less clear that it must be done also to avoid scandalizing them and setting a bad example; this is a charity God requires of us, since the love of God requires us to love our neighbor.

[15] Part of this letter was published in *Esoterism as Principle and as Way*, chap. "What Sincerity Is and What It Is Not".

When so-called sincerity breaks the framework of traditional—or simply normal—rules of behavior, it betrays thereby its prideful nature; for the rules are venerable and we have no right to scorn them by placing our subjectivity above them. It is true that saints sometimes break these rules, but they do so from above, not from below—by virtue of a divine truth, not a human sentiment. Be that as it may, if a man of tradition effaces himself behind a rule of behavior, this is certainly not out of hypocrisy, but out of humility and charity: humility, because he recognizes that the traditional rule is right and that it is better than he is; charity, because he does not wish to impose on his neighbors the scandal of his own faults, far from it: he intends to manifest a salutary norm, even if he is not yet personally up to its level.

August 20. The noble man is one who dominates himself and loves to do so; the base man is one who does not dominate himself and has a horror of doing so. The spiritual man is one who transcends himself and loves to do so; the worldly man remains horizontal and hates the vertical dimension. And this is important: one cannot subject oneself to a demanding ideal—nor seek to transcend oneself for the sake of God—without bearing in one's soul what psychoanalysts term "complexes"; this amounts to saying that there are "complexes" that are normal for a spiritual man or simply for a decent man and that, conversely, the absence of "complexes" is not necessarily a virtue, to say the least. Doubtless, primordial man, or deified man, no longer has any complexes, but it is not enough to be free of complexes to be a deified or primordial man.

The root of all true sincerity is sincerity towards God, not towards what suits our own good pleasure; in other words, it is not enough to believe in God, one must also draw all the consequences of this in our outward and inward behavior; and when we aspire to a perfection—since God is perfect and wants us to be perfect—we seek to manifest it even before we have realized it, and in order to realize it.

A man who submits to outward and inward norms, and thus who is striving in the way of perfection—or striving to eliminate imperfections—is well aware that among those who do not make this effort there are some who surpass him in natural qualities; but being endowed with intelligence, otherwise he would not be man, he cannot fail to note that, whether he likes it or not, he is necessarily better than worldly men with respect to metaphysical truth and spiritual effort, and that any effort made for the sake of God is worth infinitely more than a mere natural quality that is never turned to spiritual account. For the rest, worldly people are always looking for accomplices in their dissipation and their ruin, and this is why spiritual people part company with them as much as possible, unless they have an apostolic mission; but, in this case, they will be most wary of imitating the bad behavior of the worldly and thus of going against what they preach.

I write all of this since you brought up the thorny—or double-edged—problem of sincerity, and I do so without referring to concrete cases that I have not seen for myself.

P.S. I do not know whether I stated clearly enough that the content of sincerity is our tendency towards God and our consequent conformation to the rules that this tendency requires, and not our nature pure and simple with all of its defects. And hypocrisy consists not in adopting a superior mode of behavior with the intention of realizing it, but in adopting it with the intention of seeming to be more than one is. If the mere fact of adopting a model behavior were hypocrisy, it would be impossible to strive for the good.

—·:·—

"*Fundamental Elements of the Esoteric Path*"
Pully, November 21, 1975 to a reader

There is indeed but "one thing needful",[16] and it is impossible to avoid it within the framework of the human vocation, given on the one hand that our intelligence is made for the Truth, and on the other hand that we have a soul to save.

To understand a religion in depth, one must understand religion as such: now the religious phenomenon is identified in its essence with the one and universal wisdom, hence with esoterism or the "primordial tradition", or if one prefers with the *Philosophia perennis.* In other words, esoteric wisdom is based, doctrinally and methodically, on what is common to all religions, or on what underlies each of them. If I am repeating here something that is obvious, it is to emphasize

[16] Luke 10:42.

that one must never lose sight of this fact—for experience proves that the temptation to do so is great—when engaged in the practice of an orthodox spirituality, that is to say, when one is surrounded by a framework of formalism or mythology.

There are three planes to consider in the human microcosm: namely intelligence, will, and soul. The spiritual function of human intelligence—hence its essential function—is discernment between the Real and the illusory, the Absolute and the contingent, the Infinite and the finite, the Permanent and the impermanent; this is the one and universal Doctrine, hence the quintessence of all theology and all metaphysics. Then, there is the will: the spiritual function of the human will, which is free, is essentially the in principle continuous concentration of the mind on the Real, the Absolute, the Infinite, the Permanent, or on the avataric Manifestation of the Real, which in practice amounts to the same; this is the Method, and it is the quintessence of all possible paths, for "prayer" is everything and according to Saint Paul one must "pray without ceasing".[17] Finally, there is the soul, the character, sensibility, affectivity, the capacity to love: the spiritual function of the soul is essentially the quasi-existential conformation to the Real, namely virtue; this is Morality, not of course merely extrinsic and social, but intrinsic and contemplative; without beauty of soul—I would even say without the sense of beauty—no spirituality is possible, displeasing as this may be to the ignorant and the pedants who imagine that for metaphysical realization all that matters is "technique", that is to say, a kind of coldly mechanical *yoga*. Discernment, concentration, virtue: it is these elements and nothing else that one must seek when one has entered a spiritual path as a metaphysician; when practicing such a path, one must not be "converted" to a given theology or mythology, though one must love the symbols and their beauty, in one's own religious cosmos as in that of others.

Christianity is a bhaktic esoterism become religion; hence it is exoteric by its literalist and dogmatist interpretations, and not by its symbolism or its means, which are initiatic in their essence. Baptism and Confirmation taken together constitute Christian initiation; according to Guénon, the sacraments later lost their initiatic character, but this is impossible in principle and in fact: in principle, because God never gives less than He promises—it is rather the reverse that is

[17] 1 Thess. 5:17.

true—and in fact, because it is technically impossible to bring about such a change, if only due to the Christians having been dispersed since the first centuries. From the point of view of the method, the central means is the ejaculatory orison containing the sacramental Name of Jesus, or possibly that of Mary or both at once; the central *mantra* of Christianity—the support for concentration—is therefore *Jesu*, or *Jesu Maria*, in Latin or Greek. Whoever wishes to practice this method, which dates back to the origins of Christianity, must solemnly promise the Holy Virgin to do so—in the form of a vow—in a sanctuary dedicated to her; he must also ask the Virgin's permission and implore her assistance, and this will have to be kept secret, at least *a priori* and under normal circumstances. And he will then have to renounce all the dispersing and degrading trivialities of the modern world; we must await death in a little spiritual garden and do so in the midst of our family life and worldly duties, as the case may be. God wants our soul and nothing else; if He demands something more from us, we will know this with certitude by giving Him our soul.

As there are hardly any valid sacraments left in the Post-Conciliar Church,[18] ejaculatory orison—the "Jesus Prayer" or "prayer of the heart" of the Orthodox—can suffice, for "God knows His own" and the Name of Jesus can serve as a substitute Mass, since one has no other choice; unless the Tridentine Mass is still accessible, depending on where one lives. With respect to the invocation: since it is impossible in practice to pronounce the orison without ceasing, we must do so at least three times a day, and at all other moments if we reasonably can; we must have an underlying rhythm, but the rest of the time we are free.

I write you all of this, Madame, out of duty, so as not to overlook anything; therefore, I must tell you in addition that Islamic esoterism is also accessible in the West, but I have no reason *a priori* to go into further details regarding it. That said, let us return to the essential. There are two moments in life that are everything, and these are the present moment, when we are free to choose what we would be, and the moment of death, when we no longer have any choice and the decision belongs entirely to God. Now if the present moment is good, death will be good; if we are now with God—in this present that

[18] Schuon is referring to the effects of the changes introduced by the Second Vatican Council.

ceaselessly renews itself but always remains the only actual moment—God will be with us at the moment of our death. The remembrance of God—ejaculatory orison—is a death in life; it will be a life in death.

Between the present moment, when we remember God, and death, when God will remember us—and this reciprocity exists already in each prayer—there is the rest of life, the duration extending from the present moment to the last moment; but duration is merely a succession of present moments, for we live always "now"; thus it is, concretely and operatively speaking, always the same blessed instant when we are free to remember God and to find our happiness in this remembrance.

P.S. Metaphysical truth and perpetual prayer, together with intrinsic virtue—virtue considered in terms of beauty—are the fundamental elements of the esoteric path and in the final analysis of all spirituality. And the divine Name contains in principle the totality of all sacramental means.

—·⁝·—

"*An Understanding between Religions*"
Pully, February 22, 1976 to a reader

I am completely against ecumenism as it is envisaged today, with its ineffective "dialogues" and gratuitous and sentimental gestures amounting to nothing. Certainly, an understanding between religions is possible and even necessary, though not on the dogmatic plane, but solely on the basis of common ideas and common interests. The common ideas are a transcendent, perfect, all-powerful, merciful Absolute, then a hereafter that is either good or bad depending on our merits or demerits; all the religions, including Buddhism—Buddhist "atheism" is simply a misunderstanding—are in agreement on these points. The common interests are a defense against materialism, atheism, perversion, subversion, and modernism in all its guises. I believe Pius XII[19] once said that the wars between Christians and Mus-

[19] Pope Pius XII (1876–1958), the last traditional Catholic pope before the official onset of modernism with Vatican II.

lims were but domestic quarrels compared to the present opposition between the world of the religions and that of militant materialism-atheism; he also said that it was a consolation to know that there are millions of men who prostrate themselves five times a day before God.

—— ·:· ——

"*Esoterism Is Not Syncretism*"
Pully, April 30, 1976 to a reader

The Father in question has the immense merit of being a traditionalist, and this has nothing to do with his inability to understand things situated outside of Catholic tradition. It is deeply illogical and unfair to reproach integralists for opinions that from the point of view of tradition are a matter of indifference; I prefer the narrow-mindedness of an integralist—he is entitled to this theologically—to the possible broad-mindedness of a modernist. For the modernist who accepts Islam does so on the basis of modern errors, in other words, for philosophical and psychological reasons that Islam itself does not accept; whereas the integralist bases himself either on truth as such—which obviously includes the Islamic perspective—or at least on a form of this truth, namely Catholicism, precisely. Better to hold to a truth that is narrow but offers salvation, than to be broad-minded while betraying the essential.

The "rigidity of dogma" can be transcended, but only metaphysically and mystically, thus from within, not from without; on the theological plane the dogma must be rigid, otherwise it disappears; there is here also a question of collective psychology, which Providence—or the Holy Spirit—always takes into consideration. Esoterism is not syncretism; forms are what they are and they have a right to exist. Dogmas, while being exclusive and thus "narrow" and "rigid", are sacred; and what they exclude on the plane of form, they include on the plane of the metaphysical essence that is one.

—— ·:· ——

"*The Catholicism of All Time*"[20]
Pully, July 21, 1976 to a reader

At the time of Saint Pius X,[21] Catholics of integrity were those who accepted the directives of this pope and who, like him, rejected modernism; the modernists called them "integralists". Thus, from the point of view of the modernists there are "integralists", but from the point of view of the non-modernists there are only Catholics; "integralism" is not a specialty, it is simply the Catholicism of all time. Consequently, it is wrong to think that there are two kinds of Catholicism and that there are mistakes on both sides; there is but one single Catholicism, the one defined by Pius X; and those who do not accept this definition place themselves outside of Catholicism; they are the modernists, precisely.

P.S. In principle, Catholicism could be open to other spiritualities; but on condition that it be Catholicism and not something else! Now modernism is something else, and thus its "tolerance" is worthless.

—·:·—

"*The Name* Hari Om"
Pully, November 27, 1976 to Martin Lings

One of the disciples in Basel married a Hindu woman whom he met in Bombay, where he was working at the time; this Hindu woman had received the *mantra Hari Om* from a *guru*; on that basis, she would now like to be my disciple, which I accepted. She thus made a *khalwah* in Basel with the name *Hari Om* and reading from the *Bhagavad Gītā*.

This brings to mind that for many years I have had a particular and completely involuntary relationship with the name *Hari Om*; I

[20] This is the first of four letters regarding the effects of the Second Vatican Council on the Catholic Church. See also the letter dated February 27, 1978, titled "Traditionalist Catholics and Modernist Heretics", the letter dated June 30, 1982, titled "Intrinsic Orthodoxy", and the letter dated July 21, 1984, titled "Disorders in Today's Church".

[21] Pope St. Pius X (1835–1914) vigorously opposed modernism in the Catholic Church, notably implementing an oath against modernism.

pronounce these words fairly often, but only notice it afterwards. It is like a trace of the Hindu *barakah* that overwhelmed me in Chemin de Lucinge.[22] It goes without saying that I would not allow anyone to imitate me on this point, all the more so as the initiative does not come from me.

—— ·:· ——

"*When a Spiritual Experience Is Authentic and Profound*"
Pully, July 6, 1977 to a disciple

You ask me whether this event requires a particular attitude on your part. Yes and no. When a spiritual experience is authentic and profound, it leaves a trace in us; now one must be faithful to this trace. He who has benefited from such a grace knows exactly what he must and must not do; he can no longer be exactly the same man as before. He must not seek to do extraordinary things; from the point of view of the spiritual method and social comportment, nothing changes, unless there was in this comportment something improper. What Heaven wants of us is our soul; it invites us therefore to inwardness. "The kingdom of God is within you", Christ said.[23] "I am black, but beautiful", says the Song of Songs,[24] and this saying is attributed to the Holy Virgin; once again, this is about contemplative inwardness. A major spiritual event, comprising a kind of vision, cuts us off in a certain way from the world; it is as if we were living henceforth in a kind of invisible sanctuary belonging already to the hereafter; or as if we were in a little garden that is already celestial, whose happiness is no longer terrestrial. If we have the impression that we are unfaithful to the vision, we must make a prayer to the celestial Personage come to meet us.

—— ·:· ——

[22] Schuon's former residence in Lausanne.

[23] Luke 17:21.

[24] Song of Sol. 1:5.

"*Difficulties in Contacts between Whites and Indians*"
Pully, October 5, 1977 to Joseph Brown

The difficulties in contacts between whites and Indians are easy to understand. First of all, the white man does not have a sense of the sacred to the degree that he is a modern man, which almost all whites are; if he asks an Indian questions, he usually does so out of curiosity, without realizing that the Indian has no motive for responding to an interrogation he considers indiscreet and pointless.

To say that modern man does not have a sense of the sacred amounts to recognizing that he is full of false ideas; intellectually and morally, he is unaware of the axioms of the traditional spirit—or in other words of spirituality as such; he does not know about metaphysics, cosmology, or mysticism. Metaphysically, modern man is unaware that everything is a manifestation of the Self, which is at once transcendent and immanent; he knows nothing of the doctrine of *Ātmā* and *Māyā*, even if he has read some Hindu books, for in this case he thinks it is merely a question of concepts having a historical, psychological, or phenomenological interest—in short, things that can be put aside. Cosmologically, he does not realize that the world is made of a hierarchical series of regions—beginning with the Self and extending to matter—and that the evolutionist error is simply a "horizontal" substitute for "vertical" emanation, which begins unfolding with the archetypes and passes through the animic or subtle world. That being the case, modern man also knows nothing of the sacred and its laws, and nothing of the psychology that is derived from it and bears witness to it.

Question: how can one study the metaphysics, cosmology, and spirituality of a people without having any idea what it means? This is the whole problem. And this is why people go around in circles indefinitely, while developing by way of compensation finely drawn or charitable considerations that are beside the point. I repeat: the white man does not offer the Indian a sufficient, satisfying, or acceptable motivation for answering the questions he asks, nor in the eyes of the Indian does he exhibit a state of spiritual readiness meriting the answers he seeks. From the point of view of any traditional discipline, one does not have the right to speak of sacred things without a sufficient reason or outside the relationship between a master and his disciple; or again, there are things that lose their "power" if discussed without a plausible motive.

But there is more: beyond the fact that the Indian has no motive for answering questions whose justification he does not perceive, he cannot see the value of the white man's need for logical explanations; and if in spite of this the Indian answers, he is unable to do so by means of the abstract categories of classic, European dialectics. He therefore responds in a symbolic language that the white man in turn cannot comprehend, given that the modern mind does not understand symbolism, its principles, and its methods. If the Indian has gone to a university, there is a very good chance he will have accepted uncritically the errors and mental habits of white people and that the abstract and differentiated language he makes use of will therefore be of no help to him when explaining the Indian mysteries. In a similar way, there are Easterners who think with two separate brains, a traditional one and a modern one, so that their thinking is either impeccable or absurd depending on the brain they are using.

One might object that academics who study the Indians are no longer so ignorant because of the work of Eliade[25] and others; I reply that they remain ignorant and incompetent enough to meet the description I gave above, if only because they draw no serious conclusions from whatever real knowledge they may possess.

In any event, "the Indians as they really are" are only rarely the Indians as they are in their substance and as they were still at the beginning of the twentieth century; first because everything has been done to transform the Indians into cowboys, and then because one wants to attribute to the "authentic Indian" the cowboyism that has been inflicted on him. The aristocratic and more or less primordial simplicity of the Indian is not at all the same thing as the simplifying and democratic mindset of the average American; to be simple and natural is not to be mentally a barbarian. I draw these remarks from my own experiences.

So, you visited the Blackfeet; we are glad to learn that Tradition is being maintained, or is even awakening, in this tribe.

October 7. How does one explain to an academic that Black Elk,[26] in his subtle form, was reabsorbed into the world of the archetypes, passing through the subtle state and stopping at the threshold of the

[25] Mircea Eliade (1907–86), the influential Romanian historian of religions.

[26] Schuon is referring to the visionary experiences of the Lakota holy man, which are described in *Black Elk Speaks*.

archangelic world; that certitude of the cosmic degrees and all the more so of the Principle resides in the very substance of the Intellect, which inserts itself into the individuality while remaining universal and in essence principial; that human ignorance is derived from both the accidental and providential scission between the Intellect and the ego; that Revelation has for its purpose the actualization of immanent knowledge, hence a knowledge that is connatural with the Intellect; that the goal of spiritual methods is the abolition of the scission between the individual consciousness and the universal Consciousness; how does one explain this to academics, and how can one understand the wisdom of the Indians without knowing all of that?

—·⁝·—

"*Traditionalist Catholics and Modernist Heretics*"
Pully, February 27, 1978 to a reader

You allude in your letter to the Council,[27] whose causes must be known in order to have an opinion of it—unless one were to say that the fruits suffice. One cannot say that it produced a "reversal of tendencies", for rather it is itself the product *a priori* of all the tendencies that are contrary to Catholicism in particular and to Tradition in general. It was convoked in the name of the cult of man and with the intention of destroying the Catholic Church by falsifying it; a stratagem made possible by the fact that the majority of the prelates were more or less converted to modernism, and that Roncalli,[28] who was himself a modernist, hastened to create as many modernist cardinals as possible. There is nothing mysterious about this; from the nineteenth century onward, and even before, rationalism on the one hand and scientism on the other could not but influence Catholics who, like all Westerners, were *a priori* imbued with progressivist "civilizationism"; the errors current in the nineteenth century gave rise within Catholicism itself to this movement called "modernism". This false ideology was

[27] The Second Vatican Council of 1962–65.

[28] Angelo Giuseppe Roncalli (1881–1963), known as John XXIII, convoked the Second Vatican Council.

masterfully analyzed and defined by Pius IX,[29] then by Saint Pius X; the latter erected a protective wall against modernism by introducing the anti-modernist oath, and he did not fear to proceed with numerous suspensions and excommunications, which was the normal thing to do, though it required a certain amount of courage. The following popes up to and including Pius XII recalled more than once the definitions and condemnations proclaimed by Pius IX and Pius X; but, unfortunately, they contented themselves with that and on average avoided taking punitive measures. They contented themselves with making theoretical declarations and relied on the anti-modernist oath; and since they themselves were anti-modernists—which is obvious, since heretics cannot be popes—the government of the Church remained orthodox.

Upon the death of Pius XII, the modernists went on the attack; revenge would be taken for the fact that, in order to avoid scandal, Pius XII had omitted to excommunicate Roncalli, Montini,[30] and others; Roncalli was elected in order to allow the modernists to occupy the Church, as a foreign army occupies a defenseless country. However, Roncalli's election was invalid owing to the fact that he was strictly speaking a modernist; the election of Montini—an extreme and blatant heretic and a destroyer of the Mass—was so *a fortiori*; this is to say that the Council is null and void. I think it is unnecessary to tell you that already several centuries ago the greatest theologians—Saint Alphonsus de Liguori, Saint Robert Bellarmine, Cajetan, and others—envisaged the possibility that a pope could lapse into heresy, or that he could be a heretic even before his election, which would annul the latter; the question they faced was uniquely whether such a usurper is *depositus ipso facto* or if he is *deponendus*, the first point of view being principial, hence irrefutable, and the second being juridical, hence open to discussion. And all of this of course has absolutely nothing to do with the question of infallibility, which arises only in the case of *ex cathedra* declarations; it is only too obvious that a false pope can declare nothing *ex cathedra*, so infallibility does not apply to him.

You say that the Council started "from a position of complete exclusion against that which was not strictly and dogmatically Catholic"; however, it did this in order to save appearances and to fool the

[29] Pope Pius IX (1792–1878) condemned a total of eighty modernist errors or heresies in his "Syllabus of Errors" (*Syllabus Errorum*).

[30] Giovanni Battista Enrico Antonio Maria Montini (1897–1978), known as Paul VI.

traditionalist or hesitant Conciliar fathers. This "position of complete exclusion" is the normal position; no traditionally sound council has the right to manifest another position, whatever esoteric knowledge individuals may have in private. Exoterism exists and has a right to exist; a council is there to define and to defend it, and nothing else. It is a fact that religions contradict one another formally and there can be no question of manifesting esoterism on planes that are strictly reserved for exoterism; it would not be an esoterist attitude, because esoterism is realistic and does not confuse different planes; it puts each thing carefully in its place. The world is what it is and esoterists are the first to know this.

Traditionalists—Msgr. Lefèbvre[31] notably—are sometimes reproached for being closed to esoterism, when in fact esoteric knowledge has absolutely nothing to do with the issue; what is at stake is to defend the Catholic religion, as it is a religion, and nothing else. What certain traditionalists can be reproached for—but this, too, has nothing to do with the question of orthodoxy—is calumniating Muslims; but not for refusing Islam. Msgr. Lefèbvre respects Muslims but does not accept their religion, something he clearly cannot be reproached for, and which, I repeat, has nothing to do with the question of Christian orthodoxy—the only question that needs be raised when considering the opposition between traditionalist Catholics and modernist heretics. Hence, there is nothing appealing about the Council's openness towards non-Catholic and non-Christian traditional forms, first because this is absurd on the plane where it occurred, and then because an opening that, for psychological reasons, accepts everything in a jumble and on the basis of a false humanism presents no concrete interest.

Your letter contains allusions to the spiritual life. Clearly it is never too late to start a life dedicated to the "one thing needful".[32] But to start such a life, it is necessary to affirm the intention of doing so in a prayer addressed to the Holy Virgin, to ask for her help and blessing by promising her to remain faithful to this commitment, that is to say, the commitment to practice the invocation of a specific sacred Formula.

[31] Msgr. Lefèbvre (1905–1991) was a French Roman Catholic archbishop who played a leading role within the conservative bloc during the Second Vatican Council. Lefèbvre would subsequently gain prominence in opposing the modernist innovations within the post-conciliar Church.

[32] Luke 10:42.

Since a life of prayer must have a fundamental rhythm from which we never depart, one should practice the invocation three times a day no matter what the length of each session is; when one has the time and strength to do so, however, one can also recite the specific Formula or Name at each moment. If one cannot practice the invocation while seated, one can recite the Formula while walking in a street, and even mentally; but one must never neglect one of the three daily moments, even if it is as short as only a few minutes if time is lacking. Apart from the initial prayer addressed to the Holy Virgin, one should start with a little retreat of at least two hours in order to pronounce the Formula without interruption, for it is necessary to have a beginning in everything; and this retreat can be repeated from time to time. We must never ask whether we are "worthy" of such a path, nor whether we are sufficiently gifted for it, for we have no choice; we have an immortal soul, and we do what we can.

I am not telling you what you must do, I am telling you what my Christian friends are doing and what I advise them to do; moreover, what I advise is self-evident if one has a deep understanding of the issues.[33]

—·⁝·—

"*Remain in the Little Garden*"
Pully, May 19, 1978 to a disciple

"To sense an illness is not to have it anymore", Lao Tzu said.[34] In other words, the remedy against something harmful lies in the awareness we have of it; the remedy is provided by this awareness itself.

I want to start by telling you two things: first, that you have nothing to fear; secondly, that the trial you are undergoing is providential; what happened to you had to happen, and it is for your good. Because you had too much self-assurance and as a result not enough

[33] Schuon summarizes his advice on invocatory prayer to Christian seekers in the letter dated September 6, 1970, titled "Metaphysical Truth, Unitive Concentration, and Heavenly Beauty", and the letter dated November 21, 1975, titled "Fundamental Elements of the Esoteric Path".

[34] *Tao Te Ching*, chap. 71.

prudence; you also had too much intellectual curiosity without enough faith; too much critical sense without enough of a sense of proportion.

Aurobindism[35] is not a tolerable heresy and one must keep away from it like the plague. There is no need for me to go into details about this senseless and frankly vile ideology; intellectually speaking, it is one of the most foolish philosophies there is; Shri Ramana Maharshi made fun of it when people brought it up to him.

You were obviously under a bad psychic influence, but this must not scare you, for despite your sufferings such an influence belongs to the contingent, whereas the divine Name pertains to the Absolute. Next, our *Tarīqah* is called *Tarīqah Maryamīyyah*, which means that it is placed under the protection of the Holy Virgin; I remind you in this respect of this verse of the Koran: "I have named her Mary, and I commend her and her offspring to Thy protection from Satan the outcast."[36] Now the "offspring" of the Holy Virgin also encompasses our *Tarīqah*, by spiritual adoption.

One must recite the three final *sūrahs* of the Koran often, recite the *Shahādah* much, and also practice personal prayer, the *du'ā*: in it one describes one's state, and by describing it before Heaven, one as it were exhausts it, and one attracts heavenly aid. One must also recite in Arabic the following formula: "Sufficient for us is God, and He is the best Disposer of affairs";[37] at each session seventy-two times, tradition says. A similar practice is the invocation *yā Latīf* one hundred twenty-nine times, or five hundred, or one thousand times a day.

And one must realize holy monotony, holy poverty, holy childlikeness; knowing that you know the essential principles of metaphysics, you must remain in the little garden of the remembrance and of the Holy Virgin, without any curiosity and without any ambition.

You ask me in your letter if your interpretation of Aurobindism is correct; it is entirely accurate; it is an evolutionism wherein man makes himself practically speaking God. The encounter with those forces of darkness was, I repeat, a providential experience for you; do not regret it, and tell yourself that you were bound to have this

[35] That is, the modernist movement surrounding Aurobindo Ghose (1872–1950), a Hindu philosopher and *yogin* propagating a theory of spiritual progress and evolution.

[36] *Sūrah* "The Family of Imran" [3]:36.

[37] This popular Islamic prayer, based on *Sūrah* "The Family of Imran" [3]:173, was written in Arabic in the original letter.

experience so that you would be forever cured of certain temptations and certain risks in your nature. I will think of you in my prayers, God willing.

—— ·⁝· ——

"*The Sciences Need Metaphysics*"; "*Jewish Esoterism*"
Pully, August 19, 1978 to a reader

Harmonics—or musical science in the broadest sense—must like all traditional sciences be linked in some way to metaphysics and mysticism; but this is really all I can grant it on the basis of universal metaphysics or esoterism. In any case, there is no metaphysics and no mysticism that would represent harmonics as something spiritually essential. Metaphysics has no need of the sciences, though the sciences need metaphysics. The latter is nothing other than the doctrinal discrimination between the Real and the unreal, the Absolute and the relative, God and the world, together with the whole fabric of gradations and reflections that this discrimination entails. Mysticism is the inner realization of this intellection by means of a traditional method, thus within the framework of a religion; with it come various technical, psychological, moral, and aesthetic conditions; I am speaking here of esoterism, not of outward religion. I mention all this in order to emphasize what is indispensable with regard to the ultimate goal.

Jewish esoterism can ultimately teach nothing other than what every other esoterism teaches, for Truth is one. Differences of principle—like the one mentioned in your letter—can only be on the surface.

P.S. Universal Reality has many dimensions, if one can so express it, and harmonics corresponds to one of them; this is already a great deal, but it is not right to see in harmonics the "nucleus of doctrinal wisdom". Note intervals and numbers form one category among others; one cannot enclose Reality in any distinct category of existence.

There is in Judaism not only a metaphysical-mystical numerology, but also a doctrine of letters, which is just as important. Moreover, the *Torah*, and with it the *Zohar* and the *Sepher Yetzirah*, infinitely surpass every partially scientific interpretation.

—·:·—

"*A True Traditionalist*"
Pully, December 19, 1979 to a publisher

I have just received the list of your publications and I note that for the most part they are racist, fascist, and Nazi in spirit and thus in no sense traditionalist in the proper and authentic sense of this word. I do not wish to appear in such a context, and I cannot give my consent to the publication of one of my books under your imprint. The public would place me in a modern political category, whereas I am engaged in nothing of the kind, being a true traditionalist and thus identified with a scale of values that escapes modernists, even those of the right.

7. To the Far West
Ages 72–88

"Settling in Bloomington"[1]

Pully, June 12, 1980 to Martin Lings

I must now speak to you of something most important. We have taken a very serious resolution, and I must say that I have had a premonition of this for quite some time already. We have the intention of settling in Bloomington.

There are for this—that is to say, for this project—inward as well as outward reasons. I am no longer young, and do not have so much time left to live; now, I feel that there is a dimension that is missing in my life, and that Bloomington could be its framework. I long for a vast and quiet ambience away from the pressures and dispersions of the world; I also have the sense that the Bloomington community, which is ever growing in number, has need of me, and I will even say that the Far West has a certain right over me. But in this, as in all things, I intend to submit entirely to God's Will.

Another factor is that I am becoming more and more known and in Pully I am too accessible; I do not want to become inaccessible, but I would like nevertheless to have an ambience that is both quieter and better organized. You know the geography of Bloomington: a vast, forested landscape with pure air, few people, and little noise; and young people who are full of zeal and have plenty of free time at their disposal.

As you can well imagine, I did not take this decision lightly, and I am more than aware of what our departure will mean for many disciples in Europe; but as I said, our intention is not to leave them totally, and we hope, moreover, that our friends will come and visit us; they will always be welcome, this is obvious. And we certainly do not intend to leave them without news from us.

[1] See *Frithjof Schuon: Messenger of the Perennial Philosophy*, chap. 20, "The Move to America".

June 13. A thought that came to mind is the following: the fact that we were solemnly adopted by the Lakota tribe indicates a certain destiny; the Indians are America, and they are at the same time virgin nature, primordiality, the *Religio perennis.* I have carried this dimension in myself since my childhood, and my work bears its imprint.

Destiny did not want for me to retire in the Maghreb, which is the Far West for the Muslim world; now America is the Far West as such. Destiny wanted for me to have in this country a large *zāwiyah* situated well outside of town—and this town itself is a kind of garden—and destiny offered us near the *zāwiyah* a piece of land where a small house can be built for us, with Heaven's help. Everything is in God's hands.

—·:·—

"*Since My Arrival*"[2]
Bloomington, September 21, 1980 to Hans Küry

When I was staying with the Indians over twenty years ago, an old Lakota asked me where I came from, and when I answered him that I came from far away, from the other side of the ocean, from Switzerland, he said to me that "Switzerland is everywhere, it is also here". I have experienced this quite distinctly since my arrival here—much more distinctly than I would have thought; when I close my eyes during the invocation, whether sitting or walking, I am then in Pully, in my *khalwah*, or my study, or my garden; I do not only imagine being there, it is as if I really were there, I sense no difference at all; this to the extent that I may happen to think of my outward surroundings. I experienced something similar with the call to Bloomington while I was still in Pully; during the invocation, it was as if the forested landscape where I now live was calling to me; it was like an inward music that had something of the silvery mountain air about it.

It is strange that the landscape here reminds us of the Alps, despite there being no mountains; but the peaceful clearings, the mysterious forests, the completely pure air, the rugged ground, all these things could be in the Alps.

[2] This is the first letter written after Schuon's immigration to America.

September 22. The houses of the friends here have a distinct Japanese touch, shown already by the fact that the sliding doors (*shoji*) and certain lamps were made by a Japanese carpenter; this has for me a profound meaning, in that the Japanese art of building and furnishing bears witness in its fashion—through Shinto, which has always been close to me—to the primordial tradition, as does the Indian tradition.

The forest has something sacred about it, and likewise the stag, which belongs to the forest; the stag combines gentleness with strength, and its antlers—the German word for "antlers" (*Geweih*) even reminds one of "consecration" (*Weihe*)—recall the branches and crown of the trees. There is somewhere in northern Germany a region called "Saints' Forest" (*Heiligenwald*), and this not only has a beautiful ring to it, but a profound meaning as well; the forest is in itself a sanctuary, and bears witness to the *Religio perennis*. Here in our region there are deer, and the day before the building of my house began, a stag came to the spot where my house was to stand.

—— ·:· ——

"*A Moving Towards the* Religio Perennis"
Bloomington, October 19, 1980 to Leo Schaya

Here the woods are lit up with glowing autumn colors, from the most delicate yellow to the most fiery red, and when a light wind blows, the leaves glide to earth as if it were raining gold, as in a fairy-tale. A few days ago it rained, and afterwards, at sunset, the whole landscape was plunged in a rosy and golden light; there was a sweet inebriation in the air as if all had turned into singing wine; rarely in my life have I seen something of such fairytale-like beauty.

October 20. Hans Küry wrote me that there is surely a correspondence between my book on Sufism[3] and my change of residence; I am indeed very conscious of this correspondence. It is a question of a moving away from the *Religio formalis* by virtue of a moving towards the *Religio perennis*; both are apparent in the last article I wrote in

[3] *Sufism: Veil and Quintessence* (Bloomington, IN: World Wisdom, 1981; 2006).

Pully, shortly before my departure, and in the first article I wrote in Bloomington, shortly after my arrival.

Early this morning, the Yellowtails left after having stayed two weeks at the Fitzgeralds, whose house is nearby. The Indians were present twice at one of our prayer gatherings, and every evening at the Fitzgeralds there were healing rites with long prayers, in the course of which Yellowtail touched and stroked those being treated with his eagle fan.[4] I was the first he treated, and this contact with the *barakah* of his eagle feathers had a special meaning for me: it was an encounter, through the medium of the Indian world, with the *Religio perennis*, and this at the beginning of my stay on this continent. When we showed the Indians our new house, Yellowtail said a long prayer in our prayer room and so to speak consecrated it, and this had again a meaning similar to that of the above-mentioned event.[5]

October 21. And this leads me to mention the following: the fact that Islam as an *upāya*—as the Buddhists would say—is a *Religio formalis* does not prevent it, as the last of the revealed religions of the Semitic world, from being in a certain way especially close to the *Religio perennis*, namely through its emphasis on the One, the quintessence, and then on the essential, the universal; thus through its simplicity, which comes from its essentiality. On the other hand, Islam emphasizes—as indeed does every religion—particular values of the primordial religion, and this is manifested not only through its evident beauties, but also through the virtues of the Muslims; through their centeredness on God, their surrender to God, their fervent faith, their generosity. Moreover, it depends how one understands a dogma, a rite, a moral precept: whether outwardly or inwardly, formally or supra-formally, according to the law or according to the spirit, the essential. If on the one hand the primordial religion lies in pure Truth and its

[4] Patrick Laude has rightly observed that "The Crow Medicine Man and Sun Dance leader Thomas Yellowtail performed healing ceremonies pertaining to 'white magic' during his regular visits to the Schuons in Indiana. These sessions were in no way part of the spiritual method of Schuon's *tarīqah*" ("Quintessential Esoterism and the Wisdom of Forms: Reflections on Frithjof Schuon's Intellectual and Spiritual Legacy", *Sacred Web* 20 [2007]:190n).

[5] The Yellowtails were also the first visitors to stay in the Schuons' new home in Pully in 1954.

universal applications, it manifests itself on the other hand through the inwardness or essentiality of our actions.

I have often repeated the following: when in the *Fātihah* I ask for right guidance, I do so not because I wish to pray in an Islamic fashion, but in order to tell God what I sincerely desire and what all men should desire, namely: "Lead us on the straight path." Someone once told me that when he entered a mosque he felt constricted by the religious form; this is obviously nonsense, for if this were the case one could never take pleasure in a beautiful color, but would appreciate only pure light; one would not see that a pure color also transmits light, even if in a particular way. When I enter a sanctuary, of whatever religion, I perceive with gratitude the particular *barakah* and then, in and through it, the primordial *barakah*. And this takes nothing away from the fact that the sanctuary proper to the *Religio perennis* is God's free nature.

Our house stands in a large clearing on which there are also several clumps of trees; on one side is the road, then comes the field on which the Perrys' house is being built, and then comes more forest—everywhere there is wild, ravine-riven forest, for it goes up and down as in the mountains; yet the landscape around Bloomington is quite flat and has the charm of southern England. Quite close to our area there is a lake with numerous branches, similar in size to a smaller Swiss lake; and then comes forest and more forest towards the south. The day before yesterday, Yellowtail blessed the building-site of the Perrys; he stood there with his peace pipe and prayed to the four cardinal directions.

October 22. There are people who because of the symbolism and beauty of a religion take on its dogmatic narrowness, its theological eccentricity and bias of soul; and conversely there are people who because of these same characteristics reject the symbolism and beauty of a religion. And yet there are both beauties and narrownesses in every religion, even in those that are in their way prolongations of the primordial religion; with these, too, there are all kinds of adaptations and renewals. The *Religio perennis* is the body, the *Religio formalis* is the garment; each has its meaning, and each can be combined with the other in various ways.

—·:·—

"*Even Good Translators Easily Forget*"
Bloomington, January 28, 1981 to Leo Schaya

Enclosed is your corrected translation; first a general remark: a translator does not have the right either to clarify or comment; this means that the translator as such is not authorized to write something that the author could also have written in his own tongue, but did not write; I mention this because even good translators easily forget this. For example, one does not have the right to make something understandable or easy to grasp for the English reader that I did not want to make understandable or easy to grasp for the French reader; the opinion of some that a translation ought to be a commentary, and that the more one follows the words, the farther one strays from the meaning, is properly absurd, or in any case applies only in exceptional cases or conditionally.

—·:·—

"*Not a* Tarīqah *Like the Others*"
Bloomington, May 18, 1981 to Hans Küry

Life is like a dream; who would ever have thought that one day I would be meeting with you and other old friends in America! And at the same time, this new world here has something about it that in some way resonates with images of my earliest childhood; day after day I experience this anew; this or that suddenly strikes me as wonderfully familiar.

I must often reflect that our *Tarīqah* is not a *Tarīqah* like the others; or rather that it cannot be so; that God could not want it to be a *Tarīqah* like all the others. One should be clearly aware of the reasons for this: there is first of all our purely esoteric perspective; then the fact of our contents of consciousness given us by our Western origin; and then the *Vedānta* as a metaphysical foundation; and lastly also the end of the cycle in which we live, and the role entrusted to us, namely with regard to the needs of our contemporaries.

As I say, our point of departure is the search for esoterism and not for a particular religion; for the pure and total Truth, not for a sentimental mythology. To renounce and forget the religion of our forefathers simply in order to immerse ourselves in another religion—as certain Guénonians do, without even noticing it and in the name of esoterism!—this could never be our perspective.

In the second place: given that by far the majority of the members of our *Tarīqah* are Westerners, hence non-Muslim born, it follows that they have contents of consciousness that they cannot in all honesty disown; one cannot in the name of the highest Truth behave as if one were not what by rights one really is; and it would be a gross offense to believe that God does not know what we are and that He takes no account of the circumstances of our native temperament. What I said previously about Westerners applies to the Jewish *fuqarā'* as well: they cannot be expected to forget the *Torah* and no longer to know how immensely precious the Psalms are; and finally it also holds in a certain measure—or where applicable in equal measure—for those *fuqarā'* of Eastern descent who are familiar with Western culture and possibly with Hinduism and Buddhism; they, too, have contents of consciousness that must be taken into account, and they, too, have a need for pure esoterism and therefore seek more than a religiously-colored mysticism. Our *Tarīqah* is by no means there purely for Westerners; it is even there expressly for those Easterners who have given up their religion under Western influence; for them there can be no mere going back, but our *Tarīqah* offers them more than what they left behind.

Thirdly: I have said that in some way we take our stand on the *Vedānta*, notwithstanding the fact that the whole of metaphysics is perfectly contained in the *Shahādah*; but as regards doctrinal exposition, we take our stand on Shankaracharya, not on someone like Ibn Arabi; the latter we accept only insofar as we find in him something of the *Vedānta*. Now Shankara is altogether clear and unambiguous; Ibn Arabi on the contrary is uneven, tortuous, obscure, and ambiguous, despite all his merits. Quite generally we recognize in Hinduism the great echo of the primordial religion; while on the other hand the Red Indian world shows us that the holy scripture of the primordial religion is to be found in God's virgin Nature, and this is no small teaching.

From all this results the following: we understand and love all sacred symbols, all sacred art; in this domain, too, we cannot and may not disown the contents of consciousness that we indelibly possess and that to some extent have shaped us.

It is because all these factors or conditions are present in our case that our *Tarīqah* could not be a *Tarīqah* like all the others; something therefore had to happen from Heaven to make this clear and to set a seal upon it, and such was the coming of the Themes of meditation, and then the coming of the Holy Virgin.

The peculiarity of Muhammad is to be the synthesis of all spiritual possibilities; this makes his image, seen from without, somewhat unintelligible in comparison with the formal distinctness of other prophets; Muhammad's distinctness lies precisely in his many-sidedness. Christ represented quite distinctly—in relation to the Jewish cult of the Law—spiritual inwardness; and therefore he has this meaning for the Sufis too; he is the Prophet of the Heart, not of outward works; and Mary has the same meaning, with the difference that she founded no religion and is "Mother of All the Prophets", hence well-spring of all the religions. An Arab friend said to me this morning that he has a special love for Christ; I answered him that where Maryam is, there, too, shines Isa; precisely because of the mystery of inwardness.

The primordial doctrine and the invocation: therein lies everything. *Advaita Vedānta* and *Japa-Yoga*. Doctrine and way; the doctrine radiates *a priori* from Shankara; the way I received from the Shaykh al-Alawi; and both gifts, and all further gifts and graces, come from God.

The image of the Prophet is clear and distinct—provided one has the key to it—insofar as he is an open fan of all the virtues.

—— ⁛ ——

"*My Paintings of the Virgin*"
Bloomington, October 11, 1981 to Max Schray

I write you today because I have long had the intention of explaining the symbolism of my paintings of the Virgin; I may already have done this in part in earlier letters, but I do not recall the details and I would rather mention the essential in a new letter.

First this: the image of the Holy Virgin conveys a heavenly presence, namely the presence of the protectress of our *Tarīqah*. This is a "making present" but not yet symbolism. As to this latter, its first content is femininity in general and virginity in particular: femininity expresses a divine aspect, namely Mercy—and in the highest sense Infinity—while virginity expresses a created perfection, namely the purity and receptivity of the contemplative soul striving towards God; therein lies the imitation of Mary. According to the teaching of Krishnaism, every soul is a *gopī*; every creature is female and virginal in relation to God. And the beauty of the Holy Virgin is the beauty of the purified soul, standing before God and receiving the divine Light.

In my paintings of the Virgin—as in representations of the Buddha—the eyes are closed; this symbolizes inwardness, interiorization. For in a sense, the first thing one must do before God is this: to close one's eyes to the trifles of the world; for "the Kingdom of God is within you".[6] This is one thing. The other is the erect—or vertical, upright—posture of the Holy Virgin; this is her presence, her actuality; also, her inner activity, her consciousness of God; her invocation. For if the posture of man is upright and not horizontal, it is so because he is created for the God-conscious "Now"; this is why he is *ibn al-waqt*, "son of the Moment"; the eternal "Now".

As in images of the Buddha, the erect posture of the Virgin also refers to motionlessness; to recollectedness before the motionless Center; also, to resignation to the divine Will. Inwardness, resignation, and recollectedness.

Then the nudity: from the point of view of *gnosis* it means pure, total Truth; the *Haqīqah*. The *Sharī'ah* is veiling, the *Haqīqah* is unveiling. *Māyā* and *Ātmā*. But nudity also has another meaning that is mystical: namely the self-revelation of the deepest Interior; when the soul abides in the deepest Interior, this Interior then becomes outwardly visible; sacred nudity is as it were the visibility of the Heart. Or the Heart permeates and encompasses the entire man and becomes thereby visible. For that reason, the saint Lalla Yogishwari danced naked, having discovered and realized the deepest Interior.[7]

With the Holy Virgin of my paintings, the uncovering means not only the *Haqīqah*, but also the *Rahmah*; not only the self-revealing

[6] Luke 17:21.

[7] Lalla Yogishwari was a fourteenth century Kashmiri poetess and saint; among the gems of her poetry often quoted by the author are the lines: "My guru spake to me but one precept. He said unto me, 'From without enter thou the inmost part.' That to me became a rule and a precept, and therefore naked began I to dance."

pure and total Truth, but also the self-giving and liberating Mercy. The mystical *lactatio* has this meaning; so do the representations of feminine divinities in Hinduism and the *Mahāyāna*.

Without thinking in the least of the black Madonnas, in many of my pictures I painted the Virgin in a dark color, so to speak unconsciously or supraconsciously. "I am black, but beautiful":[8] this verse of the Song of Songs I have often cited and explained.

And what is the meaning of the Child? First, as *Haqīqah* or *Sophia*, Mary is Mother of all the Prophets. Secondly, as *Rahmah*, she is the virginal and maternal protectress, helper, savioress of those who take refuge in her protection; as it is written in the Koran: "And I (Mary's mother) have named her (the little child) Mary, and I commend her (Mary) and her offspring to Thy (God's) protection from Satan the outcast."[9] "Her offspring": those are her protected followers, those who entrust themselves to her protection; hence also the *Tarīqah Maryamīyyah*. And why is the Child in the pictures male, when the soul is feminine in relation to God, as I said above? Because the question here is—purely symbolically speaking—no longer that of the relationship of the soul to God, but that of the *faqīr* to the *Rahmah*; and the *faqīr* is *mujāhid*, fighter in the *jihād*, the holy war; in the *jihād al-akbar*. This relationship thus corresponds to that of the old Germanic heroes, who were borne by the Valkyries to Valhalla; for the *mujāhid* must somehow experience spiritual death, he must "die before he dies".[10] The *dhikr* is a death, and to this answers the *Rahmah*; there is no Mercy without invocation, no *Rahmah* without *dhikr*. This is also one of the meanings of the saying: "I am black, but beautiful."

October 12. The closed eyes symbolize the mystery of *khalwah*, holy "inclusion" or "seclusion", and the open eyes—in two or three of my earliest icons—mean the mystery of *jalwah*, holy "radiation". And as I have already said, *jalwah* is illustrated through uncovering, and *khalwah* through covering; this symbolism of clothing and nudity can also be compared—as often mentioned—to the contrast of *Sharī'ah* and *Haqīqah*.

[8] Song of Sol. 1:4.

[9] Koran, *Sūrah* "The Family of Imran" [3]:36.

[10] A *hadīth* of the Prophet Muhammad.

In almost all of my paintings, the Holy Virgin has her eyes closed, as does the Child; they close them before an inner paradise; and since uncovering means the exteriorization of the inward, uncovering manifests the inward paradisal state. The closing of the eyes is first of all night, but then it becomes day; it is "black" with regard to the world, but "beautiful" with regard to the inner "Kingdom of God". "Verily, with hardship cometh ease."[11]

—·⁝·—

"*Nature's Winter Miracle*"
Bloomington, January 18, 1982 to Hans Küry

You are right, it looks like a Christmas tale here: everywhere heavenly pure snow and solemn stillness; this brings me back to my childhood, when winter was for me a kind of other-worldly experience. This snowy solitude that surrounds us now is once again a message of the mystery of "Peace", hence also of serenity and spiritual liberation; not for nothing are the German words for "peace" ("*Friede*") and "liberty ("*Freiheit*") similar sounding, and "joy" ("*Freude*") as well; and this makes me think of the goddess Freya—not for nothing does this word mean "woman" ("*Frau*")—the feminine-divine archetype of happiness, love, beauty, and fertility; the Hindu Lakshmi corresponds to this. Expressed in Islamic terms one can say that the mystery of expansion, exhalation, and the breast, thus of *inshirāh*, is derived from the mystery of *salām*; or from that of *islām* when this word is understood in its original meaning. I have often referred to this.

The blanket of snow presently covering our region reminds me of the spiritual significance of snow as a crystalline element: it illustrates a heavenly blessing, a heavenly descent—falling snow has indeed something paradisal about it—and then of the purifying heavenly Presence, far removed from all the struggle of passions; this is how in Islamic countries I experience the call to prayer, as it floats down from Heaven and extinguishes as it were all earthly noise.

In connection with nature's winter miracle, I would also like to say something about the other forms that water takes: first of all rain,

[11] Koran, *Sūrah* "The Expansion" [94]:6.

which the Koran compares to life-bestowing grace; it symbolizes vertical enlightenment, which comes down from Heaven directly, in contrast to horizontal tradition, which conveys the sacred only indirectly and whose symbol is the river. The river in turn comes from the spring—this is the historical Revelation that occurs once—whereas rain has no determinable earthly origin; "the wind bloweth where it listeth";[12] in this way, rain signifies the timeless or ever-actual grace of the Spirit. This grace "falls from Heaven", and this Heaven is "within you".

The lake conveys a message similar to that of the snow that blankets all in its peace: it is heavenly Presence, the *Sakīnah*, somehow even nearer to life and less distant from earth than the blanket of snow and yet altogether holy in its contemplative quietness and stillness. The water lily and swan are related to the lake, as are rushes and weeping willows; so, too, the moon reflected in it, and by day the sun's golden path.

And then there is the sea, which bears witness to the Infinite itself; it is divine primordial Power and yet also Peace in its immeasurable motionlessness; it is not for nothing that all rivers flow into the ocean.

To these reflections, I would like to add the following: all directly or indirectly necessary sensory experiences or activities, whether physical or psychic, have a so-to-speak sacramental value and a corresponding effectiveness, at least in principle; with the primordial man or enlightened sage, in actual fact as well, for this results from the nature of things. Meister Eckhart said that whoever has grasped this mystery—that is to say, whoever has realized it—receives the Eucharist each time upon eating or drinking; this indicates the sacredness of food and of eating and drinking; consequently, there are peoples or tribes that remain reverently silent while eating, and therein also lies the deeper significance of grace at mealtimes. The same holds true for other sensory experiences that are noble in themselves, above all for love; then also for seeing and hearing, since both can be either worldly or sacred, exteriorizing or interiorizing. Sanctity of the natural; sanctifying of the natural; sanctification through the natural; therein lies the spiritual nobility of man. One can also say that this nobility is devotion, thus the direct or indirect remembrance of God. Gratitude goes together with this, for the noble man does not allow habit to jade

[12] John 3:8.

him, he experiences symbols and beauty ever anew, as on the first day of encounter; hence his soul does not age, it remains in timeless childhood and becomes ever more true to itself.

—— ·:· ——

"*An Inner Contact*"; "*Purely a Man of Nature*"
Bloomington, March 8, 1982 to Leo Schaya

Before I wrote my article on the nature of the Prophet,[13] I had an inner contact with his being; it was a spiritual state that lasted for three days. Immediately thereafter I wrote my article. Praise be to God and thanks be to God.

March 9. After having lived for weeks in a fairytale-like landscape of crystalline snow, spring finally wants to arrive. Much earlier, I was necessarily a man of the city: I had to work in cities, and my dreams were interwoven with ancient streets; later, I had a garden and withdrew from time to time to the Alps; now, I am purely a man of nature and even have no other choice: there are no more dream-streets here, only country roads with a few fields and then nothing but forests wherever one looks. This now is my world, which Heaven gave to me. Yet something of this world is accessible everywhere, if one has the eyes and the grace to see it.

—— ·:· ——

"*A Sufficient Sense of Esoterism*"
Bloomington, April 22, 1982 to Martin Lings

The *Tarīqah* is not there to offer the happiness, or sentimental satisfaction, of belonging to a religion; one must therefore neither encourage nor seek to retain people who finally are not seeking for more than this, or who do not have a sufficient sense of esoterism, of the essential, the universal. I bless the happiness of those who are happy in a

[13] See *In the Face of the Absolute*, chap. "The Mystery of the Prophetic Substance".

religious faith, but they should not seek to impose their limitations on us.

All told, only those disciples who have profoundly assimilated our perspective are qualified to visit us, not those who, lacking in experience or imagination, do not know how to go beyond the framework of religious conventionalism, and because of that are above all seeking for *barakah.* Their conventionalism cannot but be shocked or disappointed in our midst, all the more so as they are not likely to be receptive to values of another order; it would be much more regrettable for them than for us. And I will say with the Buddhists: "May all beings be happy!"

—·:·—

"*The Problem of Protestantism*"[14]
Bloomington, May 25, 1982 to Martin Lings

I was glad to read in your letter your thoughts on the problem of Protestantism. Regarding this subject, I would like to specify further the intention of my first paragraph—I am referring to the chapter in my book[15]—with the help of the following image: imagine that two people with their child and a cat board a ferryboat to cross a river; it costs one franc per person, hence three francs total because it costs nothing for the cat. If the crossing were to cost one franc per "adult", the child would pay nothing; but it is per "person", and hence one must pay for the child; if it were per "creature", then one would also have to pay for the cat. Now in speaking of three "denominations", it is as if I were speaking of three "persons"; but this does not mean the child is an "adult" just because he is administratively a "person". Protestantism is the child; liberal Protestantism is the cat: a child is a "person"; a cat is not a person.

[14] Schuon's 1981 article, "The Question of Protestantism", sparked a number of questions from disciples and long-time readers. This is the first of three letters in this volume dealing with Schuon's views on Protestantism. See also the letter dated June 30, 1982, titled "Intrinsic Orthodoxy", and the letter dated July 2, 1982, titled, "The Power of a Spiritual Archetype".

[15] "The Question of Protestantism" in *Christianity/Islam: Perspectives on Esoteric Ecumenism* (Bloomington, IN: World Wisdom, 1985; 2008).

Hence, according to a certain relative aspect, I place Protestantism on the same plane as that of the two old Churches, but only according to this extrinsic aspect because I take care to add: "a Christian possibility—a limited one, no doubt, and excessive through certain of its features". Hence there is a difference in level. I depended completely on the words "a limited one, no doubt" to make the reader understand that even though there is a certain extrinsic equality, there is nevertheless a certain intrinsic inequality on another plane; but since Protestant piety is nevertheless a possible path—it is only liberal Protestantism that is not a path—I am obliged to take note of the existence of a third "denomination". I did not say that Catholicism is limited, nor that Orthodoxy is limited; I said that Lutheranism is so.

"For where two or three are gathered together in my name, there am I in the midst of them," Christ said.[16] Among all the possible meanings of this saying, there could also be this one: the first two who are gathered are Catholicism and Orthodoxy, and the third that joins them is Protestantism. Indeed, Christ could have said "where three are gathered", thus placing the three confessions on the same plane, but he said "two or three", thus indicating a certain difference in level; you see the nuance.

In any case, an Orthodox would tell me that the demonstration is not yet complete; I return now to the image of the ferryboat with the three persons. He would say that the two adults are of different sexes since they are the parents; if one supposed the child were a girl, then one would have a new division: only one person would be a male; the other two would be women. You see the conclusions that could be derived from this point of view with regard to the definition of the denominations: if the masculine sex symbolizes legitimacy, then only one denomination would be completely legitimate; the other two—despite the difference in age—would be more or less illegitimate, age representing here the denominational level, precisely. A Catholic could make the same argument against Orthodoxy, but I grant preeminence to the latter.

I fear I may have tired you with a demonstration that is perhaps quite useless, but after hesitating somewhat I allowed myself to do it because of the problem of my first paragraph. This is a mere question of emphasis, hence of dialectics.

[16] Matt. 18:20.

May 26. Christ told the apostles (Matt. 23:8–12): "But be not ye called Rabbi: for one is your Master, even Christ; and all ye are brethren. And call no man your father upon the earth: for one is your Father, which is in heaven. Neither be ye called masters: for one is your Master, even Christ. But he that is greatest among you shall be your servant. And whosoever shall exalt himself shall be abased; and he that shall humble himself shall be exalted." In light of this text it is easy to grasp the justification for the Orthodox and Protestant protest against the papacy.

Without Protestantism there would not have been the Council of Trent and therefore no Catholic Counter-Reformation; now the functional necessity of Protestantism proves its relative—and confessionally sufficient—legitimacy; without it the Catholic Church would not have found the necessary impetus to pull itself together again.

The etiquette surrounding an Orthodox patriarch is sacerdotal; that surrounding a pope is imperial; Dante had noticed this very well, he who wanted the pope to become a priest again.

—— ·⁞· ——

"*Visual Assimilation*"; "*The* Mudrā"
Bloomington, June 9, 1982 to Marco Pallis

Since I have just alluded to museums, I would like to add the following: since my childhood, I have loved museums, and I could spend hours visually assimilating the messages of the diverse traditional worlds. For me, visual assimilation came before conceptual assimilation; and here I have in mind not only sacred art, but handicrafts as well, including the most modest; for it can happen that an artifact may vehicle as much spirituality as does sacred art in the strict sense of the term.

Man is "made in the image of God";[17] hence I have always been interested in man, in races, castes, astrological and other types, costumes, the arts; in religions and wisdom traditions, of course, but this pertains to the divine order as much as it does to the human order; the knowledge of Heaven does not *a priori* depend on the knowledge of earth, it is rather the other way round. I have taken interest in man,

[17] Gen. 1:26.

but not first and foremost; there is a universal phenomenology of which man is indeed the center, but not necessarily the key.

From time to time, we have the visit of Yellow Tailfeather, who is the great shaman of the Crow and is considered one of the spiritual leaders of the Indians of North America. He attends our *majālis*—seated in the back of the sanctuary on a buffalo hide—and we sometimes attend his ritual gatherings, where he treats those who are sick with his fan of eagle feathers. He stays with one of our friends who is an adopted member of the Crow tribe.

P.S. One of the part-human, part-divine phenomena that has fascinated me ever since my childhood is the *mudrā*; the one in which the hand is vertical, the thumb holding the middle finger so that they form a circle, the ring finger being half inclined, the other two fingers remaining nearly vertical; in short, that *mudrā*-synthesis which seems to present a pearl, a jewel, a *cintamāni*, an elixir; a *mudra* that teaches and communicates, not through a word, obviously, but through a divine or nirvanic gesture, precisely. A gesture that seems to extract—or to have extracted—what is most precious, most directly salvific, from a complex Message; which brings to mind that other *mudrā*, what for the Buddha was the "Flower Sermon".

—— ·:· ——

"*Intrinsic Orthodoxy*"[18]
Bloomington, June 30, 1982 to Jean Borella

I appreciate very much the trouble you have taken to inform me in detail about the various currents of opinion in the integralist universe. This calls right away for a remark: regarding the papacy, the notion of a "vacant seat" immediately requires under present conditions that of a "usurped seat", otherwise this notion remains insufficient and inoperative; because not every vacancy is alike. It is true that, as Saint Robert Bellarmine deems, a pope cannot lapse into heresy and that no pope has ever done so; but precisely the pseudo-pontiffs of the

[18] Part of this letter was published in *In the Face of the Absolute*, chap. "Christian Divergences".

"Conciliar" and "Post-Conciliar" Church are not popes who lapsed into heresy, because they were heretics before being "popes" and were elected for that very reason.

That said, I am surprised by the intolerance, pettiness, belligerence, and also by the lack of realism of the integralists; because these are people who, after all, are always talking about humility and charity, and who take communion and pray; there is in this a mystery of the absurd, not to mention the collective stupidity of the world, in particular the Catholic world; it is as if words had become meaningless.

As for the Protestant problem, it is wrong to try to define Protestantism—"orthodox" and not "liberal" Protestantism—in terms of Catholic logic alone; I say "to define" because if it were merely a question of demonstrating the incompatibility between Protestantism and Catholicism, and of affirming Catholicism's right to remain true to itself in face of the Protestant provocation, I would have nothing to object; for I never thought that the intrinsic legitimacy of the Lutheran phenomenon—I will speak about this thorny issue further on—meant that Catholics would be obliged to give up any of their rights, extrinsic as well as intrinsic.

Moreover, even from the specifically theological viewpoint—which is not enough to resolve the problem—Catholic logic is not absolute since there is also the logic of the Greek Church; I see no reason to prefer Catholicism to Orthodoxy, to say the least, for the latter's positions are very sound and enable one to see better that if there is something absolute and inviolable about the Catholic point of view, there is nevertheless something relative and debatable about it as well. If from the Roman Catholic point of view there are elements of heresy in Greek Orthodoxy, the reverse is equally true: Catholicism appears to the Orthodox as a heterodoxy; both points of view have, esoterically speaking, their respective justification. But what I want to call attention to here is first of all that some of Luther's reproaches coincide with those of the Orthodox Church, and secondly that the attitude of the Orthodox Church with regard to Lutheranism is surprisingly indulgent, which is not without meaning.

I come now to the crux of the matter. Religious phenomena are ruled by two great principles, namely "apostolic succession" and "mandate from Heaven"; to the first pertains "sacramental technique" and to the second "attribution of grace", that is to say, the intervention of an "extra-canonical" grace. The "mandate from Heaven" is a Confucian notion: it means, as you no doubt know, that the authority or investiture descends directly from Heaven, without the intermediary of a sacramental means, and according to certain conditions of which Heaven alone is judge; such was the case of the emperors of China and also, as Dante observed in his treatise on monarchy, that of the Roman and later the Germanic emperors. This investiture, of which moreover the papacy is itself quite paradoxically an example—and this is a reason for the Greeks to reject it, since they only accept sacramental, hence "traditional", consecrations—this investiture derives all of its authority from the spiritual archetype that under certain providential conditions must manifest itself in the human world, with the ontological necessity of "possibilities of manifestation", as Guénon might say; but here it is a question not of just any manifestation, but of positive manifestations "willed by Heaven".

The Lutheran phenomenon, exactly as is the case with other analogous manifestations, notably in Hinduism and Buddhism, depends entirely on the principle of "mandate from Heaven", hence on the "intervention of a salvific archetype"; on that basis, this phenomenon is altogether independent of the rule of "apostolic succession" and "sacramental technique", and this independence—the human and confessional mentality being what it is—explains precisely the vehemence of the Lutheran denials and, above all, its "extrinsic heterodoxy"; not "intrinsic" since the perspective is determined by an archetype *in divinis.* I might be asked this question: how could a Catholic, even an esoteric one, accept the "intrinsic orthodoxy"—not "extrinsic"—of Protestantism? And someone might ask, with all the more apparent reason, this other question: how could a Catholic accept the intrinsic orthodoxy of Islam? Because Islam rejects Christianity, just as Protestantism rejects Catholicism, but even more fundamentally so; and if esoterism allows one to understand why and how Islam can do this, then esoterism allows one also to understand why and how Protestantism can do so likewise, *mutatis mutandis.* The apparently naive and crude nature of the arguments plays no role in this domain; it is symbolism, no more no less.

To say that Catholicism is "intrinsically orthodox" is not to say that it has no limitations and that it is perfect; no *upāya* is. There are three betrayals in Catholicism that are almost unbelievable: the first is the savage and irresponsible anathematization of the Orthodox Church; the second is the Renaissance; the third, which is obviously the worst, is the so-called "council"[19] with its consequences; none of this would have been possible without an abuse in the papacy; it was an "orthodox" abuse, no doubt, but an abuse nevertheless! This is the "human margin", which claims its rights—much more natural than supernatural—even in the midst of religions or confessions. And I will say that one of the most glaring and visible proofs of all of this is the horrible and stupid world of baroque art; if the Catholic confession alone represented the Christian *barakah* in the most faithful way, such an aberration at the level of forms would never have been possible; especially not at the level of sacred things.

—— ·:· ——

"*The Power of a Spiritual Archetype*"
Bloomington, July 2, 1982 to Jean Borella

In pure metaphysics, exclusive accentuations—namely "points of view" and "aspects"—are not admissible; seeing things through a colored glass is not metaphysics. But in exoterism accentuations or colorations are not just allowed, they constitute the very principle of the exoteric outlook; and they inevitably assert themselves unsparingly and with vehemence. According to Islam, the only sin that will certainly not be forgiven is that of associating partners with the one God; in this perspective of Unity, the Trinity appears as almost the worst of aberrations; and this perspective has its rights since exoterism does. According to Protestantism, it is the Mass that is an abomination, since it seems to substitute itself—given that it presents itself as a sacrifice—for the unique Sacrifice of Calvary; here, too, the accentuation of an exclusive point of view has its rights, those of exoterism, precisely. For Christianity, the worst of abominations is the rejection of Christ—not believing that Christ alone saves or thinking there could be other ways than his. For Judaism, the ultimate blasphemy is to believe that the *Torah*, which is meant for all of eternity, could be practically abolished and replaced by something else.

Whether we understand it or not, whether we like it or not, we have to accept the fact that exoterism exists by the Will of God—for

[19] That is, the Second Vatican Council of 1962–65.

He knows what men are—and that therefore exoterism has certain rights. Now Protestantism is a fruit of the exoteric perspective; it is not a fundamental fruit, but a secondary one, which however is inevitable and legitimate on its plane. One of the extrinsic proofs of this is the lightning expansion of Protestantism in the Northern countries among believers, namely those who, precisely, were Catholics; it is impossible to admit that all of these men, several million in other words, would have been essentially bad and that the others, those who remained Catholic, would have been essentially good; the extremely serious disorders in the Catholic world of that time are all too well known. Of course this argument applies only in connection with a truly religious ideology; it loses all value when it is applied to an obviously false ideology, such as Catholic modernism—not to mention the political ideologies—because in those cases the motive for success is altogether different; it does not stem from the power of a spiritual archetype, but from the seduction of error and from men's weakness.

But what is the meaning of the fact that Protestantism rejects Tradition and intends to base itself on Scripture alone? It means that this is a question, quite paradoxically, of a religious possibility that is marginal and not fundamental: the argument here is that Scripture alone is absolutely stable, whereas Tradition is variable and therefore not absolutely trustworthy; proof of this is that the Catholics, Orthodox, and Protestants are in agreement on the subject of Scripture, but not on that of Tradition; in Islam as well, the abrupt divergences between Sunnis and Shiites concern Tradition and not Scripture. The Gospel—the New Testament—is one, but the liturgies are diverse and some are even of doubtful authority. The Catholics are quite obviously right to maintain their point of view, but that of the Protestants corresponds nevertheless to a possibility within a particular theological, mystical, and moral context, and not outside it.

"*As If Inborn in Me*"

Bloomington, August 11, 1982 to Leo Schaya

I have described in a recent letter how I went first through Protestant and then Catholic Christianity, and how then for about ten years, before I entered Islam, I was fully under the spell of Hinduism, without however being able to be a Hindu in the literal sense; but I lived in that time no other religion than that of the *Vedānta* and the *Bhagavad Gītā*; this was for me the first experience of the *Religio perennis*. Now one could ask whether the American Indian world, which in its manner likewise manifests the *Religio perennis* directly and indirectly—as does Shinto for example—one could ask whether this world did not play a similar role in my life; to which I must answer: there was neither the possibility nor the necessity for me to experience it as a religious framework and practice; neither the nature of the Indian spiritual message, nor my own spiritual needs required this. Having said this, it is also true on the one hand that I was adopted at a certain moment into the Indian world—into the Lakota tribe—and on the other hand that belonging to the Indian world does not exclude the practice of another religion—somewhat as Shinto and Buddhism are compatible with one another. I could not have been adopted outwardly into Hinduism, as it would have excluded the practice of another religion, whereas I could be adopted outwardly into the Indian world without this conflicting with my practice of another form of religion. The Indian world entails first and foremost the reading of the primordial doctrine in the phenomena of nature—each one reads what he understands—and the experiencing of nature as the holy, primordial home that everywhere manifests the Great Spirit and everywhere is filled with Him; and this awareness gives to the Indian his dignity made of reverence for nature and self-domination; it accounts also for the unique grandeur of his artistically richly-accented appearance, in which eagle and sun combine and which, in the archetypal realm, belongs to the divine prototypes.

And then I felt early on a certain community of destiny or comradeship-in-arms between the Indians and myself, in the sense that they had to fight at every step against an all-desecrating power that was contemptuous of nature and dedicated to its exploitation and ultimate annihilation, and that I too was engaged in a similar battle since my youth; I wanted to preserve a seemingly vanishing paradise, in myself at least, against the rush of a superior force that flowed all around me, threatening the very kernel of my being while belittling, debasing, and disfiguring everything; and when I was a youth I was nearly shattered by it. That this battle was not in vain, we all now know.

Long after the Six Themes had come to me, I found that they correspond to the directions of space and thus also shed light both on the Indians' worship of these directions as well as on the rite of the Sacred Pipe, which is of such importance in their religion and in which lies in principle the whole primordial doctrine, hence the *Religio perennis*. "And unto God belong the East and the West, and wheresoever ye turn, there is the face of God."[20]

In Islam, I found a home in the biblical world, which in a sense transported me back to my childhood, to the Protestant and not the Catholic period; for the Catholic world is "ecclesiastical", not "biblical" as is the Protestant, despite the fact that Christ himself belonged to the biblical and not the ecclesiastical world. I should perhaps mention here that Islamic "legalism"—to which a Sufism that is aware of its own nature is not, and cannot be, in the least obligated—was from the very beginning foreign to me; by this term I mean the overemphasis of the Law, taken as literally as possible, so that obedience to the least regulation is substituted for virtue, in the belief, moreover, that such obedience leads to the highest knowledge. This prejudice, which is partly theological and partly sentimental, contradicts the inwardness stressed by Christ, just as it contradicts the metaphysical truth taught by the *Vedānta* and of which pure Sufism is fully aware since this truth follows from the nature of things. For esoterism must be there wherever there is a spiritual culture; and esoterism is always esoterism wherever it may be; the modern world alone has managed to exclude this mystery totally, and this largely because the spiritual organ of esoterism has gone astray in worldly philosophy.

In Hinduism, it is not only the *Vedānta* that was and is important to me, but also *Japa-Yoga* and the cult of Krishna so often linked with it; in Buddhism, similarly, the way of Amitabha has for us a special meaning. No less significant for me in my youth before entering Islam was Ramakrishna's relationship with Kali under her gentle and merciful aspect, which in looking back I now see as a precursor sign.

Certain modalities or forms of expression in Hinduism are profoundly related to my nature, as if inborn in me; thus, the concept of *Ātmā* and *Māyā*, words such as *Om* and *Shānti*, symbols such as the *mudrā*. I could also say the same, however, of the *Shahādah* and

[20] Koran, *Sūrah* "The Cow" [2]:115.

everything in Islam that expresses divine and spiritual Peace; magnanimity and peace.

—·:·—

"*Why I Paint*"
Bloomington, December 27, 1982 to Leo Schaya

If I were asked why I paint images of the Holy Virgin, I should answer: to transmit, thus to make accessible to others, an inward vision and to make possible a participation in this vision.

—·:·—

"*The Real Link between Christianity and Islam*"
Bloomington, January 28, 1983 to a disciple

Since you have been baptized and confirmed and have assimilated the one and universal metaphysics, there is no reason for you to fear that the Christian form does not contain a sufficient esoteric virtuality, nor to ask yourself what Christianity on the one hand and Islam on the other can give you; it is enough to practice the invocation with sincerity and perseverance, and God will take care of the rest. There are only three things that matter: metaphysical discernment, invocatory practice, nobility of character; there is nothing else.

There is nothing preventing a Christian from invoking God alone; Saint Teresa of Avila's confessor would repeat in Spanish the Name *Dios* for hours at a time; likewise, and obviously, Arab Christians—there are many in Lebanon and Syria—can repeat the Name *Allāh*, which does not belong exclusively to Islam when considered in this manner. Although you normally pronounce the avataric Names of Jesus and Mary, your intention is to go towards God; God knows your intention, and it is He who decides on our degrees and stations.

But you must get rid of the confused opinions expressed in your letter. There can be no question of esoteric Islam playing the role of a "spiritual coronation" in relation to a "Christian foundation". It is only too obvious that Muslim sages have something to offer Christians—and the reverse is true likewise—but Islam as such has nothing to add to Christianity; a traditional form is a closed system and is by definition perfect in its kind. Thus, there is no possible "traditional complementarity" between the two religions; there can be no question of "grafting" the esoterism of Islam onto Christian practices. One must take great care to abstain from ambiguous speculations that risk compromising the efficacy of spiritual practices; and one must not needlessly complicate matters.

When invoking God, we must not analyze the degrees of the Absolute, if one may say; we are addressing That which transcends us infinitely, and this is all. The fact that certain invocatory modes are less direct than others does not prevent the results from being the same, especially since recourse to Mercy is more necessary than ever.

The real link between Christianity and Islam is the Holy Virgin; she personifies at once primordial Wisdom and Mercy. In and through her, we have the same religion. And there is only one God.

—— ·:· ——

"*Dwelling in the Supreme Name*"
Bloomington, March 23, 1983 to Leo Schaya

After forty years of Lake Geneva and the world of the Alps—in fact, after more than seventy years of Western Europe—I have suddenly been transplanted into quite another environment and into another part of the world; hence the question of surroundings—in connection with our sense of happiness—preoccupies me with a particular intensity and immediacy. That the remembrance of God is our true and happiness-giving home, I discovered long ago, and it was this that an old Indian meant when he said to me, many years ago, that Switzerland was everywhere; nevertheless, I have had to experience this truth here with renewed emphasis, and also in connection with habits of the soul that came unexpectedly to the fore, though without presenting too much difficulty for me; but the experience—or the discovery—has in any case been instructive. For it is living in the supreme Name that turns our destined surroundings into something golden; earthly things make us happy only insofar as they are given to us by God, or insofar as we understand them in this light; here I am speaking of spiritual and not worldly people. In other words: an environment is truly our home only to the extent that the supreme Name has become our home. This presupposes, however, that the environment is sufficiently a symbol, which is always the case with virgin nature, or in general with things we can assimilate without harm; other things we must overlook; the ability to do so is part of life. We must be patient towards the world—except towards error—because the world must also be patient towards us. There can be no happiness without gratitude, and without joy in little things.

Our relationship to God brings with it a certain solitude, because God is not the world, and the world is not God; and in this solitude there is an otherworldly sweetness, because God is the Sovereign Good. This is the meaning of an old saying: O *beata solitudo, o sola beatitudo*. The same is true of the invocation, which encloses us in a beatific lotus bud, a bud that is neither of this world nor of the next and yet is of both at once. It is not of the next world, because we are still on earth; and it is not of this world, because in God's Name we are already in Heaven; and thus it is of both at once.

Khalwah is by definition solitude, it is being alone with God; and *khalwah* is wherever there is the invocation. It is the lotus bud that exists already in the next world, and through which we, too, are already in the next world. Name and invocation form a kind of *yin-yang*: the Name is situated *a priori* in the next world, and the Invocation, on the contrary, in this; at the same time, through the Invocation, the Name is in a certain way in this world, and the Invocation, through the Name, is in the next.

The Holy Virgin embodies *khalwah*, as it says in the Koran: "When she withdrew from her people to a place towards the East and put a veil between herself and them. . . ."[21] One of Mary's names is *Hortulus Conclusus*, and I have in fact often spoken of this blissful little garden of *faqr*, for *khalwah* is not a prison, but a garden separating us from the world; though *a priori* it may be dark, *a posteriori* it is golden: "I am black, but beautiful."[22] Such was the great mystery or spiritual experience that came upon me when, many years ago, I was on the way from Port Vendres to Tangier; it was on the sea that

[21] Koran, *Sūrah* "Mary" [19]:16–17.

[22] Song of Sol. 1:4.

the Holy Virgin's grace came. Not without reason is she called *Stella Maris*.

In Mostaghanem, I met this mysterious Ahmad, without knowing whether he was an earthly saint, or Al-Khidr, or the Prophet himself. When shortly thereafter I saw him again in the *zāwiyah* in Oran, he gave a *mudhākarah* on solitude with God, and it made an indelible impression on me; it made me happy, and I felt boundless trust in this mysterious man. I cannot but recall this now in connection with all that I have written in this letter.

Golden solitude with God: such is also the *barakah* that lies upon our landscape here. The forest that Heaven has given me is a symbol of and a support for this holy solitude, which in a certain way I have longed for since my youth; and this is why my present environment is closer to my soul than all that I was accustomed to before.

In your letter, you mention this passage from the Psalms: "Be still, and know that I am God."[23] Therein lies everything.

—— ·:· ——

"*The State of Childhood*"
Bloomington, June 11, 1983 to Titus Burckhardt[24]

"Except ye become as little children", Christ said.[25] What is good about the state of childhood is that the soul is still unspent: there is gratitude for even the most modest gifts of this world and life and, moreover, an unconscious but genuine trust in God. The aging person tends to see everything in relation to a whole universe; whereas when a child takes joy in a flower, only the flower is there. Both kinds of experience—for each has its justification—are joined in the spiritual person's sense of the sacred, of the heavenly and divine archetypes.

—— ·:· ——

[23] Psalm 46:10.

[24] Written to Titus Burckhardt during what proved to be his final illness before death.

[25] Matt. 18:3.

"*A Feathered Headdress*"
Bloomington, October 13, 1983 to William Stoddart

At the time of my adoption, the Indians gave me the gift of a feathered headdress, which I did not put on for eight or ten years; then I put it on two or three times, but never in front of several people. One of the most detestable things is the vanity or triviality of insignificant people who wear such a headdress; who do it in a manner that excludes all dignity and all intelligence. I thus instinctively protested, in myself, against this frequent profanation.

When I arrived in America—at the time of our emigration—one of the friends from Bloomington, the adopted son of Yellowtail since many years, gave me the gift of another headdress, of Sioux origin and ornamented with a feathered train; I wore it just once, outdoors near my tipi. This gift was like the welcome from the red race in this continent that fundamentally belongs to it; at least this is how I experienced it, since anything out of the ordinary must have a meaning.

—— ·:· ——

"*Adopted Into An Indian Tribe*"
Bloomington, November 25, 1983 to a disciple

You ask me about the significance of being "adopted" by the American Indians. These adoptions have always existed among the Indians; there have always been whites—or sometimes men of other races—who have been adopted into an Indian tribe, or into a family, which amounts to the same thing practically speaking. From the point of view of the Indians, this means that they consider you henceforth as one of theirs; and this implies for the person who is adopted a sufficient understanding of the mentality and spirituality of the Indians. In my personal case, this has even more meaning, given my spiritual function; this indicates a certain bond with a form—late as it may be but nevertheless real—of the primordial Tradition; and it is also like a marriage with virgin nature.

—— ·:· ——

"*We Organized An 'Indian Day*"
Bloomington, December 7, 1983 to Titus Burckhardt

Yellow Tail was recently here; we organized an "Indian Day" in which many friends, both men and women, participated in Indian dress;[26] Yellow Tail, too, wore Indian dress, even the feathered headdress. He showed the women how they should dance; after the midday meal—outside on our meadow near the forest—the women did a round dance, according to his instructions, while he drummed along and sang. I, too, very exceptionally wore my headdress for this occasion, but stayed only for a short while at the celebration; I watched it afterward from a window. At the end, the friends, both men and women, sat around Yellow Tail and listened reverentially as he explained many things to them about the Sun Dance and other Indian mysteries. "It was like in the old times", he told us afterward and he was very happy.[27]

—— ·⁞· ——

"*In Memory of My Friend*"
Bloomington, January 21, 1984 to Hans Küry

I enclose for you a copy of the last letter I received from Titus Burckhardt. Now that he is in the next world, I feel that he is even closer to me than before.

As you are aware, I have known Titus Burckhardt since I was twelve years old; at school, we competed in drawing pictures of Greek heroic myths. Our real friendship began in Riehen,[28] in the house of Frau von Dechend; there we had a long conversation about Guénon, Islam, and the Maghreb. What was precious in him, humanly speaking,

[26] The dances and the manner of dress at the Indian Days were inspired by traditional Plains Indian pow-wow dance costumes and material culture. Schuon noted that "our Indian dancing is not a rite", and further affirmed that "the fact that we practice from time to time Indian dances . . . [is] independent and outside" of our spiritual method (personal papers dated 1991 and March, 1997). For more information see *Frithjof Schuon: Messenger of the Perennial Philosophy*, chap. 20, "The Move to America".

[27] Yellowtail continued to attend such celebrations each year until his death in 1993. On one of these occasions in 1987, Yellowtail adopted those present into his family.

[28] A town on the outskirts of Basel.

was the conjunction of an unusually acute and profound intelligence with a great artistic talent; since he could not become a creative artist—and it is fortunate that he was prevented from doing so—his talent was placed wholly into the service of the spiritual life; all the more so as he was at the same time mystically inclined to a very high degree.

I had much esteem also for his mother, a Rhinelander, who was likewise very gifted spiritually and artistically, and whom my father knew in his youth; and also for his sister, who resembled him in some traits of character.

There was something eternally young and liberating about Titus Burckhardt; one never felt constricted in his presence. He was certainly not lacking in humor, and he also had a sense of adventure and was enterprising and adaptable; at the same time, he was kind-hearted and had a childlike innocence and purity about him. To this I would add that he was an excellent writer, as we all know.

Like myself, he lived for many years on the shores of Lake Geneva; and he was also familiar with our area near Bloomington. He led several gatherings here, and for the local friends he is unforgettable.

I mention all this because I feel the need to say it here in memory of my friend.

P.S. His brahmanical side came to the fore only later, when he was grown up; as a boy, he was half firebrand and half dreamer, this dreaminess being a prelude to his contemplativeness to come. It is characteristic of him that, along with his brahmanical nature, he was a great friend of the American Indians; he had *Black Elk Speaks* published in German and was a friend of Yellow Tail's. The combination of the heroic and the priestly in the Indians must have appealed to him, as being in a certain way akin to his own nature.

—— ·⁝· ——

"*Disorders in Today's Church*"; "*Yellow Tail Dictated a Book*"
Bloomington, July 21, 1984 to Erich Schuon

You should not brood too much over the extravagances of the new liturgy etc. etc.; and there are several reasons for this. First, for the most general and fundamental reason that evil cannot not exist and one must accept its existence as a metaphysical necessity; and God will not call us to account for things beyond our care. Secondly, if we must accept "evil as such" because it is ontologically necessary, we must also accept "such and such an evil" because it enters into our destiny; this is what one calls "accepting God's Will". One need not make oneself ill because one cannot change others; and in any case, life does not last forever. We would like to be in Paradise, but we must resign ourselves to the fact that we are not there yet, and we must leave no stone unturned to arrive there; moreover, we are there already in and through prayer, to which we have access at every moment.

Certainly, the disorders in today's Church have causes that we may know or not know; our opinions will not alter this; but we cannot avoid noticing the phenomenon. Monks readily believe that evil is to be found only in their monastery; they are often unaware that evil is everywhere. Be that as it may, one must not have too simplistic a notion of the "Church", a notion that Christ did not have. That the Catholic Church cannot disappear—nor the Orthodox Church moreover—this is obvious, but there is a wide margin between "everything" and "nothing"; when confronted with the question of knowing "where the Church is", one should not answer it in too schematic a fashion, and one must not lose sight of certain elements of the Apocalypse. The final victory belongs to God, this is what matters. One can find consolation in reading the Psalms.

Yellow Tail (= Hawk with Yellow Tail Feathers) dictated a book that in a certain way completes the two books of Black Elk; I will send you a copy when the book is published, which may still take several months. The book's title is: "Yellow Tail: The Medicine Man and Sun Dance Chief Speaks of the Sacred Ways of the Crow".[29]

—— ⁘ ——

"*What I Owe to Guénon*"
Bloomington, July 25, 1984 to Jean Borella

If in my books—except in the first edition of *The Transcendent Unity of Religions*—I never mentioned Guénon—although it would have

[29] This book was subsequently published as *Yellowtail: Crow Medicine Man and Sun Dance Chief.* Schuon signs this letter, "These few lines with all of our best wishes, Hau, Wichahpi Wiyakpa."

been logical to do so—there are two reasons for this: the first is that Vâlsan—the recognized spokesman for strict Guénonism—in offering me peace after certain well-known dissensions, and in requesting my renewed collaboration with *Études traditionnelles*, beseeched me never to criticize Guénon in my writings, and I myself finally thought that such criticism would do more harm than good; therefore, rightly or wrongly, I refrained in the end from publicly expressing my grave objections to certain Guénonian opinions, as well as to certain dialectical shortcomings; but for that very reason, I found it impossible to mention Guénon at all, since people would then have attributed to me all the opinions that I reject, notably his theory on the sacraments. For the rest—and this is the second reason for my silence on Guénon—I owe more to the Vedantic doctrine than to the work of Guénon; what I owe to Guénon is the crucial ideas of pure metaphysics, intellectual intuition, traditional orthodoxy, esoterism, and initiation, as I owe to him the explanation and condemnation of the modern world—although in truth I hated this world already since my childhood. However, I owe to Guénon metaphysical science only in the sense that he transmitted to us the Vedantic doctrine; moreover, I was able to study the Hindu doctrines in non-Guénonian books—whether "orientalist" or not—which furnished me with supplementary information, the merits of which cannot be underestimated. In a word, I owe the essential points of reference of metaphysics to Shankara, the providential interpreter of the *Upanishads*; and no one can reproach me for not having paid my debt of gratitude by referring to the *Vedānta* and by making use of its terminology in my books. As for enlightening *anamnesis*, which is humanly incommunicable, it is always a gift from Heaven.

—·⁞·—

"*Black Elk's Dictation*"
Bloomington, August 8, 1984 to William Stoddart

I received the book *The Sixth Grandfather*,[30] which contains the notes taken by Neihardt during his meetings with Black Elk; it is thus the almost literal dictation—or the rough draft—of *Black Elk Speaks*.

[30] Edited by Raymond DeMallie (Lincoln: University of Nebraska Press, 1984).

Neihardt shortened and simplified things quite a bit; he also inserted a few passages that do not come from Black Elk, but that could come, psychologically speaking, from him. Nevertheless, all of this creates certain problems.

In favor of Neihardt, one can affirm that Black Elk received him, right from the first meeting, with a kind of impatient and surprising fervor, as someone whom he had been expecting for a long time; there was thus, on the part of Black Elk, a kind of intuition regarding the American writer's qualification; that is to say, Neihardt's arrival was providential in the eyes of the old Indian. Indeed, Neihardt had certain special gifts; he was like a "medium" of the Indian soul; Black Elk sensed that Neihardt could express better than he could himself what he, Black Elk, intended to say. Quite paradoxically, the American could add a vibration of the Red Indian psychism in instances where the Indian's dictation was completely dry and parsimonious.

But this does not completely excuse the American writer. In both of his prefaces—depending on the edition—he presents his book as a document, without accounting for two points: first of his literary collaboration, and secondly of Black Elk's adherence to the Catholic Church; both of those things should have been explained. Correlatively, if Neihardt already had the intention of presenting a document—Black Elk's dictation was a real message—it would have been better, after all, to have renounced all attempts at stylization and amplification; he should have presented his notes as they were. As for the Catholic dimension, it is true that the Indian author did not utter a word about this, and was even evasive when the American asked him a question on this subject; nevertheless, the American should have mentioned this reticence as well as the problem itself.

Like many Indians, including shamans, Black Elk followed both the ancient religion and Christianity, with differences in degree depending on the epochs: in his youth, he was a fervent catechist; towards the end of his life, he inclined more and more towards the ancient religion—*The Sacred Pipe* dictated to Brown is ample proof of this—but he nevertheless died fortified with the rites of the Church. It was the same for his son, whom I knew well.

The reason why so many Indians—including the famous medicine-man Fools Crow,[31] whom I met at Wounded Knee—practice

[31] See Thomas Mails, *Fools Crow* (Lincoln: University of Nebraska Press, 1979).

both religions at the same time, or rather add the Christian religion to their own—is that the person of Christ strikes them as an irresistible spiritual reality, and they see no reason not to integrate him into their religious life; they see no contradiction in this. I am speaking here of the Indians who practice both religions, not of those who are entirely converted to Christianity, nor of those who totally reject it.

P.S. Neihardt felt obliged to simplify the "great vision"—he was always worried about overlong passages and complications—and in that respect future commentators will have no choice but to resort to the original version given in *The Sixth Grandfather*. Be that as it may, *Black Elk Speaks* is above all a biography; for the doctrine, one has to refer to *The Sacred Pipe*, all the more as this book is strictly faithful, word for word, to the account given by the Indian author.

August 9. I would like still to emphasize the following point: *Black Elk Speaks* is a providential book, and because of this it is all that it must be. Black Elk welcomed Neihardt with a kind of prophetic enthusiasm; and this, moreover, is also how he welcomed Brown. This means that he sensed that these two men were exactly what he needed for his message; *Black Elk Speaks* is one dimension, *The Sacred Pipe* is another.[32]

—·:·—

"*A Path of Christian Esoterism*"
Bloomington, September 15, 1984 to a reader[33]

Your letter finally reached us. So, having become aware of the doctrine—metaphysics, cosmology, eschatology—you wish as far as possible to put it into practice, and to do so upon the formal basis of Christianity; in other words, you aspire to follow a path of Christian esoterism. You know that pure metaphysics is 1. essential, 2. primor-

[32] Schuon's letter contains a lengthy discussion of the conflict between European civilization and the American Indians, which is published in more complete form in an Appendix to Harry Oldmeadow's book, *Black Elk: Lakota Visionary.*

[33] The recipient was a Hungarian.

dial, and 3. universal: being essential, it is independent of all religious or confessional formulations; being primordial, it is the truth that existed prior to all dogmatic formalism; being universal, it encompasses all intrinsically orthodox symbolism and can therefore be combined with every religious language. Next, comes method, which is quintessentially prayer in the widest as well as deepest sense; the practice of the Hesychasts and the life of the "Russian Pilgrim" are examples of this in the Christian setting. And all of this requires in an imperative manner first the fundamental virtues and then, extrinsically, a corresponding comportment, namely one in conformity with the doctrine and way.

Metaphysics is not a religion, but it gives a profound and universal meaning to the ideas and phenomena of every religion: thus it teaches *a priori* the distinction between the Absolute and the relative, *Ātmā* and *Māyā*, the Principle and manifestation; now the phenomenon of Christ—or the metaphysical truth that determines it—means that "God became man that man might become God", according to a famous Patristic saying, which however is not to be taken literally, since man as such could never "become God"; but this is not the place to specify what this reservation entails, which in any case I have explained in my books. "God became man": *Ātmā* became *Māyā*; owing to this, Christ is a bridge between *Māyā* and *Ātmā*, and as a result—this is the mystery of the *Avatāra*—his name contains a saving power; and likewise the name of the Holy Virgin, for she, too, is an avataric phenomenon, in the sense that she embodies the feminine aspect of the *Logos*.

Ejaculatory orison is altogether fundamental; it has a function that is in fact eucharistic; and yet man also has need of individual and ordinary prayer: it is necessary from time to time—whenever one feels the need—to speak to God and ask for His help; this can be done through a celestial intermediary, the Holy Virgin in particular.

Before entering a path of prayer—before undertaking to invoke God three times a day and, insofar as one can, in every available moment—one must promise Heaven to persevere in this path until death; this is equivalent to the monastic vows. As for the classic vows of "poverty", "chastity", and "obedience", they have, aside from their literal meaning that concerns monks, a spiritual import that concerns all men.

You mention in your letter a man who is convinced he saw Christ; not having heard his story, I cannot express an opinion. But it is essential for you to know this: a vision never confers a spiritual authority; no one is a master owing to a vision. Certainly, the vision of a personification of the *Logos* is in itself a very rare and lofty experience; but circumstances compel us to be neutral with respect to this particular incident.

In the meantime, I assume that you will have received our letter regarding the invocatory practice and containing Christian formulas. A person whose confession is Protestant could recite in Hungarian the beginning of the Our Father, and also the "Jesus prayer". A very appropriate reading material is that of the Psalms, from which the monastic offices are drawn.

When one devotes oneself to a spiritual practice, it is important to have the right intention; one must not have intentions that are beneath the purpose of the practice. God accepts that we invoke Him for several motives, and for these alone: first of all, He accepts that we invoke Him to save our soul, and this is the intention of fear; next, He accepts that we invoke Him because we love the celestial climate, so to speak, and this is the intention of love; "I love because I love", as Saint Bernard said; finally, He accepts the intention of *gnosis*, which is based on the metaphysical evidence of the Real or the Absolute. But God will never accept the intention of obtaining sensible graces, or of having experiences, or of making an experiment, or of realizing a particular virtue or some other distinction, or of becoming this or that, and so on. And when a man experiences a spiritual state or a grace, or when he has a vision or audition, he must never desire that it happen again and, above all, he must not base his spiritual life upon such a phenomenon nor imagine that it has conferred some kind of distinction upon him. All that matters is that we practice what brings us closer to God, while heeding the conditions that this practice requires; we do not have God's measures, and it is not for us to ask ourselves what we are. Life is a dream, and to think of God is to awaken; it is to be already in Heaven, even here below.

—— ·:· ——

"*Outward Manifestations of Universality*"
Bloomington, November 18, 1984 to William Stoddart

A true metaphysician could not identify himself unreservedly with a religious *upāya* and take pleasure in it with a kind of nationalism, but obviously he must identify with what is essential—hence both universal and primordial—in the *upāya*, and this is "Islam" *a fortiori.* Needless to say, what is essential transcends the *upāya.* I am saying all of this simply because I happen to think of it right now, in connection with the problem of the outward manifestations of universality.

I want to give two examples of confessional limitation, although you already know what I will talk about. For Christianity, man is a "sinner"; this is the definition of man, and it entails the idea that the entire world is bad and that there exists only the alternative between the "flesh" and the "spirit"; it goes without saying that this perspective has a certain relative justification, but its disadvantage is that it presents itself as absolute. For Islam, man is not totally corrupted by the fall—a total corruption would be contrary to the very definition of man—but he is totally a "servant" or "slave", which metaphysically is in fact an aspect of his nature, but which could not sum up human nature as such; to believe the contrary is to deny the specifically human intelligence and dignity, and it is thus to deny what constitutes the very reason for the existence of *homo sapiens.* In the case of Islam as in that of Christianity, theology tends to push the respective dogmatic image to the point of absurdity, and most mystics identify *de facto* with these pious excesses, something a consequential metaphysician—hence one who is aware of the nature of things—would never do.

If in Muslim thought the axiom "He hath no associate"[34] gives rise to the most abusive of conclusions in various domains, in Christian thought on the contrary it is hypostatic diversity—the Trinity—that functions as the absolute, and the absence of the idea of *Māyā* is particularly noticeable; now, a true metaphysician could not possibly identify himself with such positions, and hence could not commit himself to what I call "religious nationalism". It is with good reason that Guénon defined the "religious point of view"—the word "religious" having for him the meaning of "exoteric"—as a "sentimental attachment to an idea". And one should not forget all the secondary excesses—sometimes very troublesome—to which confessional sentimentalism gives rise.

Personally, I am very sensitive to the following argument: when you say that you are a "Muslim" or a "Christian", you exclude an immense part of humanity; you separate yourself from it and reproach

[34] Koran, *Sūrah* "Cattle" [6]:164, passim.

it for not being what you are; you proclaim before the entire world that only you have the truth, unless you speak with tacit Guénonian understandings that no one can presuppose *a priori*. Nothing of the kind is to be found with the American Indians: "the Great Spirit has given you your way of praying, and has given us our way of praying"; and that is all.

—·⁞·—

"*A Deadlock in the Orthodox Tradition*"
Bloomington, March 11, 1985 to a reader[35]

You write me that you have reached a deadlock in the Orthodox tradition and do not know how to proceed. This comes from the fact that you are not sharply enough aware of what truly matters; and since you look to the authority of pure metaphysics and esoterism—otherwise you would not be writing to me—this gives me a reason to illustrate the essential points.

For us there are three things that count, all the rest is a matter of form: first, discernment between the Real and the unreal, the Absolute and the relative, *Ātmā* and *Māyā*, the Eternal and the ephemeral, God and the world; secondly, the constant—in principal unceasing—consciousness of the Real, the Fundamental, the Divine; thirdly, the conformation of our inner life and our actions, our conduct, to the Real and to our effective relationship with it. In other words: metaphysical Truth; then continuous invocation; and lastly beauty of soul, hence virtue. The main emphasis here is on the invocation; the Desert Fathers and Saint Mary of Egypt did nothing else. In the Orthodox Church, the "Jesus Prayer" is used for this purpose; however, the Name of Jesus can suffice. The Name of Jesus ultimately signifies the highest Reality—for here the essential is the Divine and nothing else—whereas the Jesus Prayer is addressed more particularly to the Mercy that is inherent in the Divine. This Mercy is also expressed by the Name of Mary.

In light of the above, what the priests or laymen one meets in the Orthodox Church do or do not do, understand or do not understand, is a matter of indifference. Even Orthodox theology is finally not

[35] The recipient was an Orthodox Christian.

relevant to our needs, since for us what counts is the metaphysical Truth, whose most direct expression is in fact the *Vedānta*; then the invocation, thus our effective relationship with that Truth; then the nobility of our inner life, our freedom from worldliness, egoism, presumptuousness, and pettiness. For whoever has a sense of the Truth has also a sense of the sacred, and whoever has a sense of the sacred bears in a certain manner the sacred in his soul. As Plato said: "Beauty is the splendor of the True."

The whole of Christian doctrine and spirituality lies, in fact, in the saying of Saint Irenaeus: "God became man that man might become God." There are various versions of this saying, but the essential is in any case in the form I have cited, which should not of course be taken literally. In Vedantic terms: "*Ātmā* has become *Māyā* that *Māyā* may become *Ātmā*", or "may return to *Ātmā*"; for it is not the mode or degree of the union that matters, but the fact of union, whether it is a question of the "beatific vision" or something else. The way to this is the quasi-Eucharistic invocation of Jesus; the other sacraments are supplementary means of grace, but—as Meister Eckhart said—in the last analysis we carry them within us; whether or not they are *de facto* accessible to us is another matter. In any case, that man as such cannot become God every metaphysician knows.

Many years ago, I attended a service in the Athens Cathedral and know how endlessly long the Orthodox liturgy can be; this has strictly speaking nothing to do with the spiritual Way, and one who practices prayer—or invocation—as a method certainly need not reproach himself if he attends only the most essential services; after all, the Desert Fathers went for years without going to church, and the spiritual life of the "Russian Pilgrim" was likewise not dependent upon attendance at church. Esoterism, as far as we are concerned, is indeed much less bound to the outer world of forms than exoterism is. One should, however, have no feeling of inner opposition to the Church, for one ought not to expect from it what it cannot give. The Church, in fact, offers only an altogether general framework, which is not fully binding in every respect; and it represents only a very particular *bhakti*, which is inevitably sentimental and limited, and not a thoroughly comprehensive spirituality. With Islam it is of course *a priori* the same, *mutatis mutandis*, and likewise with Judaism.

You ask me whether there are criteria by which one can recognize whether one is on a wrong path. Certainly, there are such criteria, but here the question arises as to whether the wrong path is an objective or a subjective one. Meister Eckhart—whom you mentioned in your letter—taught that there are as many paths to God as there are men; this only means, however, that an objectively valid path, for him who subjectively actualizes it aright, is at the same time a unique path, for the simple reason that each human being is in a sense distinct from every other human being and therefore stands alone before God.

—— ·:· ——

"*A Moralist and An Aesthete*"
Bloomington, March 15, 1985 to Jean Borella

As far as I am concerned, I want to be both a moralist and an aesthete, and even fundamentally so; because I cannot conceive of any metaphysical wisdom or operative science outside of those two qualities. It goes without saying that I speak of intrinsic and not merely social morality, and of integral and not merely profane aesthetics. In a word, one cannot be a metaphysician with impunity without being at the same time a moralist and an aesthete in the deepest meaning of these terms, something that is proven by all traditional civilizations, the climate of which is made of virtue and beauty.

—— ·:· ——

"*An Interiorizing Effect*"
Bloomington, April 14, 1985 to Leo Schaya

From the little picture enclosed, you can see that I am still painting—when it is not Mary, then the heavenly Messenger Pte San Win; the *Rahmah* in various forms. Sometimes I ask myself the question why in fact do I bring visible things into the world; would it not be better to remain with the things that are invisible? Then I say to myself, my paintings have an interiorizing effect, not an exteriorizing one, and what I paint, no one else can paint.

What I seek to express in my paintings—and indeed I cannot express anything other—is the sacred combined with beauty. Thus, spiritual attitudes and virtues of soul. And the vibration emanating from the paintings must lead inward.

—·:·—

"*A Favorite Reading*"
Bloomington, July 22, 1985 to Marco Pallis

Echoes of Japan[36] by Shastri has just been published in French, translated by one of my disciples in France; this little book is a gem. It reminds me of a big book, *Honen the Buddhist Saint*,[37] which is a favorite reading of several of my friends; among spiritual books it is what I would call a key to happiness.

What matters in life is precisely this: to know how to combine metaphysical science with an aspect of the real that makes us happy; or rather, to discover in spiritual realities a vital aspect that coincides with happiness. Now as proven by the notion of *Ānanda* and by the appeasing and beatific dimension of *Nirvāna*, this aspect is strictly speaking not one among others, but on the contrary a fundamental reality—a reality to which we have the right, if I may say, owing to our own nature or essence, which coincides with That which is.

—·:·—

"*Spiritual Life Should Not Depend on Any Sensible Grace*"
Bloomington, September 38, 1985 to a disciple

The experience of which you speak in your letter to me contains nothing that ought to disquiet you; such experiences are normal in an esoteric climate, and they also have no relationship with dogmatisms or with syncretism; the link between our path and the Holy Virgin

[36] Hari Prasad Shastri, *Echoes of Japan* (London: Shanti Sadan, 1961).

[37] Shunjo Hoin, *Honen the Buddhist Saint: His Life and Work*, translated by Revs. Harper Havelock Coates and Ryugaku Ishizuka (Kyoto: Chion-in, 1925). For an abridged version of this 956-page work, see *Honen the Buddhist Saint: Essential Writings and Official Biography*, edited by Joseph A. Fitzgerald (Bloomington, IN: World Wisdom, 2006).

proves this. Heaven is well aware that we are of Christian origin on the one hand and of Vedantic formation on the other, which opens certain doors and gives us certain rights.

I have always loved the Curé d'Ars—I read some forty years ago an account of his life by the Abbé Trochu[38]—but without losing sight of the following factors: this saint's path is that of a penitential *bhakti* which by definition appeals to the will and to sentiment, but not to intelligence; that is to say, metaphysical arguments play no role in this path, whereas in the esoterism of *gnosis*, on the contrary, ideas are keys of primary importance; it is owing to this efficacy of metaphysical concepts that someone could say: "It is not I that have left the world; it is the world that has left me." This is what a disciple of the Shaykh al-Alawi told me.

In Christian mysticism—Catholic above all—one begins by "leaving the world"; in esoteric sapience, one begins by understanding what it is: "There is no lustral water like unto Knowledge";[39] nothing disarms seductive *Māyā* so well as the knowledge we have of it, around us as well as within us. The beginning of all *gnosis* and of all liberation is in fact the understanding of the relationship between *Ātmā* and *Māyā*; but this doctrine—and the corresponding alchemy—remain outside the bhaktic perspectives, above all those that are voluntarist and penitential. These perspectives, which are at the same time fundamentally suspicious of all that could seem to them to be quietism, also underestimate the sacramental grace of the divine Name; they place the entire burden on man's side and wish to overlook—with some exceptions—that God can put Himself in place of our weakness.

Nevertheless, sanctity is sanctity, and Paradise is Paradise, no matter which path is taken to arrive there; the metaphysician or *jnānin* will necessarily love the saints, whoever they might be, on account of the marvel of sanctity. Obviously, it is not impossible for some saint, above us in Heaven, to love us; there is nothing extraordinary in this saint's being a Catholic, while—from the point of view of form—we are in Islam, since, I repeat, we are Christian in origin. The blessed in Heaven know well why we are in Islam; they know our intellectual and spiritual motives, and they understand our quest. Ever since Islam

[38] See Abbé François Trochu, *The Cure d'Ars: St. Jean-Marie-Baptiste Vianney* (London: Burns, Oates and Washbourne, 1927).

[39] *Bhagavad Gītā* 4:38.

existed, the Blessed Virgin could not be unaware of what Islam is; the proof of this is that in Ephesus—a Catholic religious told us this in Ephesus itself—Mary works as many healing miracles for the Muslims as for the Christians, without ever trying to convert the former; and it is by praying to the Holy Virgin that certain of the disciples found their way to the *Ṭarīqah*.

So, the Curé d'Ars has helped you. Other disciples have had similar experiences with other saints, in the first place with the Holy Virgin, obviously; but given her super-eminent rank, she is situated beyond confessional denominations—not in relation to Christians, but in herself and in relation to non-Christians who have recourse to her. A question: the Curé d'Ars, to whom you addressed yourself, came to your aid; but are you certain that the benefic presence you feel since that moment does not come from the Holy Virgin? For the Curé d'Ars always placed himself under Mary's mantle, so to speak. I am not at all sure that an ordinary saint could grant an earthly person a permanent presence, whereas the Holy Virgin can, and even does so readily for those who place their trust in her, as the Curé d'Ars did, precisely. Do not wonder too much from whom the grace comes; it comes from Heaven. And I am strongly inclined to think that it comes from the heavenly Mother of our *Ṭarīqah*.

When we have outward or inward difficulties, we can always express them in a prayer addressed to God; or possibly to the Holy Virgin, if a certain *barakah* prompts us to do so, but not to another saint, whether Muslim or Christian. Hence, I am very far from encouraging prayers addressed to the blessed in Heaven; if one of the blessed has helped you, may God be praised; but if ever you feel the need to ask a favor from someone "other than God", concentrate on *Sayyidatnā* Maryam.

In any event, our spiritual life should not depend on any sensible grace; it is well and good to feel a celestial presence, but this has nothing to do with our path; our path is active, not passive, and it is based on ideas and practices, not on experiences. We should not be overly interested in whether our states of soul are agreeable or not; we can certainly accept sensible graces with respect and gratitude, but what matters in the eyes of God is what we do and not what we experience.

You ask me whether you should try to eliminate the kind of "consolation" that you experience; no, you must simply not make it a problem; if this "consolation" does not disturb anything in your spiritual practice, there is no harm in it; if on the contrary it opposes this practice, this means that you must turn away from it. One must always come back to the same fundamental certitudes, and not waver in the uncertain: now what is absolutely certain, I repeat, is that God alone is God, and that we must attach ourselves to Him; this is the meaning of life, and this above all is the reason for being of the human state.

—·:·—

"*What Is Most Basic and Most Urgent*"
Bloomington, November 11, 1985 to a reader[40]

The three fundamental constitutive elements of every religion are doctrine, prayer, virtue. Doctrine: namely the distinction between the Absolute and the relative, God and the world, *Ātmā* and *Māyā*. Prayer: this is quintessentially ejaculatory orison. Virtue: beauty of soul, the pillars of which are humility and charity; in other words, effacement and generosity; knowledge of oneself and compassion towards others.

There can be no question, under the current circumstances, of entering the Catholic Church. The Islamic traditional form is accessible, but it presents too many problems in a case such as yours. What remains is the Protestant path, which would allow you to keep all of your outward freedom while at the same time being perfectly effective according to the degree of your fervor; baptism is a sufficient initial condition from the "initiatic" and ritual point of view. The entire emphasis is on prayer; on the basis of the virtues of course, for the intention must be pure. The most universal formula—but always within the framework of Christianity—is the following: "Our Father which art in heaven, hallowed be thy name." Another possible formula—closer to *bhakti*—is the "Jesus Prayer" practiced by the Hesychasts and by the "Russian pilgrim": "Lord Jesus, have mercy on us." Closer to the specifically Catholic perspective, but also to the Hindu cult of the *Shakti*, is the *Ave*: "Hail Mary full of grace." One can practice for the ejaculatory orison either the first formula exclusively—the beginning of the Lord's Prayer—or the other two, or simply the Jesus Prayer; or all three alternatively, but granting then pre-eminence to the first, in the sense that it must be recited as often as possible.

[40] The recipient was a Protestant Christian.

One must begin with a solemn promise to God, or Christ, or the Virgin: "I want to follow this path, bless me and help me." Then one must recite the chosen prayer three times a day, and as often as possible in between those times. One must also practice individual prayer—speech addressed to God—and the reading of the Psalms at least once a week.

This is what is most basic and most urgent, expressed in Christian terms. It is clear that esoterism deepens these elements; you will find glimpses of this in my books.

—— ·:· ——

"*False Certitudes*"

Bloomington, January 30, 1986 to Martin Lings

One must take care not to have false certitudes about men, things, and situations, because there is a classic pitfall here, well known in mystical theology. The subjective phenomenon of certitude can be an illusion—all the more pernicious as the issue is important—and as for the proofs one advances, they can be a matter of interpretation, or of "projection" as one would say in psychology; they can be refuted by other proofs, these being real but which one ignores or wants to ignore.

—— ·:· ——

"*Something Mysterious in Old Age*"

Bloomington, June 26, 1987 to Marco Pallis

The more I age, the more I see that there is something mysterious in the condition of old age; I have in mind him for whom life has a meaning. Most people are passive in regard to phenomena and events, they let themselves be corroded so to speak by duration; time has the power to change them; from this stems the characteristic psychology of the average old person, who is someone tired and "disillusioned". Altogether different is the position of the man—whatever his age—who by his spiritual attitude keeps himself outside time: duration does not corrode him, he does not abandon himself to the powers of the world, he learns not to be the dupe of his own soul; he abides in the changeless freshness of the "Eternal Present". What is curious in the average old man is that certain of his youthful "illusions" were worth more than the "disillusion" of his old age; for there are experiences and evaluations that, not being wisdom, merely prove the smallness of the individual; the man who knows how to age soundly, on the contrary, always keeps some of the happiness of childhood. The key to his happiness is to a large extent gratitude.

It could be said that space disperses us, whereas time enslaves us; in the first respect, the worldly man is someone agitated; in the second respect, he is someone passive. To know the meaning of life and to take it seriously is to keep one's freedom; it is to rest at the Center and in the Present. Obviously, there is a certain fatigue in old age, but it need not determine our personality; and alongside it there is a perfume of holy childlikeness and second youth.

—— ·:· ——

"*In the West by a Westerner for Westerners*"
Bloomington, September 13, 1987 to Harald von Meyenburg

Our *Tarīqah* was founded in the West by a Westerner for Westerners; we did not start with the idea that Easterners would need us. The great majority of the disciples were *a priori* seekers coming from Christianity, who based themselves on the *Vedānta*, and who wished to enter the *Tarīqah* because of the initiation and the invocation; they were not Muslims who wished to deepen their religion esoterically. In any event, it is not possible that the passage into Islam be for God the only solution offered Western seekers, since that would be an incomprehensible negation of Christianity—which however is willed by God—and just as incomprehensible a victory of Islam; on the other hand, it is perfectly possible that the form of pure esoterism in the West—at the end of times—must be Islamic, but on condition that this community of Islamic form have a character distinguishing it from all other Muslim communities. And it is precisely this particular character—which is absolutely necessary—for which certain people, keenly bent on "orthodoxy", reproach our *Tarīqah*.

—·:·—

"*My Message Is in My Books*"
Bloomington, January 6, 1988 to Seyyed Hossein Nasr

As for the radiation of my work, I want to place the accent on my books and not on the *Tarīqah*; more than once I had the intention of closing it—that is to say, of no longer receiving anyone—because I had doubts about the possibility of maintaining it intact, and especially of having it grow, given the average man's inferior character and the absence of an environment that educates him; and I see more and more that experience corroborates this impression. Be that as it may, what I would like to repeat here—because of its importance—is that my message is in my books; it is not in the *Tarīqah*, at least not *a priori* so; what I mean by this is that my books constitute a "predication", they are directed to the public, whereas the *Tarīqah* is not the object of any propaganda. I could say that the *Tarīqah* is only a message in terms of my books and inasmuch as it extends my written message; this means that aspirants to the *Tarīqah* must be readers who understand my books and are convinced by them. There can be exceptions—there are some inevitably, and it is for me to decide about these—but then these are people who in any case accept all that I represent and that I manifest. If the *Tarīqah* spreads in the world, this is fine, but it must not spread at all costs; all the more as I have no interest whatsoever in expansion for the sake of expansion.

—·:·—

"*Another Kind of Sufism*"
Bloomington, March 16, 1988 to Harald von Meyenburg

One could come to the conclusion that the treatises and practices of average Sufism constitute an essential element for our *Tarīqah* given that they refer to the elements of "total Truth" and "invocatory Way"; but this is not the case since the purpose of my writings is to help one understand what is essential in all possible doctrinal formulations, and also since the quintessential practice that the invocation represents renders all secondary ascetic or religious practices superfluous—and this was in fact the opinion of the Shaykh al-Alawi. The teachings of average Sufism—we can employ this expression to specify that there is another kind of Sufism, without forgetting that not all *Tasawwuf* has been expressed in books—have even less of a character of essentiality in that they are mixed with theological speculations and confessional "mythology", in short with things that are not derived from pure esoterism and because of this remain foreign to the reason for being of our *Tarīqah.* I am not of course saying that we do not have the right in our midst to read Sufi writings; I am simply saying that these writings do not constitute for us expressions of what is absolutely essential, on average at least, and that these kinds of readings present in fact certain dangers regarding the clarity of ideas; not to mention the inconveniences of religious sentimentalism.

What I received in Mostaghanem, by way of teachings, was the legal minimum of the *sharī'ah* and, from the Shaykh al-Alawi, the Initiation. As for the metaphysical ideas, I "heard" them in Mostaghanem—at least in a certain form—but did not "receive" them, for they were already familiar to me, thanks to the *Vedānta* on the one hand and to the celestial gift of pure intellection on the other. Likewise, my function of *murshid* and my quality of *Shaykh al-barakah* are gifts from Heaven; my title of *muqaddam* was only an administrative measure, which moreover was unnecessary according to Guénon. As for the Method, namely the invocation, it is a gift from Heaven through the intermediary of the *barakah* of the Shaykh al-Alawi; it comes with another gift: the Six Themes of Meditation, which in all that they imply constitute the very substance of our Way.

—— ·:· ——

"*A Person's Traits of Character*"

Bloomington, March 31, 1988 to a reader[41]

We should not be astonished if we notice defects of character, or even vices, in a person whose parents are normal or virtuous, for if there were saints whose parents were bad people, the reverse must

[41] The recipient was a mother whose son had become a criminal.

also be possible, namely that there may be bad people whose parents were saints. A person's traits of character have two possible sources: either the individual substance—the origin of which no one knows—or heredity; when a character cannot be explained by heredity, this means that it is entirely specific to the individual. For a child is not just the product of his parents; he contains something new that comes from himself, otherwise there would never be exceptional men, and otherwise a quality or defect would always belong to the entire paternal or maternal line, all the way up to the ancestors and to Cain and Abel. The root of the problem, metaphysically speaking, is All-Possibility; evil cannot not exist since the world is not God; "for it must needs be that offences come",[42] though there is also the parable of the prodigal son.[43] All that we can do in such cases is to pray for the person who has gone astray; this is what Saint Monica did, the mother of Saint Augustine; you could also pray for your grandchildren.

What matters for us is to practice resignation on the one hand and trust on the other: resignation to God's Will and trust in God's Mercy.

Summer 1988

The individual substance, which "transmigrates", is linked to the potentialities of the divine All-Possibility and has nothing to do with the genes transmitting hereditary dispositions; these dispositions are superadded to the substance of the individual. They do not begin to be actualized until the moment the substance enters the body, more or less at the third month of growth; this combination constitutes the soul. It is perfectly unnecessary to investigate the origin of the empirical soul; the individual is what he is thanks to All-Possibility on the one hand and heredity on the other; when an individual cannot be reached through reason, one may always pray for him. One must not try to understand the mysteries of fatality.

The worth of an individual is absolutely independent of the question of knowing whether his conception is the result of a transgression or of a moral or legal behavior on the part of his parents. It has happened that the fruits of transgressions were saints.

We live in a horrible epoch and one must not be surprised at the horror of its manifestations. One obviously must not accept or

[42] Matt. 18:7.

[43] See Luke 15:11–32.

approve of a particular evil, but one must be resigned to evil as such; while discerning and refusing the absurd, one must accept its existence, otherwise one becomes immersed in a state of revolt against God, unconsciously no doubt, but nevertheless really. Therefore, do not be overly astonished by the evils that cannot but exist; and pray! For every encounter with God has its value.

—— ·⁝· ——

"*My Oldest Friend*"
Bloomington, April 11, 1988 to Max Schray

Lucy von Dechend is my oldest friend,[44] for I met her in my earliest childhood; then you came—I knew you already from the Sternenmühle period—and after that came Titus Burckhardt and Jakob Jenny. I met all the other friends only when they were adults; I speak of those who are in our community. I was told then that like other people I, too, would lose sight of my childhood friends in the "seriousness of life", something I did not believe, and I was proven right. I was also told that like "everyone else" I, too, would be converted to "reality"; yet for me it was the "dreams" that became reality, which had to happen precisely because they were not dreams, but realities.

I was often told in my childhood: "Just wait till you are grown up, you will see well enough then . . .". Now I waited my entire life for this grown-up state, but never noticed its coming; I do not know what it is all about. This has its basis in the fact that on the one hand I was already grown up as a child, and on the other hand never ceased being a child.

—— ·⁝· ——

"*A Friend Has Left This Station*"
Bloomington, July 8, 1989 to Richard Nicholson

Thank you for your two letters with the precious information concerning our friend Marco Pallis. His name evokes all kinds of memories

[44] This letter was written shortly after Lucy von Dechend's death.

for me, the unforgettable meeting with Swami Ramdas,[45] a memorable visit at Hari Prasad Shastri's home; without forgetting the essential, namely our numerous stays in the house at Egerton Terrace, and your repeated visits through the years in our home in Pully. I saw him for the last time in your apartment in London; if I am not mistaken, this was my last visit to England.

If I am sending you the enclosed picture, it is because of the robe I am wearing; it belonged—you know this very well—to the holy Lama of Lachen, and Pallis gave me this treasure as a gift.

One certainly has no right to complain about living on this earth, but when one learns that a friend has left this station of the *samsāra*, one cannot help feeling happiness for him; this is what I feel when I think of Marco Pallis. "Gone, gone, gone to the other shore, attained the other shore, O Enlightenment, be blessed!"[46]

—— ·⁝· ——

"*All Phenomena Are Reference Points*"
Bloomington, October 2, 1989 to Wolfgang Smith

As promised, I have reread your letter in order to find out which point in it, at first reading, seemed to me not altogether satisfying. I believe the difficulty—if there is one—lies in the fact that the question remains open as to what exactly is to be understood by "physics"; a simple question of terminology in the end. I readily accept that in physics—in the usual scientific sense—there is a domain that has as yet hardly been touched upon, a domain that properly speaking no longer wholly belongs to what is understood empirically as "physics"; on the other hand, however, this cannot mean that an empirical science could as it were find its way into the domain of metaphysics, meaning that in metaphysics discoveries *ab extra* would be possible. Now, in no way do you say this, but the reader accustomed to

[45] Swami Ramdas (1884–1963), a devotee of the Hindu *avatāra* Rama, described the practice and fruits of invocatory prayer in his spiritual autobiography *In Quest of God* (Mangalore: P. Ganesh Rau, 1925). For more on the "unforgettable meeting" between Schuon and Ramdas, see *Frithjof Schuon: Messenger of the Perennial Philosophy*, chap. 15, "Noteworthy Encounters".

[46] From the *Heart Sutra*.

thinking in Vedantic terms could, independently of your intentions, fear—rightly or wrongly—that such a conclusion is "in the air". In any event, it is important never to lose sight of the fact that in metaphysics the knowing subject can only be the Intellect in the Eckhartian sense; an extraordinarily high requirement, rooted in the supernatural. Which of course should not be taken to mean that empirical discoveries could not be reference points for a metaphysical awakening; this, however, only concerns the situation of the knowing individual and not metaphysics as such, which of course every man bears within his deepest self—a self *de facto* difficult to attain or in most cases unattainable; nevertheless, easily attainable for the born pneumatic. The pneumatic is the man for whom all phenomena are reference points or keys; things for him are metaphysically transparent—he can in a way "touch" the divine archetypes; he "sees" the ontological radius and not merely the cosmological circumference that does not touch the center. With all this, I am surely telling you nothing new.

—— ·:· ——

"*Walk Above the Clouds*"; "*To the Far West*"
Bloomington, October 13, 1989 to Ruth Michon

When one is seventy years of age, one has the feeling of being old; when one is over eighty, one no longer knows whether one is old or young, at least so it is with me. This is not just a matter of years, for people are different, and the experience of age also differs. I feel all of a sudden much closer to my childhood than I did in earlier years; one grows slowly into the timeless. And what constitutes our personality stands out quite clearly before us; we see what fundamentally we always have been, despite all the ruses of the *Māyā* surrounding us that seeks to estrange us from our true nature. I had from childhood four ideals: the True, the Beautiful, the Sacred, the Great; and this in a world of error, ugliness, profanity, and pettiness; it made me ill, and being ill made adapting to the world around me difficult. I am frankly amazed that I was able to survive it all.

Something particularly hard to learn is to bear the absurd; the ability to walk above the clouds and leave the world below, in fact and not just in theory. There are not only the vexations of the world, but also the rifts and knots in one's own soul, and then—on quite another plane—possible health difficulties that react upon the soul. I repeat over and over that it is part of natural wisdom and also of virtue to surrender to God's Will and to trust in God's Goodness. "The Lord is my shepherd, I shall not want."[47]

I had terrible trials to go through, but at the same time divine Providence guided me in a marvelous way. And now at last I have come here, to the Far West on the other side of the ocean; surrounding our house are meadows and vast wild forests; had I seen this in my childhood, I would have been overjoyed.

P.S. Many years ago, a Moroccan Shaykh said that I would end my days in the "Far West", and that this would be good for me. Now for the Arabs, the "Far West" is Morocco, since it is the westernmost land in the Islamic world; in itself, however—for us of the Old World—the Far West is America; the old Shaykh spoke the truth without knowing it. In the Koran it says: "And unto God belong the East and the West, and wheresoever ye turn, there is the Face of God. Lo! God is All-Encompassing, All-Knowing."[48]

——·⁝·——

"*Only Individuals Can Be Saved from Modernism*"
Bloomington, October 26, 1989 to Jacob Needleman

In your Preface to the second edition of *The Sword of Gnosis*,[49] you say that what is needed is not only truth, but also a shock that makes it acceptable to modern man. Now this presupposes that modern man is open, not to any shock, but to an *interiorizing* one, which precisely is not the case. The French Revolution, then Communism, Fascism, and Nazism, were shocks, but these shocks were *exteriorizing*. What does it mean that Judaism, Christianity, and Islam operated with shocks?

[47] Psalm 23:1.

[48] *Sūrah* "The Cow" [2]:115.

[49] *The Sword of Gnosis: Metaphysics, Cosmology, Tradition, Symbolism* (Baltimore: Penguin, 1974; Baltimore: Arkana, 1986) is an anthology of perennialist articles edited by Jacob Needleman.

It means that the human collectivities for which they were intended possessed a natural qualification for such a therapy; that it was possible to interiorize them through a shock, precisely. The very definition of modern man is that a shock will reach him only on condition that the shock will be exteriorizing, not interiorizing; that it must have something demagogic about it, for instance. All this amounts to saying that in our century only individuals can be saved from modernism, not collectivities; in a way, modern man is the creature that stubbornly does not want to be saved.

All this means that we have information to give, but nothing to preach. The idea that one should find a shock-idea, or shock-formulation, acceptable for the average modern man, is contradictory in itself; the illuminating or interiorizing shock cannot work any longer, there is no longer receptivity for it. The cosmological reason for being of modern man is the monstrous possibility of intellectual and spiritual incurability; in other words, the reason for being of the ending *Kali-Yuga* is the exhausting of the worst possibilities of the human cycle; it is an ontological necessity, very limited, but unavoidable. Let us not ask: what can we do to convert the devil? Let us ask: what can we do to convert, or inform, those who are qualified. And this is exactly what we do!

—— ·⁞· ——

"*The Quasi-Collapse of Communism*"
Bloomington, November 22, 1989 to Erich Schuon

The quasi-collapse of Communism—of which the newspapers are speaking—can be explained by its fundamental lack of realism, namely by the sheer excess of bureaucratic centralization and by the abolition of religion. Without religion, individuals no longer have moral conscience; Napoleon deemed that religion was absolutely necessary for a human society, since according to him "the best of monarchs could never govern a population of scoundrels". As for centralization, its effect is that no one takes responsibility for anything; wheat is harvested, not when it is ripe, but when the bureau in Moscow decides it is; or, when the harvest is gathered, it rots where it is because there are no vehicles available to fetch it, and so on and so forth.

Religion is natural to man. The religious phenomenon is by definition supernatural; artificial religions are ineffective. In other words: the "supernatural" is "natural" for man. There are certainly religions that have degenerated due to man's fault—the paganisms in the Bible are an example of this—but there are no religions as such without a divine origin. It is futile to "construct" a human society without religion; the construction will not stand. And when religion is rationalized, it is destroyed. Marxism forgets that society is made for men and not conversely, and that religion enters into the very definition of the human being.

—·:·—

"*The Average Modern Man*"
Bloomington, March 1, 1990 to Jacob Needleman

You were using the word "shock" in your Preface.[50] The meaning of my previous letter[51] was that this shock is inherent to truth itself and that in the modern world as a whole there is no longer receptivity for it; blind to the truth, the average modern man is also insensitive to the shock. The shock comes from the truth; the truth does not come from the shock; it would be a tautology to say that we need a shock besides that of the truth. Man is *a priori*, and by definition, a thinking creature; intellectual, spiritual, and moral health begins with ideas, thus with thinking; otherwise our spiritual attitudes would have no sufficient reason. All this is obvious, but I say it because I am thinking of it in the context of this letter.

You ask in your Preface, "And which people are needed?" The people needed exist—people saying the truth and saintly people—but the majority of "modern men" do not listen to them. This is, I repeat it, the main problem. *Et pax hominibus bonae voluntatis*![52]

[50] That is, to the second edition of *The Sword of Gnosis.*

[51] See the letter dated October 26, 1989, titled "Only Individuals Can Be Saved from Modernism".

[52] Luke 2:14.

—— ⁛ ——

"Nudity in Catholic Art"
Bloomington, February 6, 1992 to William Stoddart

I write to you today to share with you my responses to certain objections regarding nudity in Catholic art. It has been argued—and you surely know this—on the one hand that Michelangelo and Cellini were homosexuals, and on the other hand that Renaissance art is not the traditional art of Catholicism; now what matters is not the question of knowing whether Michelangelo, Cellini, and others—who made sculptures of completely nude Christs—were homosexuals or not, but the fact that the Church accepted them and that their works could be found, or are still found, in monasteries and churches; and as to the argument that the Renaissance does not represent traditional Catholic art, I will say that "traditional art" is a Guénonian notion, not a Catholic one. For Catholicism there is only religious art, and this art can be anything, as shown by the Vatican with its Sistine Chapel and its statues, and by thousands of churches from the Renaissance up to our times; not to mention the "surrealist" horrors that the Church, despite a warning from Pius XII, tolerates in its sanctuaries. I have to insist on this: the Renaissance, with or without Michelangelo and Cellini, was not a product of Protestantism or Islam, it was a product of Catholicism alone.

Doubtless, the Renaissance popes and those of the Baroque period did not themselves intend to produce works that would be incompatible with conventional Christian moralism, but they were not upset that others did so, to say the least; and if they accepted nude works of art, it is because they were intelligent enough to understand that there has to be an element of nobility in the human body, hence something ennobling. Saint Nonnus, upon beholding Saint Pelagia entering the baptismal font naked, praised God for having put in human beauty not only the occasion of a fall, but also the occasion of an elevation towards God.

If there is an ennobling element in the human body, this aspect must be able to manifest itself in certain settings and certain circumstances, according to the degree of contemplativity of men; this is shown by the Hindu world, and is found also in other traditional worlds in one way or another. In any event, total suppression of nudity—which is advocated and practiced by some Semitic moralists—results in repressions and complexes that are the cause of all kinds of unhealthy deformations; not for saints, surely, but for common mortals. An example of this, in the Christian world, is the strange ugliness of too many types of dress, starting from the end of the Middle Ages; it is as if one wished to replace the body's absence with a caricature of the soul.

February 7. Regarding sacred nudity, I will say it is based on the analogical correspondence between the "most outward" and the "most inward": the body is then seen as the "exteriorized heart", and the heart for its part "absorbs" so to speak the corporeal projection; "extremes meet". It is said in India that nudity favors the irradiation of spiritual fluids; and also that feminine nudity in particular manifests Lakshmi and for that reason has a beneficial effect on the ambience. In an altogether general way, nudity expresses—and "realizes" virtually—a return to the essence, the origin, the archetype, hence to the celestial state: "And this is why, naked, I dance," as Lalla Yogishwari said.

P.S. To return to the mystery of the human body: the most outward, as I have said, corresponds to the most inward; and likewise for traditional worlds: what is most immediately convincing, most irrefutable—most fascinating, if one will—is the aesthetic appearance of these worlds; their artistic expression in the fullest sense of this word. *Corpus, anima, spiritus*: between the sensible unfolding and the metaphysical essence there is the moral beauty characteristic of religion; for instance, resignation to God's Will and trust in divine Mercy.

—— ·:· ——

"*My Life's Work*"

Bloomington, January 31, 1996 to André Gerth

The question of my possible religious affiliation, touched upon in your letter, is intentionally not discussed in the writings of Professor Hossein Nasr and others for this reason: being *a priori* a metaphysician, I have had since my youth a particular interest not only in *Advaita*

Vedānta, but also in the method of realization of which it approves; this practice is based above all on exercises of metaphysical or mystical meditation, combined with the pronunciation—or invocation—of sacred formulas or names. Since I did not find these methods—in their strict and esoteric form—in Europe, and since it was impossible for me to turn to a Hindu *guru* because of the laws of caste, I had to look elsewhere; and since Islam contains that method *de facto*—in Sufism—I finally decided to look for a Sufi master; the outer religious form did not matter to me. It should be mentioned here that in my childhood I was first Protestant and then Catholic; however, under the influence of Indian metaphysics I soon gave up religious practice. Concerning my relations with an Arab Shaykh and his dervish order, I kept them secret as far as possible, so as to avoid the false impression that I had converted to a religion. The renowned Professor Louis Massignon[53]—a believing Catholic—knew my position and certainly did not think badly of me for it; perhaps you know his great work on the Sufi Al-Hallaj? My late brother, a Trappist Father, was also very understanding towards me.

If I sharply reject the modern world as such—I am, however, only partly in agreement with Guénon's *East and West*—it is because I am fundamentally opposed to philosophical rationalism and also to artistic naturalism; both are hallmarks of "classical" Greece and appeared anew as the "Renaissance". Here I would note two things: first, that it is false to see in Plato a rationalist in the modern sense; Anaxagoras and Protagoras could not stand farther apart from him; secondly, that influenced by Egypt, Plato also criticized naturalistic art. Paradoxically, there was also renewed interest in Plato and Plotinus in the Renaissance; also good poetry and good music. Be this as it may, the fact that I reject modernism as a general phenomenon obviously does not mean that I do not recognize isolated instances of individual worth in these latter times. But no one, in full awareness of the facts, could deny that the main characteristic of our time is a desacralization of the whole world.

P.S. I have difficulty accepting that the rigor of my outlook could give serious scholars occasion to simply pass over my life's work in

[53] Louis Massignon (1883–1962) was a French Islamicist, best known for his magisterial study *La Passion de Husayn Ibn Mansur al-Hallaj* (1975).

silence. An author's uncompromising stance does ultimately have its documentary value. Our salvation does not depend on whether we understand something or not—apart from the principal doctrines of metaphysics that we must know—rather it depends on what we do spiritually. We should put things that are enigmatic to us in parentheses, since it suffices that God knows the answer. The important thing is that we have found and understood the essential, thus the liberating, in life; beside this, everything else is indeed insignificant. God is what He is, and the world is what it is, whether we understand it or not. We must adhere with gratitude and faith to the liberating Truth; to the Truth and to the Way.

AFTERWORD

"Life Is Simple"[1]
Bloomington, January 20, 1991 to Erich Schuon

At our age, one thinks much about what lies behind us, and one easily reproaches oneself with mistakes and blunders; much, however, is due to our ambience, which from the time of our childhood harms our character—that is to say, it prevents it from developing normally. This is far from being a general rule—of course!—but it was the case with both of us, at least to a very great extent. It brought about an inner conflict that has had its value in the spiritual life.

When all is said and done, life is simple: one stands before God from birth to death; the important thing is to be aware of this and to draw the consequences from it. Consciousness of the Sovereign Good is the greatest of consolations, it should keep us in equilibrium always. What results from this consciousness is first of all the quality of resignation, the constant acceptance of God's Will; this virtue is difficult to the extent that we wish to force the world to be other than it is, to be logical for example. The complement of resignation is trust; God is good and everything is in His Hands. There is also gratitude, for every man has reasons to be grateful; one must remember frequently the good things we enjoy and not forget them because we lack something else. Finally, one must do something in life, for man is an acting being; and the best of acts is the one that has God as its object, and this is prayer.

[1] Written to his older brother during what proved to be his final illness before death.

APPENDIX

"*What You Should Do To Be Saved*"[1]
Bloomington, July 22, 1986 to a reader

Dear Mr. Albert,

You ask me in your letter — which I received in January — what you should do to be saved.

I am very old and I cannot write long letters any more. So I must be short.

The answer is: Pray. For if you practice prayer all your life, you cannot be lost.

Of course, you must abstain from sin and also from the manyfold perversions of the modern world.

You may be a member of the ancient, traditional, Tridentine Catholic Church, or of an Orthodox Church, or of a traditional, not sectarian evangelical Church. But the main thing is prayer; to understand this, it is good to read the Psalms.

The most important practice is ejaculatory prayer, for instance the Prayer of Jesus: "Domine Jesu Christe miserere nobis." Or the beginning of the Lord's Prayer: „Pater noster qui es in caelis." Or just „Jesu Maria."

This is all I can say in a few words.

With all my best wishes,

Frithjof Schuon

[1] This facsimile is one of the few letters written by the author in English.

GLOSSARY OF FOREIGN TERMS AND PHRASES

A fortiori (Latin): literally, "from greater reason"; used when drawing a conclusion that is inferred to be even stronger than the one already put forward.

A posteriori (Latin): literally, "from after"; subsequently; proceeding from effect to cause or from experience to principle.

A priori (Latin): literally, "from before"; in the first instance; proceeding from cause to effect or from principle to experience.

Ab extra (Latin): literally, "from outside"; proceeding from something extrinsic or external.

Ab intra (Latin): literally, "from within"; proceeding from something intrinsic or internal.

Adab (Arabic): in Islam, traditional politeness, propriety, spiritual courtesy.

Ādi-Buddha (Sanskrit): in Buddhist cosmology, the universal or primordial Buddha, in whom is personified supreme suchness or emptiness, and from whom come forth both the *Dhyāni-Buddhas* and the historical Buddhas, including Siddhartha Gautama.

Advaita (Sanskrit): "non-dualist" interpretation of the *Vedānta*; Hindu doctrine according to which the seeming multiplicity of things is regarded as the product of ignorance, the only true reality being *Brahma*, the One, the Absolute, the Infinite, which is the unchanging ground of appearance.

Aham Brahmāsmi (Sanskrit): "I am *Brahma*"; in *Advaita Vedānta*, one of the four principal "great sayings" (*mahāvākyas*) of the *Upanishads*.

Allāh (Arabic): literally, "God"; a term used by both Muslims and Arab Christians to refer to the One God.

Anamnesis (Greek): literally, a "lifting up of the mind"; recollection or remembrance, as in the Platonic doctrine that all knowledge is a recalling of truths latent in the soul.

Ānanda (Sanskrit): "bliss, beatitude, joy"; one of the three essential aspects of *Apara-Brahma*, together with *sat*, "being", and *chit*, "consciousness".

Anima (Latin): soul; see *corpus* and *spiritus*.

Apara-Brahma (Sanskrit): the "non-supreme" or penultimate *Brahma*, also called *Brahma saguna*; in the author's teaching, the "relative Absolute"; see *para-Brahma*.

Arqān ad-Dīn (Arabic): literally, "pillars of the religion"; the five pillars of Islam are: (1) the testification of Unity (*shahādah*); (2) the canonical prayer (*salāt*); (3) the fast (*sawm*) during Ramadan; (4) almsgiving (*zakāt*); and (5) the pilgrimage (*hajj*) to Mecca, if one has the means.

Āshram (Sanskrit): in Hinduism, a center for meditation and religious study, often associated with a saint or *guru*.

Ātmā or *Ātman* (Sanskrit): the real or true "Self", underlying the ego and its manifestations; in the perspective of *Advaita Vedānta*, identical with *Brahma*.

Avatāra (Sanskrit): the earthly "descent", incarnation, or manifestation of God, especially of Vishnu in the Hindu tradition.

Ave Maria (Latin): "Hail, Mary"; traditional prayer to the Blessed Virgin, also known as the Angelic Salutation, based on the words of the Archangel Gabriel and Saint Elizabeth in Luke 1:28 and Luke 1:42.

Barakah (Arabic): "blessing", grace; in Islam, a spiritual influence or energy emanating originally from God, but often attached to sacred objects and spiritual persons.

Barzakh (Arabic): as used in the Koran, a "barrier" or "separation" between paradise and hell, or this life and the next, or the two seas (fresh and salt); in the interpretation of Sufism, an "isthmus" connecting different planes of reality.

Basmalah (Arabic): traditional Muslim formula of blessing, found at the beginning of all but one of the *sūrah*s of the Koran, consisting of the words *Bismi 'Llāhi 'r-Rahmāni 'r-Rahīm*, "In the Name of God, the Clement (*Rahmān*), the Merciful (*Rahīm*)".

Bhakta (Sanskrit): a follower of the spiritual path of *bhakti*; a person whose relationship with God is based primarily on adoration and love.

Bhakti, *bhakti-mārga* (Sanskrit): the spiritual "path" (*mārga*) of "love" (*bhakti*) and devotion.

Brahma or *Brahman* (Sanskrit): the Supreme Reality, the Absolute.

Brahma nirguna (Sanskrit): *Brahma* considered as transcending all "qualities", attributes, or predicates; God as He is in Himself; also called *Para-Brahma*.

Brahma saguna (Sanskrit): *Brahma* "qualified" by attributes and predicates; God insofar as He can be known by man; also called *Apara-Brahma*.

Brāhmana (Sanskrit): a brahmin or member of the highest of the four Hindu castes; a priest or teacher.

Buddhānusmriti (Sanskrit): "remembrance or mindfulness of the Buddha", based upon the repeated invocation of his Name; central to the Pure Land school of Buddhism; known in Chinese as *nien-fo* and in Japanese as *nembutsu*.

Cintamāni (Sanskrit): literally, "wish-jewel"; in Hinduism, a magical jewel associated with the gods Vishnu and Ganesha and having the capacity to grant every wish; in Buddhism, this same jewel is carried by the *Bodhisattva*s Avalokiteshvara and Kshitigarbha.

Chit (Sanskrit): "consciousness"; one of the three essential aspects of *Apara-Brahma*, together with *sat*, "being", and *ānanda*, "bliss, beatitude, joy".

Corpus (Latin): body; see *anima* and *spiritus*.

Dār al-harb (Arabic): literally, "abode of war"; geographically, those areas where Islam is not the predominant religion, or where conditions are unfavorable or hostile for the practice of Islam.

Dār al-islām (Arabic): literally, "abode of Islam"; geographically, those areas where Islam is the predominant religion.

Darshana (Sanskrit): a spiritual "perspective", point of view, or school of thought; also the "viewing" of a holy person, object, or place, together with the resulting blessing or merit.

De facto (Latin): literally, "from the fact"; denoting something that is such "in fact", if not necessarily "by right" (*de jure*).

Deponendus (Latin): "required to be deposed".

Depositus (Latin): "deposed".

Deva (Sanskrit): literally, "shining one"; in Hinduism, a celestial being; any of the gods of the *Vedas*, traditionally reckoned as thirty-three.

Dharma (Sanskrit): in Hinduism, the underlying "law" or "order" of the cosmos as expressed in sacred rites and in actions appropriate to various social relationships and human vocations; in Buddhism, the practice and realization of Truth.

Dharmakāya (Sanskrit): literally, "*dharma* body"; in *Mahāyāna* Buddhism, the supreme and non-manifest form of the Buddhas, personified as the *Ādi Buddha*; see *Sambhogakāya* and *Nirmānakāya*.

Dhikr (Arabic): "remembrance" of God, based upon the repeated invocation of His Name; central to Sufi practice, where the remembrance is often supported by the single word *Allāh*.

Dīkshā (Sanskrit): in Hinduism, a rite of initiation performed by a *guru*, or spiritual director, and typically involving the gift of a *mantra*, or sacred formula.

Dios (Spanish): God.

Du'ā (Arabic): literally, "call, plea"; in Islam, individual, personal prayer, as distinguished from canonical (*salāt*) and invocatory (*dhikr*) prayer.

Et pax hominibus bonae voluntatis (Latin): "And peace to men of good will" (cf. Luke 2:14).

Ex cathedra (Latin): literally, "from the throne"; in Roman Catholicism, authoritative teaching issued by the pope and regarded as infallible.

Ex voto (Latin): an offering to a saint or divinity, given in fulfillment of a vow; derived from the Latin, *ex voto suscepto*, "from the vow made"; placed in churches or chapels where the worshipper seeks grace or wishes to give thanks.

Fanā' (Arabic): "extinction, annihilation, evanescence"; in Sufism, the spiritual station or degree of realization in which all individual attributes and limitations are extinguished in union with God.

Faqīr (Arabic, plural *fuqarā'*): literally, the "poor one"; in Sufism, a follower of the spiritual Path, whose "indigence" or "poverty" (*faqr*) testifies to complete dependence on God and a desire to be filled by Him alone.

Fard (Arabic, plural *afrād*): "alone"; in Sufism, one who realizes the truth on his own and without membership in a *tarīqah*, or even without belonging to a revealed religion, receiving illumination directly from God.

Farḍ or *fard* (Arabic): "indispensable, obligatory"; in Islamic law, all actions fall into one of five categories: (1) prohibited (*harām*); (2) discouraged (*makrūh*); (3) neutral (*mubāh*); (4) recommended (*mustahabb*); and (5) obligatory (*fard*); see *harām* and *makrūh*.

Fātihah (Arabic): the "opening" *sūrah*, or chapter, of the Koran, recited in the daily prayers of all Muslims and consisting of the words: "In the Name of God, the Beneficent, the Merciful. Praise to God, Lord of the Worlds, the Beneficent, the Merciful. Owner of the Day of Judgment, Thee (alone) we worship; Thee (alone) we ask for help. Show us the straight path, the path of those whom Thou hast favored, not (the path) of those who earn Thine anger nor of those who go astray."

Fedeli d'Amore (Italian): "the faithful of love"; a group of Medieval poets, including Dante, who transposed the courtly ideal of love for the earthly beloved—in Dante's case, Beatrice—into a means of deepening one's love for God.

Gnosis (Greek): "knowledge"; spiritual insight, principial comprehension, divine wisdom.

Gompa (Tibetan): a Buddhist complex typically containing a fortification, monastery (or nunnery), and university; located in areas of Tibet, Ladakh (India), Nepal, and Bhutan.

Gopī (Sanskrit): literally, "keeper of the cows"; in Hindu tradition, one of the cowherd girls involved with Krishna in the love affairs of his youth, symbolic of the soul's devotion to God.

Gopuram (Sanskrit): massive ornamental entrance structures of South Indian temples in the Dravidian style; typically ten or more stories high and in the form of enormous pyramids, each story decorated with a wealth of sculptures.

Guna (Sanskrit): literally, "strand"; quality, characteristic, attribute; in Hinduism, the *guna*s are the three constituents of *Prakriti*: *sattva* (the ascending, luminous quality), *rajas* (the expansive, passional quality), and *tamas* (the descending, dark quality).

Guru (Sanskrit): literally, "weighty", grave, venerable; in Hinduism, a spiritual master; one who gives initiation and instruction in the spiritual path and in whom is embodied the supreme goal of realization or perfection.

Hadīth (Arabic, plural *ahādīth*): "saying, narrative"; an account of the words or deeds of the Prophet Muhammad, transmitted through a traditional chain of known intermediaries.

Hadīth qudsī (Arabic): "divine, holy narrative"; an extra-Koranic saying in which God Himself speaks through the mouth of the Prophet.

Hadrah (Arabic): "divine Presence"; also designates the sacred dance performed by Sufi dervishes.

Haqīqah (Arabic): "truth, reality"; spiritual or esoteric truth, in contradistinction to the formal and exoteric law of the *Sharī'ah*; in Sufism, the inward essence of a thing, corresponding to an archetypal Truth in God.

Harām (Arabic): "forbidden, prohibited"; in Islamic law, all actions fall into one of five categories: (1) prohibited (*harām*); (2) discouraged (*makrūh*); (3) neutral (*mubāh*); (4) recommended (*mustahabb*); and (5) obligatory (*fard*); see *fard* and *makrūh*.

Hari Om (Sanskrit): in Hinduism, a sacred formula or *mantra*.

Homo sapiens (Latin): literally, "wise man"; the human species.

Hortulus conclusus (Latin): "enclosed garden" (cf. Song of Sol. 4:12).

Ibn al-Waqt (Arabic): literally, "son of the Moment"; in Sufism, a spiritual station of complete surrender to the present moment, the eternal "Now".

'Īd as-saghīr (Arabic): literally, "lesser feast"; a holiday in the Islamic calendar celebrating the end of the month of fasting in Ramadan; also known as *'Īd al-fitr*, "the feast of breaking fast".

Ijtihād (Arabic): literally, "exertion"; in Islamic law, an independent judgment concerning a legal or theological question, arrived at by those possessing the necessary qualifications through a reinterpretation of the Koran or *Sunnah*.

Imām (Arabic): in Islam in general, the "leader" of the congregational prayer; in Sufism, a spiritual representative of the *shaykh* or master.

In divinis (Latin): literally, "in or among divine things"; within the divine Principle; the plural form is used insofar as the Principle comprises dimensions, modes, and degrees.

Inshirāh (Arabic): literally, "solace, comfort"; the peace resulting from the spiritual opening or "expansion" (*sharh*) of the breast; also the name of the ninety-forth *sūrah* or chapter of the Koran.

Ipso facto (Latin): by that very fact.

Islām (Arabic): "submission, peace"; the peace that comes from submission or surrender to God.

Jalwah (Arabic): spiritual radiation; see ***khalwah***.

Japa-yoga (Sanskrit): method of "union" or "unification" (*yoga*) based upon the "repetition" (*japa*) of a ***mantra*** or sacred formula, often containing one of the Names of God.

Jejunium (Latin): "fasting, abstinence from food".

Jihād (Arabic): literally, "exertion", "striving"; the "holy war" fought against the enemies of Islam.

Jihād al-akbar (Arabic): "the greater holy war"; in Sufism, the inward fight against the ignorance and passion of the ego; in contradistinction to the "lesser holy war" (*jihād al-asghar*) or outward fight against the enemies of Islam.

Jīvan-mukta (Sanskrit): one who is "liberated" while still in this "life"; a person who has attained to a state of spiritual perfection or self-realization before death; in contrast to ***videha-mukta***, one who is liberated at the moment of death.

Jnāna or *jnāna-mārga* (Sanskrit): the spiritual "path" (*mārga*) of "knowledge" (*jnāna*) and intellection; see ***bhakti*** and ***karma***.

Jnānin (Sanskrit): a follower of the path of *jnāna*; a person whose relationship with God is based primarily on sapiential knowledge or ***gnosis***.

Kali-Yuga (Sanskrit): in Hinduism, the fourth and final ***yuga*** in a given cycle of time, corresponding to the Iron Age of Western tradition and culminating in a ***pralaya*** or the ***mahāpralaya***; the present age of mankind, distinguished by its increasing disorder, violence, and forgetfulness of God.

Kalki-Avatāra (Sanskrit): the tenth and last of the incarnations of Vishnu, who is to come at the end of the *Kali-Yuga* in order to punish evildoers and usher in a new age.

Karma (Sanskrit): "action, work"; in Hinduism and Buddhism, the law of consequence, in which the present is explained by reference to the nature and quality of one's past actions; one of the principal ***mārga***s or spiritual "paths" of Hinduism, characterized by its stress on righteous deeds.

Karma-mārga, karma-yoga (Sanskrit): the spiritual "path" (*mārga*) or method of "union" (*yoga*) based upon right "action, work" (*karma*); see *bhakti* and *jnana*.

Kātib (Arabic): a writer, scribe, or secretary.

Kawkab durrī (Arabic): "shining star"; from the Verse of Light in the Koran (24:35).

Khalīfah (Arabic): literally, "successor", "viceregent"; a representative or vicar, often used in reference to the four rightly-guided caliphs, or successors, of the Prophet Muhammad; in Sufism, every man is in principle a *khalīfah* of God.

Khalwah (Arabic): spiritual retreat or seclusion; see *jalwah*.

Krita-Yuga (Sanskrit): "perfect age"; in Hindu cosmology, the pure "golden" age wherein the tenets of religion are followed naturally; see also *yuga*.

Kshatriya (Sanskrit): a member of the second highest of the four Hindu castes; a warrior or prince.

Lactatio (Latin): literally, "suckling", "nursing".

Logos (Greek): "word, reason"; in Christian theology, the divine, uncreated Word of God (cf. John 1:1); the transcendent Principle of creation and revelation.

Ma'rifah (Arabic): "knowledge"; in Sufism, the spiritual way based upon knowledge or *gnosis*, analogous to the Hindu *jnāna-mārga*; see *mahabbah* and *makhāfah*.

Maghrib (Arabic): literally, the "place of sunset" or the "west"; in Islam, the canonical prayer (*salāt al-maghrib*) performed after sunset and before nightfall; also, the Islamic Far West (*al-Maghrib al-aqsā*) comprising Morocco, Mauritania, Algeria, Tunisia, and Libya.

Mahabbah (Arabic): "love"; in Sufism, the spiritual way based upon love and devotion, analogous to the Hindu *bhakti mārga*; see *makhāfah* and *ma'rifah*.

Mahādeva (Sanskrit): literally, "great god"; an appellation of Shiva understood as the transcendent Absolute; see *deva*.

Mahāpralaya (Sanskrit): in Hinduism, the "great" or final "dissolving" of the universe at the end of a *kalpa*, or "day in the life of *Brahmā*", understood as lasting one thousand *yugas*.

Mahāshakti (Sanskrit): literally, the "great *Shakti*"; refers to the feminine aspect of *Brahma* or the Absolute; see *shakti.*

Mahāyāna (Sanskrit): "great vehicle"; a form of Buddhism, including such traditions as Zen and *Jōdo-Shinshū*, regarded by its followers as the fullest or most adequate expression of the Buddha's teaching; distinguished by the idea that *Nirvāna* is not other than *samsāra* truly seen as it is.

Mahāyuga (Sanskrit): in Hindu tradition, a "great age", comprising four lesser ages (*yugas*) or periods of time, namely, *krita-yuga* (the "golden" age of Western tradition), *tretā-yuga* ("silver"), *dvāpara-yuga* ("bronze"), and *kali-yuga* ("iron").

Majlis (Arabic, plural *majālis*): literally, "a place of sitting"; a session or meeting; in Sufism, a gathering of *fuqarā* for recitation or chanting of *dhikr.*

Makhāfah (Arabic): "fear"; in Sufism, the spiritual way based upon the fear of God, analogous to the Hindu *karma mārga*; see *mahabbah* and *ma'rifah.*

Makrūh (Arabic): literally, "hateful, discouraged"; in Islamic law, all actions fall into one of five categories: (1) prohibited (*harām*); (2) discouraged (*makrūh*); (3) neutral (*mubāh*); (4) recommended (*mustahabb*); and (5) obligatory (*fard*); see *fard* and *harām.*

Malāmatiyah (Arabic): "men of blame"; a category of Sufis that accentuated self-reproach and endeavored to conceal virtue behind a façade of ignoble action.

Mantra (Sanskrit): "instrument of thought"; a word or phrase of divine origin, often including a Name of God, repeated by those initiated into its proper use as a means of salvation or liberation; see *japa-yoga.*

Mauna-dīkshā (Sanskrit): in Hinduism, initiation (*dīkshā*) conferred by a *guru* through silence (*mauna*), as opposed to look or touch; see *dīkshā.*

Māyā (Sanskrit): universal illusion, relativity, appearance; in *Advaita Vedānta,* the veiling or concealment of *Brahma* in the form or under the appearance of a lower, relative reality; also, as "productive power", the unveiling or manifestation of *Ātmā* as "divine art" or theophany. *Māyā* is neither real nor unreal, and ranges from the Supreme Lord to the "last blade of grass".

Mleccha (Sanskrit): foreigner; member of a non-Aryan race, but not necessarily regarded as inferior to Aryans; see *Avatāra.*

Modus vivendi (Latin): literally, "mode of living"; a practical compromise or working arrangement between competing interests.

Mudhākarah (Arabic): a discourse given by a spiritual authority or functionary at a gathering of Sufi dervishes; see *majlis.*

Mudrā (Sanskrit): literally, "seal"; in Hinduism and Buddhism, a symbolical ritual gesture, most often of the hands or fingers.

Mujāhid (Arabic): one who fights in the "holy war" (*jihād*); in Sufism, understood as one who engages in the fight against his own soul; see *jihād* and *jihād al-akbar.*

Muqaddam (Arabic): the representative of a Sufi *shaykh*; authorized to give instruction and initiate disciples into the spiritual order.

Murīd (Arabic, plural *murīdūn*): "one who seeks"; a disciple of a Sufi order who has pledged allegiance to a spiritual guide or *murshid*; see *faqīr.*

Murshid (Arabic): "guide", "instructor"; in Sufism, a spiritual master capable of conferring the supreme Name and guiding disciples on the path by pointing out faults and indicating remedies.

Mutatis mutandis (Latin): literally, "those things having been changed which need to be changed".

Nembutsu (Japanese): "remembrance or mindfulness of the Buddha", based upon the repeated invocation of his Name; same as *buddhānusmriti* in Sanskrit and *nien-fo* in Chinese.

Nirmānakāya (Sanskrit): the "earthly body" or "body of supernatural metamorphosis" of the Buddha; see *Dharmakāya* and *Sambhogakāya.*

Nirvāna (Sanskrit): literally, "blowing out"; in Indian traditions, especially Buddhism, the extinction of suffering and the resulting, supremely blissful state of liberation from egoism and attachment

Noblesse oblige (French): literally, "nobility obligates"; the duty of the nobility to display honorable and generous conduct.

O *beata solitudo, o sola beatitudo* (Latin): "O beatific solitude, O sole beatitude"; a Cistercian motto, attributed to Saint Bernard of Clairvaux.

Om (Sanskrit): in Hinduism, the sacred monosyllable symbolizing *Brahma* or the Absolute; also prevalent in Buddhism as a mantric syllable.

Oratio (Latin): literally, "language, speech"; in Christian usage, words addressed to God; prayer.

Para-Brahma (Sanskrit): the "supreme" or ultimate *Brahma*, also called *Brahma nirguna*; the Absolute as such; see *apara-Brahma*.

Philosophia perennis (Latin): "Perennial Philosophy"; the one, perennial, and universal wisdom at the heart of all orthodox religious traditions.

Prājna (Sanskrit): the state of "deep sleep" in which consciousness merges with *Brahman*.

Pralaya (Sanskrit): "dissolution"; Hindu teaching that all appearance is subject to a periodic process of destruction and recreation; see *mahāpralaya*.

Pranava (Sanskrit): "primordial sound"; a designation for the sacred syllable *Om*.

Prapatti (Sanskrit): "seeking refuge"; pious resignation and devotion to God.

Pratyeka-Buddha (Sanskrit): "independent Buddha"; in Buddhism, one who attains enlightenment without a teacher and who makes no attempt to instruct disciples.

Pro domo (Latin): literally, "for (one's own) home or house"; serving the interests of a given perspective or for the benefit of a given group.

Qiblah (Arabic): in Islam, the direction of prayer towards Mecca.

Qiyās (Arabic): literally, "measure, analogy"; analogical reasoning in Islamic logic and law; a method for applying the teachings of the Koran and *Sunnah* to issues and circumstances not explicitly dealt with in the traditional sources.

Rahmah (Arabic): "compassion, mercy"; in Islam, one of the Names of God, who is supreme Compassion, Mercy, and Clemency.

Rahmān, Rahīm (Arabic): "clement", "merciful"; found in Islam in the invocatory formula *bismi 'Llāhi 'r-Rahmāni 'r-Rahīm*: "In the Name of God, the Clement, the Merciful", *Rahmān* being the compassion of God insofar as it envelops all things, and *Rahīm* being the beneficence of God insofar as it is directed toward men of good will.

Rak'ah (Arabic, plural *raka'āt*): literally, "bowing"; in Islam, one complete cycle of ritual action performed during the canonical prayer (*salāt*), each prayer consisting of either two, three, or four cycles (*raka'āt*).

Religio formalis (Latin): "formal religion".

Religio Perennis (Latin): "Perennial Religion"; the one, universal, and perennial essence underlying the formal religions.

Risālat al-Ahadīyah (Arabic): the "message of unity".

Rūh (Arabic): "Spirit"; in Sufism, either the uncreated Spirit of God or the spirit of man.

Sādhu (Sanskrit): literally, "holy man, saint, sage"; in Hinduism, a renunciate or wandering ascetic.

Sakīnah (Arabic): the divine Peace, especially as dwelling in a sanctuary or in the heart; analogous to the Hebrew *Shekhinah*.

Salām (Arabic): "peace"; in Islam, one of the ninety-nine divine Names.

Samādhi (Sanskrit): "putting together, union"; in Hindu *yoga*, a state of supreme concentration in which consciousness is entirely absorbed in the object of meditation.

Sambhogakāya (Sanskrit): the "beatific body" or paradisal "body of bliss" of the Buddha; see *Dharmakāya* and *Nirmānakāya*.

Samsāra (Sanskrit): literally, "wandering"; in Hinduism and Buddhism, transmigration or the cycle of birth, death, and rebirth; also the world of apparent flux and change.

Sanātana Dharma (Sanskrit): "eternal law"; in Hinduism, the universal or absolute law or truth underlying specific and relative laws and truths.

Sannyāsin (Sanskrit): "renunciate"; in Hindu tradition, one who has renounced all formal ties to social life.

Sat (Sanskrit): "being"; one of the three essential aspects of *Apara-Brahma*, together with *chit*, "consciousness", and *ānanda*, "bliss, beatitude, joy".

Satsangha (Sanskrit): "company of the good"; the company of persons of holy or ascendant nature.

Sayyidatnā (Arabic): "our liege lady"; a title of respect, placed before the name of a female prophet or saint; also used as a title of respect for female descendants of the Prophet Muhammad.

Sayyidnā (Arabic): "our liege lord"; a title of respect, often placed before the name of a prophet or saint; also used as a title of respect for descendants of the Prophet Muhammad.

Shahādah (Arabic): the fundamental "profession" or "testimony" of faith in Islam, consisting of the words ***lā ilāha illā 'Llāh, Muhammadan rasūlu 'Llāh***: "There is no god but God; Muhammad is the messenger of God."

Shakti (Sanskrit): the consort of Shiva; creative "power", expressed in Hinduism in the form of divine femininity.

Shānti (Sanskrit): "peace".

Sharī'ah (Arabic): "path"; in Islam, the proper mode and norm of life, the path or way willed and marked out by God for man's return to Him; Muslim law or exoterism.

Shaykh (Arabic): literally, "old man, elder"; in Sufism, one who has attained spiritual mastery through submission to the discipline and instruction of another *shaykh* and who can thus trace his lineage to the foundation of a given Sufi brotherhood (*tarīqah*).

Shaykh al-barakah (Arabic): a spiritual master who benefits from spiritual inspiration of the first magnitude; a plenary spiritual master with the mandate to direct an independent Sufi brotherhood (*tarīqah*) connected to a spiritual heritage.

Shirk (Arabic): literally, "association"; the association of something with God, or of something relative with the Absolute; in Islam, considered as the worst of sins.

Shūnyamūrti (Sanskrit): "the form or manifestation of the void"; traditional epithet of the Buddha, in whom is "incarnate" *shūnyatā*, ultimate "emptiness", that is, the final absence of all definite being or selfhood.

Sīdī (Arabic): "my lord, master"; a title of respect used in the Islamic Far West (*al-Maghrib al-aqsā*); a variant form of *sayyidi*.

Sidna (Arabic): "our lord"; a title of respect used in the Islamic Far West (*al-Maghrib al-aqsā*); a variant form of *sayyidnā*.

Silsilah (Arabic): "chain"; in Sufi orders, an initiatic chain of transmission, beginning with the Prophet Muhammad, and including an unbroken lineage of spiritual masters through the centuries.

Sine qua non (Latin): an indispensable or essential condition.

Sophia (Greek): "wisdom"; in Jewish and Christian tradition, the Wisdom of God, often conceived as feminine (cf. Prov. 8).

Sophia Perennis (Greek): "Perennial Wisdom"; the eternal, non-formal Truth at the heart of all orthodox religious traditions.

Spiritus (Latin): Spirit; the supra-individual principle of the human microcosm, with its seat in the heart; see *anima* and *corpus*.

Staretz (Russian): "old man"; in the Christian East, a spiritual father or guide.

Stella Maris (Latin): "Star of the Sea"; a traditional epithet of the Blessed Virgin Mary.

Stella Matutina (Latin): "Morning Star"; a traditional epithet of the Blessed Virgin Mary.

Summum bonum (Latin): the "supreme good".

Sunnah (Arabic): "custom, way of acting"; in Islam, the norm established by the Prophet Muhammad, including his actions and sayings (see *hadīth*) and serving as a precedent and standard for the behavior of Muslims.

Sūrah (Arabic): one of the one hundred fourteen divisions, or chapters, of the Koran.

Sūtra (Sanskrit): literally, "thread"; a Hindu or Buddhist sacred text; in Hinduism, any short, aphoristic verse or collection of verses, often elliptical in style; in Buddhism, a collection of the discourses of the Buddha.

Tālib (Arabic): literally, "seeker"; in Islam, a student seeking after knowledge; in Sufism, a disciple of a spiritual master or *shaykh*.

Tao (Chinese): literally, "way"; in Taoism, the ultimate Source of all things, from which they come and to which they return; the Way of the universe and the sage.

Tarīqah (Arabic, plural *turuq*): "path"; in exoteric Islam, a virtual synonym for *Sharī'ah*, equivalent to the "straight path" mentioned in the *Fātihah*; in Sufism, the mystical path leading from observance of the *Sharī'ah* to self-realization in God; also a Sufi brotherhood.

Tasawwuf (Arabic): a term of disputed etymology, though perhaps from *sūf* for "wool", after the garment worn by many early Sufis; traditional Muslim word for Sufism.

Tasrīh al-Ism (Arabic): in Sufism, formal authorization given by the *Shaykh* to the disciple for the practice of the invocation of the divine Name.

Tat tvam asi (Sanskrit): "thou art That"; one of the *mahāvākyas*, or "great sentences", from the *Vedas* enunciating the supreme identity, or union with *Brahma*.

Tawakkul (Arabic): complete "reliance" on God and "trust" that He alone is sufficient for all one's needs.

Terza rima (Italian): literally, "third rhyme"; a three-line stanza using chain rhyme in the pattern aba bcb cdc ded, etc., first used by Dante Alighieri in his *Divine Comedy*.

Torah (Hebrew): "instruction, teaching"; in Judaism, the law of God, as revealed to Moses on Sinai and embodied in the Pentateuch (Genesis, Exodus, Leviticus, Numbers, Deuteronomy).

Tunkashila (Lakota): "Grandfather"; the supreme, unqualified "Great Spirit" (*Wakan Tanka*) independent of manifestation; distinguished from "Father" (*Até*), the non-supreme, qualified "Great Spirit" (*Wakan Tanka*), who creates, preserves, and destroys manifestation; analogous to the Hindu distinction between *Brahma nirguna* and *Brahma saguna*.

Upaguru (Sanskrit): in Hinduism, any person or thing who incidentally performs the role of spiritual guide or instructor for a seeker; see *guru*.

Upāya (Sanskrit): "means, expedient, method"; in Buddhist tradition, the adaptation of spiritual teaching to a form suited to the level of one's audience.

Vedānta (Sanskrit): "end or culmination of the *Vedas*"; one of the major schools of traditional Hindu philosophy, based in part on the *Upanishads*, esoteric treatises found at the conclusion of the Vedic scriptures; see *advaita*.

Wakan Tanka (Lakota): the "Great Spirit", "Great Mysterious", or "Great Holy".

Walī (Arabic): literally, "friend"; in Islam, a saint.

Wasichu (Lakota): people of Western European descent; often used derogatorily to refer to the white man's "civilization" built on greed, "progress", and the exploitation of the natural world.

Wilāyah (Arabic): sainthood.

Wird (Arabic): rosary, litany; in Sufism, a collection of prayer formulas recited in the morning and the evening.

Yā Latīf (Arabic): literally, "O Subtle, Gracious"; in Islam, a supplementary prayer calling upon the aid of the divine Name *Al-Latīf* ("the Subtle, Gracious") in times of distress, particularly serious illness.

Yin-Yang (Chinese): in Chinese tradition, two opposite but complementary forces or qualities, from whose interpenetration the universe and all its diverse forms emerge; *Yin* corresponds to the feminine, the yielding, the moon, liquidity; *Yang* corresponds to the masculine, the resisting, the sun, solidity.

Yoga (Sanskrit): literally, "yoking, union"; in Indian traditions, any meditative and ascetic technique designed to bring the soul and body into a state of concentration.

Yogī or *yogin* (Sanskrit): one who is "yoked" or "joined"; a practitioner of *yoga*, especially a form of *yoga* involving meditative and ascetic techniques designed to bring the soul and body into a state of concentration.

Yuga (Sanskrit): age or eon; one of the four ages of the world in Hindu cosmology: (1) the *Krita-* or *Satya-Yuga*, (2) the *Tretā-Yuga*, (3) the *Dvāpara-Yuga*, and (4) the *Kali-Yuga*; analogous to the Greco-Roman Golden, Silver, Bronze, and Iron Ages.

Zāwiyah (Arabic): literally, "corner"; a place where Sufi initiates gather to pray together and perform their religious rites of remembrance.

For a glossary of all key foreign words used in books published by World Wisdom, including metaphysical terms in English, consult: www.DictionaryofSpiritualTerms.org.
This on-line Dictionary of Spiritual Terms provides extensive definitions, examples, and related terms in other languages.

LIST OF CORRESPONDENTS

Black Elk, Benjamin (1899–1973) acted as the interpreter for his father, the Lakota holy man and visionary Black Elk, with both John Neihardt and Joseph Brown in the interviews that formed the basis for the books *Black Elk Speaks* and *The Sacred Pipe.*

Borella, Jean (b. 1930) is a Christian philosopher and theologian who has been deeply inspired by ancient and Christian Neoplatonism and by the writings of René Guénon and Frithjof Schuon. He taught metaphysics and the history of ancient and medieval philosophy at the University of Nancy until 1995.

Brown, Joseph Epes (1920–2000) was a professor of Religious Studies at Indiana University and the University of Montana. A renowned author in the field of American Indian traditions and world religions, he was also one of the founders of Native American Studies and was largely responsible for bringing the study of these religious traditions into American higher education.

Burckhardt, Titus (1908–1984), a German Swiss, was the son of the sculptor Carl Burckhardt and the great-nephew of the famous art historian, Jakob Burckhardt. He was a leading member of the perennialist school and an expert in the fields of sacred and traditional art. He met Schuon in grammar school and later became one of his closest friends.

Coomaraswamy, Rama P. (1929–2006) was the son of the renowned perennialist writer Ananda K. Coomaraswamy. In his own right, he was an important writer on traditionalist topics, especially regarding the influx of modernist ideas and practices into the Catholic Church; he was also a practicing physician.

Gerth, André was, at the time of Schuon's correspondence, a Swiss student of theology at the University of Munich who wished to write a dissertation on Schuon's works. He came to Indiana to meet Schuon on three occasions.

Guénon, René (1886–1951) was a French metaphysician and author who was one of the founders of the perennialist school. His writings remain influential on the intellectual and spiritual bankruptcy of the modern world, on symbolism, and on spiritual esoterism. In 1930, Guénon left Paris for Cairo, where he stayed for the remainder of his life.

Iyengar, Keshavram N., was a Hindu author and editor who acted as an interlocutor between Schuon and the His Holiness the 68th Jagadguru of Kanchipuram.

Jenny, Johann Jakob (1907–1997) was a schoolmate of Frithjof Schuon's in Basel, Switzerland, and remained one of his closest and lifelong friends. He was the first person to enter Schuon's *Ṭarīqah*.

Küry, Hans (1906–1987) was a professional writer, editor, and translator who specialized in the works of Shakespeare. He met Schuon through his younger brother, Ernst, and became a lifelong friend and disciple.

Lings, Martin (1909–2005) was a leading member of the perennialist school of thought and an acclaimed author, translator, Arabist, and poet. He is best known for his writings on Islam and Sufism. Lings met Schuon in 1938 and became his lifelong disciple.

Matheson, Donald Macleod (1896–1979) was Secretary to the National Trust from 1934–45 and was awarded the Commander of the Most Excellent Order of the British Empire (C.B.E.). A translator and author of works related to the perennial philosophy, he founded The Matheson Trust, dedicated to the study of comparative religion.

Mautner, Walter (1910–1980) was a German-speaking Jewish attorney who fled from Czechoslovakia to Argentina prior to WWII, where he met a Swiss diplomat who introduced him to Schuon's writings. After the war he settled in Germany where he practiced law.

Medicine Robe was a chief of the Assiniboine people who lived in Northern Montana.

Messinesi, Aristide (c. 1892–1965) was an author, translator, and master weaver who was introduced to the works of Ananda Coomaraswamy through his involvement in the Arts and Crafts movement in England. A close friend of Marco Pallis and Richard Nicholson, he subsequently became a disciple of Schuon.

Michon, Ruth (d. 2018), of Polish-Jewish origin, fled from Poland to Basel, Switzerland, prior to WWII, where she met and became a disciple of Frithjof Schuon.

Nasr, Seyyed Hossein (b. 1933) is University Professor of Islamic Studies at the George Washington University. He is a leading member of the perennialist school and is also recognized as a spokesman for traditional Islam and Sufism, not only in North America but worldwide.

Needleman, Jacob (b. 1934) is an American philosopher, author, and religious scholar. He was the editor of several books for the Penguin Metaphysical Library, including the perennialist anthology, *The Sword of Gnosis*. He visited Schuon three times, once in Switzerland and twice in Indiana.

Nicholson, Richard (d. 1990) was a close friend of Marco Pallis and, like Pallis, was a disciple of Frithjof Schuon within the Tibetan Buddhist tradition.

Northbourne, Lord (1896–1982) was born Walter Ernest Christopher James, the 4th Baron Northbourne. He was an agriculturist, educator, translator, and writer on both agriculture and comparative religion, who introduced the term "organic farming" to the world.

Oesch, Albert was a classmate of Schuon in Basel who shared his deep interest in *Vedānta* and the great wisdom traditions.

Pallis, Marco (1895–1989) was one of the earliest Western writers on Tibetan Buddhism. His first book, *Peaks and Lamas*, describes both the course of his Himalayan mountaineering expeditions as well as the path that he took to commit himself to the Tibetan Buddhist tradition. Pallis translated into English several works by René Guénon and Frithjof Schuon.

Paterson, Adrian (d. 1940) was one of Schuon's earliest disciples, an unofficial "secretary" to René Guénon, and a close friend of Martin Lings. He died as the result of a horse-riding accident near the pyramids outside of Cairo, Egypt.

Saint-Point, Valentine de (1875–1953) was a writer, poet, painter, playwright, art critic, choreographer, lecturer, and journalist.

Schaya, Leo (1916–1985) was nineteen years old when he attended a public lecture given by Schuon at the Basel Museum, after which he immediately became one of Schuon's disciples. Schaya was the founder of the French journal *Connaissance des religions* and the author of authoritative works on Jewish mysticism.

Schray, Max (1907–1995), a textile designer, was a childhood friend of Schuon in Basel and one of his earliest disciples.

Erich Schuon (Father Gall, 1906–1991) was Frithjof Schuon's older brother. He found his calling as a monk, entering a Cistercian Trappist monastery in Belgium in his youth. He shared his brother's love of the American Indians and was adopted by Black Elk as a son and given the name *Lakota Ishnala* ("Lone Lakota").

Shastri, Hari Prasad (1882–1956) was a gifted Sanskrit scholar and author well versed in the metaphysical wisdom of *Advaita Vedānta*. He was also the founder of Shanti Sadan, the Center of Adhyatma Yoga in the West, located in England.

Smith, Wolfgang (b. 1930) was for many years a professor of physics and mathematics and is the author of several books on science and metaphysics. His works also include critiques of the so-called "New Religions".

Stoddart, William (b. 1925) is a leading author, translator, and editor of perennialist writings who was a close associate of both Schuon and Titus Burckhardt for many decades.

Vâlsan, Michel (1907–1974) was a Romanian diplomat and scholar who specialized in translating and interpreting the works of Ibn Arabi. He was a great admirer of René Guénon and became the head of an independent branch of Schuon's *Tarīqah* that exists to this day.

Von Dechend, Lucy (1899–1991) met Schuon when she was twelve years old and he was four; they remained lifelong friends. Von Dechend faithfully typed all of Schuon's articles and transcribed his most important letters prior to the advent of photocopiers. She later became the personal secretary of Titus Burckhardt.

Von Meyenburg, Harald (d. 2002) was an early companion of Schuon in Basel; he was married to the sister of Titus Burckhardt.

Yellowtail, Thomas (1903–1993) was a revered Crow medicine man and Sun Dance chief. He first met Schuon in Paris in 1953 and later traveled with him to attend Plains Indian Sun Dances in the American West in 1959 and 1963. He and his wife, Susie, were the first visitors to stay in the Schuons' new home in Pully in 1954, and the Schuons' first visitors after their immigration to America in 1980.

TABLE OF LETTERS

3. My Spiritual Father (Ages 25–27)

Table of Letters

Table of Letters

7. To the Far West (Ages 72–88)

Table of Letters

Afterword

Appendix: Facsimile Letter

INDEX

BIOGRAPHICAL NOTES

Frithjof Schuon

Born in Basle, Switzerland in 1907, Frithjof Schuon was the twentieth century's pre-eminent spokesman for the perennialist school of comparative religious thought. The leitmotif of Schuon's work was foreshadowed in an encounter during his youth with a marabout who had accompanied some members of his Senegalese village to Basle for the purpose of demonstrating their African culture. When Schuon talked with him, the venerable old man drew a circle with radii on the ground and explained: "God is the center; all paths lead to Him." Until his later years Schuon traveled widely, from India and the Middle East to America, experiencing traditional cultures and establishing lifelong friendships with Hindu, Buddhist, Christian, Muslim, and American Indian spiritual leaders. A philosopher in the tradition of Plato, Shankara, and Eckhart, Schuon was a gifted artist and poet as well as the author of over twenty books on religion, metaphysics, sacred art, and the spiritual path. Describing his first book, *The Transcendent Unity of Religions*, T. S. Eliot wrote, "I have met with no more impressive work in the comparative study of Oriental and Occidental religion", and world-renowned religion scholar Huston Smith said of Schuon, "The man is a living wonder; intellectually apropos religion, equally in depth and breadth, the paragon of our time". Schuon's books have been translated into over a dozen languages and are respected by academic and religious authorities alike. More than a scholar and writer, Schuon was a spiritual guide for seekers from a wide variety of religions and backgrounds throughout the world. He died in 1998.

Catherine Schuon was born in Bern, Switzerland in 1924. Her interest in world religions and spirituality brought her into contact with Frithjof Schuon, whom she married in May 1949. She accompanied her husband on all of his travels and helped him to receive visits and answer correspondence from spiritual seekers. Her work with her husband brought her into contact with people from diverse religions and from throughout the world. Gifted in languages, she also became fluent in English and conversant in Italian, in addition to the three languages of her youth: German, French, and Spanish. Along with her husband, Catherine Schuon was adopted into the Sioux and Crow tribes; in addition, the Lakota holy man, Black Elk, gave her the name Wámbli Oyáte Win ("Eagle People Woman"). The Schuons lived near Lake Geneva until 1980 when they moved to the United States and established themselves in the forests of Indiana. After her husband's death in 1998, Catherine Schuon spent several months each year traveling throughout the world to visit many of her late husband's admirers, each time returning to the serenity of her home in the woods outside of Bloomington, Indiana. She translated the French edition of John G. Neihardt's, *Black Elk Speaks* (1969), edited her husband's selected writings on art in the illustrated *Art from the Sacred to the Profane: East and West* (World Wisdom, 2007), and co-edited (with Michael Oren Fitzgerald), *A King James Christmas: Biblical Selections with Illustrations from Around the World* (World Wisdom, 2012), which features nine of her paintings. Catherine Schuon died in 2021.

Michael Oren Fitzgerald (b. 1949) is an award-winning author, editor, and publisher of books on world religions, sacred art, and traditional culture. He was introduced to Frithjof Schuon in 1971 through Thomas Yellowtail, the Sun Dance Chief of the Crow tribe, who also adopted Fitzgerald into his family and the Crow tribe. Fitzgerald was Schuon's neighbor for the last eighteen years of his life and is the executor of his estate. He has previously written and lectured on aspects of Schuon's life and work, notably in the biography *Frithjof Schuon: Messenger of the Perennial Philosophy* (World Wisdom, 2010). He also recorded Yellowtail's autobiography and description of the Sun Dance Religion, published as *Yellowtail: Crow Medicine Man and Sun Dance Chief.* Fitzgerald has edited twenty books and two documentary films that have received more than 45 awards. Several of his books and both of his documentary films are used in university classes. Fitzgerald has taught Religious Traditions of the North American Indians at Indiana University, an institution from which he earned a degree in Religious Studies as well as a doctorate of Jurisprudence. He lives with his wife in Bloomington, Indiana.